WEST'S LAW SCHOOL
ADVISORY BOARD

REAL ESTATE FINANCE

IN A NUTSHELL

FOURTH EDITION

By

JON W. BRUCE

Professor of Law
Vanderbilt University

WEST GROUP

Bancroft-Whitney • Banks-Baldwin • Clark Boardman Callaghan
Lawyers Cooperative Publishing • WESTLAW® • West Publishing

1997

COPYRIGHT © 1979, 1985, 1991 WEST PUBLISHING CO.
COPYRIGHT © 1997 By WEST GROUP

> 610 Opperman Drive
> P.O. Box 64526
> St. Paul, MN 55164-0526
> 1-800-328-9352

All rights reserved
Printed in the United States of America

Library of Congress Cataloging-in-Publication Data
Bruce, Jon W., 1944–
    Real estate finance : in a nutshell / by Jon W. Bruce. — 4th ed.
      p.   cm. — (Nutshell series)
    Includes index.
    ISBN 0-314-21161-6 (pbk.)
    1. Mortgages—United States. I. Title. II. Series.
  KF695.Z9B78 1997
  346.7304'364—dc21   97-9347
                                           CIP

ISBN 0-314-21161-6

1st Reprint–1998

To my wife
Barbara Edmonson Bruce

*

PREFACE

This book is a concise textual treatment of the law of real estate finance. It is designed primarily to help law students negotiate a law school course on the subject. Other members of the legal community may use this work as a general reference and starting point for research. A table of secondary authorities is included to acknowledge sources and assist readers who desire more information about a topic introduced in this volume.

The material in this book is organized into detailed outline form for two reasons. First, the format is designed to give students a thorough overview of the subject and a set of pegs upon which to hang information gleaned from classroom discussion. Second, the relative rigidity of this style helped me resist the urge to write a treatise-like work complete with mountains of footnotes. Such an approach is, of course, inconsistent with the purpose of this Nutshell Series. Exhaustive discussion, therefore, has been sacrificed in favor of summarization and clarity. Readers are requested to keep this in mind while proceeding through these materials.

One final word about the book. Real estate finance is like most property law, overgrown with rules. The rules, of course, are stated here, but so are the underlying theories. This is intended to afford readers a better understanding of the rules and an opportunity to begin critically examining them.

I wish to say thanks to the following people: my wife Barb for her patience and understanding during the preparation of all four editions of this book; John Stark and Dan Sterner of the Indianapolis bar for giving me an excellent introduction to the practice of real estate finance law; Doug Mulligan, my research assistant on the first edition, for his tireless efforts; Jim Gillespie for his encouragement and helpful comments on the first edition; Jim Ely, a Vanderbilt colleague, for his valuable suggestions about the third and fourth editions; and Scott Sartin, my research assistant on the fourth edition, for his conscientious assistance.

JON W. BRUCE

Vanderbilt University
April, 1997

OUTLINE

Page

OUTLINE

OUTLINE

OUTLINE

TABLE OF CASES

References are to Pages

TABLE OF CASES

REAL ESTATE FINANCE

IN A NUTSHELL

FOURTH EDITION

*

CHAPTER 1

INTRODUCTION TO LAW OF REAL ESTATE FINANCE

This introductory chapter presents an overview of the law of real estate finance. Because the mortgage is the cornerstone of real estate finance, it is the focal point of this chapter and for that matter the entire book.

I. MORTGAGE CONCEPT

A. DEFINITION AND DESCRIPTION

A mortgage is the transfer of an interest in land as security for the repayment of a loan or the performance of another obligation. The typical mortgage transaction is relatively uncomplicated. A landowner borrows money from an institutional lender and enters a written agreement with the lender that the landowner's real estate is collateral for the loan. In legal terminology the landowner-borrower is a mortgagor, the lender is a mortgagee, and the agreement is a mortgage. If the mortgagor fails to pay the mortgage loan, the mortgagee may enforce its security interest by using appropriate foreclosure procedures to have the mortgaged land sold to satisfy the debt. *See* Appendices A, B, and C

1

for sample mortgage forms. (In all of the illustrations in this book "MR" refers to the mortgagor and "ME" refers to the mortgagee).

B. OBLIGATION/SECURITY
DISTINCTION

A mortgage exists solely as security for an underlying obligation, typically a promissory note. Consequently, the mortgage lives, travels, and dies with the obligation.

Illustration: MR executes a promissory note and a mortgage to ME. ME assigns the note to A, but through inadvertence fails to assign the mortgage to A. Nonetheless, the mortgage follows the note into A's hands by operation of law. *See* Ch. 7, pp. 126–129 (discussing assignment of mortgage loan).

Illustration: MR executes a promissory note and a mortgage to ME. MR pays ME in full. ME returns the note to MR, but ME does not release the mortgage. ME has no further rights under the mortgage. The security interest created by the mortgage lapses when the underlying debt is satisfied. *See* Ch. 4, pp. 89–96 (analyzing discharge of obligation and mortgage).

C. STATUTE OF FRAUDS

A mortgage involves the transfer of an interest in land. Thus, mortgages must be in writing to comply with the Statute of Frauds. Equitable principles, however, may dictate that a mortgage arises by operation of law or is enforceable even though it is unwritten.

Illustration: Y asks Z for a loan to pay several bills. Z makes the loan upon Y's oral promise that Y's farm is security for the loan. Y defaults. Z seeks to foreclose and have the farm sold. Z has no right to do so, because the oral promise is unenforceable. As a general rule, simply lending money does not constitute sufficient part performance to take an unwritten security arrangement out of the Statute of Frauds. Hence, the loan is unsecured.

Illustration: C asks D for a loan to purchase a specific parcel of real estate. D makes the loan upon C's oral promise to give D a mortgage on the property to be purchased. C uses the loan proceeds to purchase the property, but refuses to execute a mortgage to D as promised. C defaults. D seeks to foreclose and have the land sold. D generally may do so, because an equitable mortgage arises by operation of law in order to permit D to obtain payment out of the product of D's loan. It is not subject to the Statute of Frauds. D also might prevail on another ground. Hardship on D, advancement of the loan proceeds, and their use to purchase the property may be considered to constitute sufficient part performance to satisfy the Statute of Frauds.

II. HISTORICAL DEVELOPMENT OF MORTGAGE

Real estate finance is best understood by one who is thoroughly acquainted with the development of the mortgage concept. An abbreviated jaunt through legal history, therefore, is in order. During this excursion, note how the legal pendulum swings first in the mortgagee's favor, then in the mortgagor's direction, and so on, back and forth, throughout history.

A. DEFEASIBLE FEE AS FINANCING DEVICE

At early English common law, a mortgage was simply a deed of a defeasible fee from the mortgagor to the mortgagee. If the debt was repaid at maturity, or "law day" in common law parlance, the mortgagee's estate terminated, and the mortgagor again owned the land. If, however, the debt was not paid at maturity, the mortgagee's defeasible fee became a fee simple absolute. Because the law courts strictly enforced the time for payment, the mortgagor lost the land even if the mortgagor tendered payment just a day late.

B. EQUITY OF REDEMPTION

1. Creation and Growth

In order to mitigate the harsh results of this common law approach, the equity courts intervened. If a mortgagor could establish a sound reason for failing to perform as agreed in the mortgage, equity would permit the mortgagor to recover the land by paying the debt after the maturity date. This right of late payment eventually was extended to all mortgagors without regard to the existence of individual equities and became known as the equity of redemption. *See* Ch. 8, pp. 169–172 (discussing equity of redemption).

2. Preservation/Clogging

Equity courts have always zealously preserved the mortgagor's equity of redemption. Any clause in the mortgage or in a contemporaneous agreement that has the effect of eliminating or impairing the mortgagor's equitable right to redeem is termed clogging and is prohibited. Otherwise a mortgage could be transformed into a defeasible fee by the use of a simple waiver clause. The courts' protective approach in this regard gave rise to the maxim: "once a mortgage, always a mortgage."

Illustration: MR executes a mortgage to ME. At the same time MR gives ME an option to purchase the mortgaged land for a nominal sum if MR defaults. The option is unenforceable as a contemporaneous clog on MR's equity of redemption. It is really a disguised waiver. *See* Ch. 6, pp. 116–117 for a discussion of when the mortgagee may properly acquire the mortgaged property.

C. FORECLOSURE

1. Strict Foreclosure

The creation of an immutable equity of redemption placed the mortgagee in a difficult position. The defaulting mortgagor's right to redeem effectively prevented the mortgagee from selling or improving the mortgaged property. The English equity courts thus came to the aid of mortgagees by developing the concept of foreclosure of the equity of redemption. After default and at the mortgagee's request, the equity courts set a time period within which the mortgagor was required to pay the debt or lose the right to redeem. If the mortgagor failed to pay within the period specified, the mortgagee obtained a fee simple absolute. This method of terminating the mortgagor's equity of redemption became known as strict foreclosure.

2. Foreclosure by Sale

Strict foreclosure was inherently unfair to the mortgagor because the value of the mortgaged land acquired by the mortgagee frequently exceeded the debt. The legal pendulum, consequently, began to swing back in favor of mortgagors. This time our state courts played an active role. The rest of this chapter deals exclusively with the evolution of real estate finance law in this country.

Equity again readjusted the conflicting interests of the parties by requiring foreclosure of the mortgagor's equity of redemption via public sale. The proceeds of the foreclosure sale were disbursed pursuant to equitable considerations. The funds were employed first to satisfy the mortgage debt. Any surplus was given to the mortgagor. *See* Ch. 10, p. 205 (discussing disbursement of sale proceeds). If the funds were insufficient to pay off the debt, the mortgagee was permitted to recover a deficiency judgment against the mortgagor. *See* Ch. 10, pp. 205–206 (treating deficiency judgments).

In the United States foreclosure by sale is the primary method of terminating the mortgagor's equity of redemption. Strict foreclosure is not widely available. *See* Ch. 10, pp. 211–212 (discussing strict foreclosure).

Two variations on the foreclosure by sale theme exist—foreclosure by judicial sale and foreclosure by power of sale. Foreclosure by judicial sale involves a court-supervised procedure that is often complex, protracted, and expensive. Nonetheless, because judicial supervision protects the mortgagor, foreclosure by judicial sale is available in all states and is the exclusive method of foreclosing the mortgagor's equity of redemption in a number of jurisdictions. *See* Ch. 10, pp. 199–206 (analyzing foreclosure by judicial sale).

Power of sale foreclosure derives its name from the fact that in many jurisdictions the mortgage may include a provision granting the mortgagee the power to sell the mortgaged property without court supervision. Ch. 10, pp. 206–211 (discussing foreclosure by power of sale). Where this type of foreclosure is available, lenders commonly employ a security device known as a deed of trust instead of a mortgage. The deed of trust provides that a trustee will conduct the foreclosure sale outside the judicial system. *See* Ch. 3, p. 49 (treating deed of trust).

D. STATUTORY REDEMPTION

Statutes in numerous jurisdictions give the mortgagor an opportunity to redeem the mortgaged property even after the mortgagor's equity of redemption has been foreclosed. This right, referred to as statutory redemption, exists in about one-half of the states. Generally the mortgagor is given a set period of time after the foreclosure sale, often one year, to pay the foreclosure sale price and redeem the land. *See* Ch. 10, pp. 212–215 (analyzing statutory redemption).

III. MORTGAGE THEORIES

Although it is generally recognized that a mortgage is a transfer of a security interest in land, controversy exists regarding the precise nature of the mortgagee's interest. During the evolution of the mortgage from a defeasible conveyance to a security device, the courts did not adequately deal with the interrelated problem of possession. Today the states handle this unresolved possession problem in three different ways.

A. TITLE THEORY

Some states, referred to as title theory jurisdictions, continue to follow the original common law view that a mortgage conveys legal title to the mortgagee. In these jurisdictions the mortgagee receives the right to possession of the mortgage property when the mortgage is executed on the theory that possession follows legal title.

Most title theory states lie in the eastern part of the country where early common law had the greatest impact. Use of the term title theory to describe the mortgage law of these jurisdictions, however, is somewhat misleading. Title theory states have departed from most aspects of the traditional English theory of mortgages, retaining it primarily with respect to possession. As a general rule, these jurisdictions consider the mortgagee's "title" to be in the nature of a security interest, rather than fee ownership.

B. INTERMEDIATE THEORY

A few states still recognize the mortgage as a conveyance of a defeasible fee in form, but limit the mortgagee's right to possession in a manner consistent with the view that the mortgage creates merely a security interest. These states, called intermediate theory jurisdictions, give the mortgagor the right to possession until default and the mortgagee the right thereafter.

C. LIEN THEORY

In the majority of states the mortgage is viewed as giving the mortgagee a lien on the mortgaged property, not legal title. Thus, in these lien theory jurisdictions the mortgagor retains the right to possession until foreclosure.

D. PRACTICAL SIGNIFICANCE OF MORTGAGE THEORIES

It is important to emphasize that even in title and intermediate theory states, the mortgagee's rights as legal title-holder generally have been eliminated where unnecessary to protect its security interest. The primary distinction among the title, intermediate and lien theories, therefore, is with respect to the right to possession. Even this difference often is obscured by a mortgage clause that spells-out the rights of the parties regarding possession. *See* Ch. 8, pp. 159–160 (discussing significance of mortgage theories).

IV. MODERN FINANCING FORMATS

Although the mortgage is still the foundation of real estate finance, many sophisticated financing variations exist today. The complex financing formats that have evolved over the past several years often involve the use of a combination of mortgages, leases, installment land contracts, or outright conveyances. In subsequent chapters, you will become well acquainted with fundamental mortgage law and will be introduced to a wide variety of other real estate financing devices.

CHAPTER 2

MORTGAGE MARKET

The principles of real estate finance law discussed in this book are meaningful only when considered in light of the practical aspects of mortgage lending. This chapter, therefore, deals with the structure and operation of the mortgage market.

I. PURPOSE OF FINANCING

A. GENERAL

The purpose of the mortgage loan is the initial point of inquiry. Distinctions in two categories are important: (1) Is the mortgage loan money to be used for construction or permanent financing? (2) Is the mortgage loan to be secured by residential or commercial property? The answers to these questions determine to a large extent the source of the loan and the terms of the mortgage agreement.

B. CONSTRUCTION/PERMANENT FINANCING

1. Description and Distinction

A construction mortgage loan, sometimes referred to as an interim loan, is a short-term loan to an owner-developer for the construction of improvements on the real estate that secures the loan.

Illustration: MR is a real estate developer who wishes to build an apartment building on land MR already owns. ME loans MR money to construct the project, to be disbursed as construction progresses. The loan is secured by a mortgage on the land and improvements and is due in eighteen months. ME collects only interest during the eighteen months. This is a simplified construction mortgage loan.

A permanent mortgage loan, sometimes referred to as a final loan, is a long-term loan to the owner of the real estate that secures the loan.

Illustration: MR obtains a loan from ME to purchase a house and gives ME a mortgage on the house as security. The loan is for a thirty-year term and is payable in equal monthly installments of principal and interest. This is a typical residential permanent mortgage loan.

2. Relationship Between Construction Lenders and Permanent Lenders

Construction mortgage loans and permanent mortgage loans often work hand-in-hand; upon completion of construction the construction lender is usually paid by funds obtained from a permanent lender. The construction lender then either assigns its mortgage to the permanent lender or releases the construction loan mortgage so that the permanent lender's mortgage has first lien priority. This, of course, has all been arranged ahead of time by the parties involved.

The following scenario is common. The borrower first obtains a loan commitment from the permanent lender, then secures construction financing. The arrangement between the borrower and the construction lender is set out in a construction loan agreement. Before construction funds are advanced, the lenders enter a buy-sell agreement whereby the permanent lender agrees to "take-out" the construction lender upon completion of construction.

3. Construction Lender's Special Risks

a. *Nature of Risk and Minimizing It*

A construction mortgage loan involves greater risk than a permanent mortgage loan. The construction lender's investment is fully secured only when the project is completed in accordance with the plans and specifications upon which the parties originally agreed. Thus, the construction lender must closely supervise construction and advance funds under the construction loan agreement as the project properly progresses. *See* Ch. 4, pp. 77–78 (discussing construction lender's dilemma). As compensation for assuming this burden, the construction lender charges a higher rate of interest than does the permanent lender.

The construction lender also attempts to minimize its risk of loss in the event the project should encounter construction difficulty. First, it takes steps to insure that its mortgage has first lien priority. *See* Ch. 4, pp. 71–79 (analyzing issues concerning future advances); Ch. 9, pp. 175–176 (treating recording statutes). Second, the construction lender may require the mortgagor to personally guaranty completion of construction. Third, often in lieu of the second alternative, it may require the mortgagor to obtain performance and payment bonds in their joint names.

b. Performance and Payment Bonds

In order to be protected by performance and payment bonds, the construction lender must be named as an obligee together with the mortgagor. When this is done the bond is called a dual obligee bond.

The dual obligee performance bond assures the construction lender that the project will be completed in accordance with the construction contract. However, the coverage afforded a construction lender by a dual obligee bond is commonly limited by a savings clause, often called a Los Angeles clause, that releases the bonding company from liability if the mortgagor breaches the construction contract. Consequently, the savings clause may operate at a critical time to eliminate the construction lender's protection under the dual obligee performance bond.

The dual obligee payment bond assures the construction lender that all charges for labor or material used in construction will be paid. This prevents loss resulting from the attachment of any mechanics' liens that might gain priority over the construction loan mortgage, but at the same time raises the possibility that the bonding company may seek to be subrogated to the rights of mechanics' lienors. *See* Ch. 9, pp. 185–189 (analyzing mechanics' lien statutes). Moreover, the bond may contain a savings/Los Angeles clause. Hence, as a practical matter, the dual obligee payment bond may afford the lender no protection at all.

c. *Liability for Construction Defects*

In the last few decades, construction lenders have faced an unexpected additional risk—liability for faulty construction. In Conner v. Great Western Savings and Loan Association (Cal.1968), the Supreme Court of California held a construction lender liable for construction defects on a negligence theory because the lender went beyond the domain of the usual lender and actively participated in the enterprise. However, almost immediately after the *Conner* decision, the California legislature enacted a statute purporting to limit construction lenders' liability for construction defects. Cal.Civ.Code § 3434 (West 1970). Although the doctrine fashioned by the California court in *Connor* has been recognized elsewhere, it has rarely if ever been employed outside California to impose liability on a particular construction lender.

C. RESIDENTIAL/COMMERCIAL PROPERTY

The distinction between residential and commercial mortgage loans is important because some lenders specialize in making loans secured by a particular kind of property. Residential mortgage loans are loans secured by any form of residential property; for example, single-family dwellings, duplexes, apartments, or condominiums. Sometimes residential mortgage loans are further broken down into loans on one-to-four-family properties called home loans and loans on larger multi-family projects. Commercial mortgage loans are merely loans made on non-residential property; for example, shopping centers, hotels, office buildings, warehouses, or manufacturing plants.

II.
ORIGINATING/SERVICING/HOLDING

In order to fully understand the mortgage market, one must appreciate the differences among originating, servicing, and holding mortgage loans. The institution that initially advances funds "originates" the mortgage loan. The organization that collects the mortgage payment from and otherwise deals directly with the borrower "services" the loan. The lender that owns the mortgage loan at any one time "holds" the loan. Many times the same entity originates, holds, and services the loan. Almost as often, the originator sells the mortgage loan to a new holder who has someone, frequently the originator, service the loan for it.

The right to service a mortgage loan is a valuable asset because of the fee involved and the possibility of earning interest on escrowed funds. Accordingly, a vigorous market for mortgage servicing rights now exists. Indeed, several different entities may service a particular mortgage loan over its lifetime, often to the consternation of the mortgagor. *See* p. 44 (discussing RESPA regulation of transfer of servicing); ¶ 19 of Mortgage in Appendix A (concerning changes in servicing agent).

III. SOURCES OF REAL ESTATE FINANCING

The institutions that make mortgage loan funds available form the foundation of the mortgage market. The most significant sources of real estate financing are described in general terms in this section.

A. COMMERCIAL BANKS

Commercial banks are depository institutions chartered by either a state or the federal government. Although commercial banks make a substantial number of permanent mortgage loans, traditionally they have limited such long-term investments in order to maintain liquidity to meet demand deposits. Construction lending is usually a more significant part of their mortgage loan operation; the yields are higher, and the bank's funds are not tied up for prolonged periods.

By 1990 numerous commercial banks were in financial difficulty. Many of their mortgage loans were in jeopardy because of overbuilding and a sluggish real estate market. Bankers and regulators took various steps to avert further trouble. Whether these efforts will succeed over the long-haul remains to be seen, but by the mid–1990s the mortgage lending situation for commercial banks had improved.

B.　SAVINGS AND LOAN ASSOCIATIONS

Savings and loan associations are also either state or federally chartered. They are specialists in housing finance and heavily invest in both construction and permanent residential mortgages. In 1995, savings and loan associations originated fifteen percent of all permanent one-to-four family residential mortgages made throughout the country. This is down significantly from well over forty percent of such loans originated by saving and loan associations in 1988.

In the late 1980s the savings and loan system entered a state of crisis. Many institutions became insolvent and numerous others teetered on the brink of collapse. As part of the Financial Institutions Reform, Recovery and Enforcement Act of 1989 Congress created the Resolution Trust Corporation (RTC) to depose of the assets of failed savings and loan associations. These assets included construction loan mortgages, permanent mortgages, and a significant amount of real estate obtained from defaulting mortgagors. The RTC completed its work in late 1995 and discontinued business the last day of that year.

C. MUTUAL SAVINGS BANKS

Mutual savings banks are state or federally chartered institutions located primarily in the northeast. They operate in the same general sphere as savings and loan associations, but tend to concentrate their mortgage investments in permanent residential mortgages acquired from other institutional lenders.

D. LIFE INSURANCE COMPANIES

Life insurance companies are state chartered and subject to local insurance law. Because of a relatively predictable flow of funds, life insurance companies are heavily involved in permanent financing of both commercial and multi-unit residential projects.

The long term nature of their mortgage investments, however, puts life insurance companies in a difficult position during periods of rapid inflation. As a consequence, they may require the right to participate in income from the project being financed. *See* Ch. 4, p. 86 (discussing revenue/equity participation).

E. PENSION FUNDS

Public and private employee pension funds are an increasing source of capital for real estate financing, particularly in the area of permanent commercial mortgages and mortgage-backed securities.

F. REAL ESTATE INVESTMENT TRUSTS

Real estate investment trusts (REITs) are a product of federal tax legislation of the early 1960s designed to give the small investor an opportunity to participate in sophisticated and diverse real estate investments. A REIT is usually formed as a business trust in which investors purchase beneficial interests called shares. If the REIT meets a number of tax requirements, it will not be taxed on income and capital gains distributed to the shareholders.

The first qualified REITs were "equity" trusts that developed or purchased income producing commercial property. They were not generally successful. In the late 1960s, however, REITs that engaged solely in mortgage lending became popular. Although mortgage REITs made permanent loans, they became important primarily as suppliers of construction financing. Consequently, the building slump of the middle 1970s hit mortgage REITs hard. Some went bankrupt, and many others barely survived.

REITs made a comeback in the 1980s and 1990s. Equity REITs led the resurgence, and by the mid-1990s mortgage REITs had regained a solid position in the world of mortgage lending.

G. MORTGAGE BANKING COMPANIES

Mortgage banking companies are incorporated and operated under state law. Although mortgage bankers are a source of some real estate financing funds, they are more important as intermediaries between borrowers and other lenders.

There are two major ways in which mortgage bankers perform their intermediary function. First, they originate home mortgage loans for sale to institutional investors and then service the loan for the investor who holds it. In 1995, mortgage banking companies originated fifty-six percent of all permanent one-to-four family residential mortgage loans made nationwide. Second, they put commercial borrowers, construction lenders, and permanent lenders in contact with one another.

In performing the latter role, mortgage bankers often facilitate the overall operation of a transaction by financing the project for a short time between the completion of construction and the sale of the loan to the permanent investor. They frequently obtain funds for this interim financing from a commercial bank under a line of credit secured by an assignment of the mortgage loan involved. This arrangement is known as mortgage warehousing. Mortgage bankers also utilize this financing technique to enable them to serve as construction lenders in their own right. In either case the mortgage banker realizes a profit from mortgage warehousing by borrowing money, often at the commercial bank's prime interest rate, and then lending it to the developer at a higher rate of return.

H. OTHER SOURCES

Credit unions, individuals, syndications, service corporations, state development agencies, and community housing authorities are other less significant sources of real estate investment capital.

1. Credit Unions

In the late 1970s federal credit unions were authorized to offer residential mortgage loans. Their impact on the mortgage market has been slight thus far.

2. Individuals

Individual sellers sometimes take back a purchase money mortgage on the property being sold. These transactions, however, constitute only a small percentage of the total mortgage loans outstanding at any one time.

3. Syndications

Syndications are groups of individual real estate investors often formed as limited partnerships. They, however, generally invest by purchasing realty rather than by making mortgage loans.

4. Service Corporations

Service corporations are organized by savings and loan associations. Their funds may be invested in real estate in a wide variety of ways.

5. State Development Agencies

State development agencies have been created by many state legislatures to deal with intrastate housing problems by financing the construction of low and moderate income housing. These development agencies generally have the power to raise funds by issuing tax exempt bonds.

6. Community Housing Authorities

Many cities have established a housing authority that finances the construction of low and moderate income housing from the sale of tax exempt bonds.

IV. OBTAINING REAL ESTATE FINANCING

A. APPLICATION AND COMMITMENT

Once a potential source of funds is identified, the borrower secures the mortgage loan through the process of application and commitment. The borrower initiates the process by making a formal or informal mortgage loan application to the lender who evaluates it in light of the risk involved.

The risk in mortgage financing is a two-tier one. The lender initially must assess the borrower's financial position with a view to predicting the likelihood that the underlying obligation will be repaid. Next, the lender must anticipate default and decide whether the mortgaged property will produce a sufficient amount at a foreclosure sale to pay the mortgage debt.

If the lender determines that the overall risk is acceptable, it will issue a loan commitment detailing the amount, term, interest rate, and other pertinent items. The length, formality, and specificity of the commitment varies from lender to lender and loan to loan. Commercial loan commitments naturally are rather complex and usually include a provision for a nonrefundable commitment fee.

A loan commitment contains numerous terms and conditions not found in the application. Consequently, the typical commitment constitutes a counteroffer to make a loan. When the borrower accepts the commitment, a binding contract for a mortgage loan is created.

B. MORTGAGE LOAN CONTRACT

Mortgage loan contracts are a frequent source of litigation. Two areas are particularly controversial: nonrefundable commitment fees and the borrower's remedy for breach.

1. Nonrefundable Commitment Fees

The commitment fee issue arises when a borrower decides not to go through with the loan and then demands return of the "nonrefundable" commitment fee on the ground the lender has done nothing to earn it. Courts have consistently rejected this contention and held that the lender is entitled to the commitment fee either as liquidated damages for breach of contract or as compensation for keeping money available for loan to the borrower.

2. Borrower's Remedy for Lender's Breach

On the other hand, when the lender refuses to complete the loan in accordance with the commitment, questions arise regarding the borrower's remedy for breach of contract. Although the transfer of a security interest in real property is an aspect of the contemplated loan, the borrower generally is not entitled to specific performance. Damages at law are normally considered adequate to compensate the borrower for any loss the borrower may have suffered by reason of the lender's failure to advance the promised funds. However, the borrower should be entitled to specific performance of the mortgage loan contract when the borrower is unable to obtain a similar loan elsewhere.

V. LOAN PARTICIPATION AND MORTGAGE–BACKED SECURITIES

A. LOAN PARTICIPATION

A lender is sometimes presented with the opportunity to make an attractive loan, but does not have the entire loan amount conveniently available. Instead of losing the loan, the lender may ask other lenders to provide a share of the funds. An arrangement of this kind is known as a loan participation. The originating mortgagee is the "lead" lender, and the others are participants. The participants' interests in the loan are usually evidenced by participation certificates issued by the lead lender who holds the loan documents, collects payments, and disburses the appropriate share of the payments to each investor. *See* Ch. 7, p. 140 (discussing forms of loan participation).

B. MORTGAGE–BACKED SECURITIES

A special type of participation involves the sale of undivided interests in a large pool of mortgage loans. The Government National Mortgage Association (GNMA), the Federal National Mortgage Association (FNMA), and the Federal Home Loan Mortgage Corporation (FHLMC) utilize such mortgage-backed securities to stimulate private investment in housing. *See* pp. 36–38 (discussing these institutions).

GNMA's "pass-through" program is an early and well-known example of this type of participation. In that program a mortgage lender issues securities backed by a pool of mortgages. The pool is comprised of mortgages insured by FHA or guaranteed by VA. *See* pp. 34–36 (discussing mortgage insurance and guaranty programs). The periodic mortgage payments made by mortgagors in the pool are distributed among the investors (participants) in proportion to their investments. GNMA guarantees that the investors will be paid even if mortgagors in the pool fail to make their mortgage payments.

Mortgage securitization has blossomed over time. FNMA and FHLMC became active in the field by issuing mortgage-backed securities and guaranteeing these securities themselves. Private issuers also entered the marketplace with a range of offerings. Various forms of mortgage-backed securities have evolved, commonly involving conventional mortgages. In sum, mortgage-backed securities have achieved a substantial position in the mortgage market.

VI. SECONDARY FINANCING

Several lenders may independently acquire separate security interests in the same property by utilizing the mortgage market technique known as secondary financing.

A. THE BASICS

1. Creation of Junior Mortgages

Because the modern mortgage is just a security interest in land, a landowner is free to mortgage the same property to as many lenders as are willing to make mortgage loans to the landowner. The placing of a second, third, or even fourth mortgage on land is termed secondary financing. The second and subsequent mortgages are categorized as junior mortgages. *See* Ch. 9, pp. 175–176 (discussing general principles of priority and recording statutes).

Illustration: MR executes a mortgage to ME–1. MR then executes a second mortgage to ME–2 and finally a third mortgage to ME–3. All mortgages are valid. MR gave ME–1 only a security interest in the land, not ownership. The second and third mortgages held by ME–2 and ME–3 are referred to as junior mortgages.

Illustration: O owns a house subject to a $40,-000 mortgage held by B bank. O desires to sell the house for $70,000. P agrees to purchase it at that price, but has no ready cash and is unable to obtain a first mortgage loan for the full amount of the purchase price. The parties, therefore, agree to the following arrangement in order to insure that the sale is consummated. O conveys the house to P subject to the existing $40,000 mortgage that P assumes and agrees to pay. *See* Ch. 6, pp. 106–125 (discussing conveyance of mortgaged property and due-on-sale clause). P gives O a $30,000 promissory note for the balance of the purchase price and a second mortgage on the house as security for its payment. B bank's $40,-000 first mortgage and O's $30,000 second mortgage are both valid liens on the property.

2. Importance of Mortgagor's "Equity"

Lenders make junior mortgage loans only if the market value of the mortgaged property exceeds the unpaid balance of prior mortgages. The difference is known as the mortgagor's equity. The use of the term "equity" in this context is really a convenient way of stating the value of the mortgagor's equity of redemption.

A mortgagor's equity may accumulate in two ways: (1) the principal balance due on existing mortgage loans may be reduced by partial payment; (2) the mortgaged property may appreciate in value.

Illustration: MR owns a house worth $100,000. MR obtains a $100,000 loan from ME–1 secured by a mortgage on the house. (Rarely will a mortgagor be able to obtain 100% financing, but it is assumed to be available here for purposes of illustration.) MR has $0 equity in the house, but still has an equity of redemption. Five years later the house has appreciated to a market value of $110,000, and MR has paid the principal on the mortgage note down to $90,000. MR, therefore, has $20,000 equity in the house. Needing cash, MR obtains a $15,000 loan from ME–2 secured by a second mortgage on the house. After this transaction MR has $5,000 equity.

The preceding illustration demonstrates the general circumstances upon which the home equity loan market has developed. A home equity loan may consist of just one advance of a certain amount as in the illustration or involve a line of credit contemplating a series of advances over time. *See* Ch. 4, pp. 71–79 (discussing future advances). Tax considerations, i.e., the deductibility of interest paid, have fueled the popularity of home equity loans. *See* Ch. 3, pp. 48–49 (noting significance of tax considerations).

3. Risk and Rate

Junior mortgage loans involve a relatively high risk because the secondary lender's security interest extends only to the value of the land in excess of prior liens. *See* Ch. 9, pp. 175–176 (discussing general principles of priority and recording statutes). Hence, lenders generally make junior mortgage loans for a shorter term and at a higher interest rate than first mortgage loans.

Illustration: Assume the same facts as in the immediately preceding illustration except that

MR fails to pay the loans to ME–1 and ME–2. Both mortgagees foreclose, and sale of the house produces $100,000 after expenses. ME–1 receives $90,000, the unpaid balance on the first mortgage loan. ME–2 receives $10,000. In reality, ME–2's $15,000 second mortgage loan was only partially secured. *See* Ch. 10, pp. 205–206 (discussing disbursement of foreclosure sale proceeds and deficiency judgment).

B.   BEYOND THE BASICS/WRAPAROUND MORTGAGES

The wraparound mortgage is a relatively recent innovation in secondary financing. This financing device can be used either to derive additional funds from mortgaged real estate or to finance the purchase of such property. In either case, the wraparound mortgage is like a typical second mortgage in that it attaches to realty already encumbered by a mortgage. Its unique feature is that the face amount of the wraparound mortgage is equal to the amount actually disbursed to the mortgagor plus the unpaid balance of the prior encumbrance. The mortgagor's payments on the wraparound mortgage, therefore, cover both the money advanced under the wraparound mortgage and the amounts due on the first mortgage. The wraparound mortgagee simply takes a portion of the payment it receives and makes the necessary payment on the original mortgage.

The interest rate on the face amount of the wraparound mortgage is generally higher than the rate on the existing mortgage. The result is that the wraparound mortgagee receives a higher than stated interest rate on the money actually advanced. This is because it collects an interest differential on the first mortgage payments as they pass through its hands in addition to interest on the funds it disbursed. At the same time, the wraparound mortgagor pays less interest than would have accrued on alternative forms of financing.

Illustration: Several years ago MR mortgaged an office building to ME–1 as security for a $1,000,000 loan at 9% interest per annum. MR has paid the mortgage loan down to $700,000 and now desires to get the $300,000 "equity" out of the project. (In this illustration it is assumed that the office building has had a constant value of $1,000,000 and that 100% financing is available.) MR could refinance by borrowing $1,000,000 at the current interest rate of 12%, paying off the first mortgage and using the $300,000 as MR desires. As an alternative, MR could obtain a conventional second mortgage loan of $300,000 at the current interest rate of 15%. MR, however, would like to avoid the significant increase in interest rate that would occur by use of either alternative. MR, therefore, obtains a wraparound mortgage loan from W–ME in the amount of $1,000,000 at 11% interest. W–ME disburses only $300,000 to MR, but receives payments from MR covering both the $300,000 advanced and the unpaid balance of the first mortgage, all at 11% interest. W–ME passes the payments on the first mortgage to ME–1 after removing the interest differential (2%). W–ME thereby receives 11% interest on the $300,000 advanced and 2% on the $700,000 balance on the first loan, an overall interest rate well in excess of the stated rate of 11%. At the same time MR pays only 11% on the $1,000,000, 1% below the current interest rate on first mortgage loans.

Illustration: O owns a farm subject to a first mortgage in favor of ME–1. MR purchases the farm from O. MR assumes the first mortgage and executes a wraparound mortgage to O in the amount of the purchase price less the down payment. This transaction is a purchase money wraparound mortgage. It is structured and administered the same as the wraparound mortgage described in the immediately preceding illustration.

VII. FEDERAL GOVERNMENT IN-VOLVEMENT IN FINANCING PROCESS

Since the Depression, Congress has made numerous attempts to improve housing conditions in this country. Its activity in this area has had a considerable impact on the mortgage market. This section discusses the federal government's involvement in the financing process via housing subsidies, mortgage insurance, secondary mortgage market support institutions, and various legislative measures.

A. HOUSING SUBSIDIES

Some Congressional action in the real estate finance area is designed to produce more and better housing for low and moderate income families through housing subsidies administered by the Department of Housing and Urban Development. The form of the subsidy varies greatly from program to program.

B. MORTGAGE INSURANCE AND GUARANTY PROGRAMS

A less direct but equally significant form of government involvement in the real estate financing process is found in the federal mortgage insurance and guaranty programs administered by the Federal Housing Administration (FHA) and the Department of Veterans Affairs (VA). These programs encourage private institutional lenders to make residential mortgage loans to borrowers who otherwise might not qualify. This is accomplished by insuring or guarantying mortgagees against loss on certain residential loans. In essence, the insurance or guaranty takes the place of a large down-payment.

Mortgage loans that are insured or guaranteed by FHA or VA are termed "FHA mortgages" or "VA mortgages" respectively. All other mortgage loans are referred to as "conventional mortgages" whether or not they are covered by private mortgage insurance.

For many years, FHA and VA were required to set a periodically adjusted maximum insurable interest rate for qualifying loans. Because this interest rate was consistently below the current conventional mortgage loan interest rate, lenders assessed a charge for making an FHA or VA mortgage loan. The charge, expressed in terms of discount points, varied depending upon the difference at the time between the conventional loan interest rate and the FHA and VA maximum insurable interest rate. *See* Ch. 4, p. 80 (discussing discount points).

In late 1983, however, Congress eliminated the maximum insurable interest rate system for FHA mortgages, thereby allowing the interest rate for such loans to fluctuate with changes in the mortgage money market as does the interest rate for conventional loans. Pub.L. No. 98–181, § 404 (1983). In 1992, pursuant to Congressional authorization, VA also stopped establishing an interest rate ceiling for its mortgages. Pub. L. No. 102–547, § 10 (1992).

Although FHA and VA mortgages are similar, they differ in at least three important ways. First, FHA mortgage loans may be obtained by members of the general public. VA mortgage loans are available only to veterans. Second, FHA insures eligible mortgage loans. VA generally issues a guaranty of partial repayment. VA borrowers, therefore, do not pay mortgage insurance premiums as do FHA borrowers. However, VA borrowers generally must pay a funding fee. Third, FHA regulations require the borrower to make a small down payment. VA regulations generally do not require one.

Private companies also have entered the field of mortgage insurance. These private mortgage insurers typically cover twenty or twenty-five percent of the unpaid mortgage debt. They became popular with lenders largely by reason of their ability to process applications for mortgage insurance in a more efficient manner than either FHA or VA. Today private mortgage insurance companies dominate the mortgage insurance business.

The growth of private mortgage insurance made ninety and ninety-five percent conventional home mortgage loans available. For many years institutional lenders were prohibited by regulation from making such high loan-to-value conventional loans. Lending institutions, however, are now generally authorized to do so, but certain types of lenders must obtain private mortgage insurance on certain kinds of high loan-to-value conventional mortgage loans in order to cover the increased risk.

C. SECONDARY MORTGAGE MARKET SUPPORT INSTITUTIONS

Congress also has created several institutions designed to maintain a national secondary market for residential mortgages. The policy underlying this secondary mortgage market approach is that the support institutions can promote the even distribution of real estate investment capital throughout the country by buying mortgages from originators and selling them to investors. Distinguish the secondary mortgage market which involves the sale of first mortgages from the separate concept of secondary financing, addressed earlier this chapter, which involves the creation of junior mortgages on already encumbered land. *See* pp. 28–33 (discussing secondary financing).

The institutions charged with responsibility for maintaining a viable secondary mortgage market are the Federal National Mortgage Association (FNMA or Fannie Mae), the Government National Mortgage Association (GNMA or Ginnie Mae) and the Federal Home Loan Mortgage Corporation (FHLMC or Freddie Mac.) Each organization plays a slightly different role in this loosely constructed system.

Created near the end of the Depression, FNMA is the oldest element of the secondary mortgage market. Originally part of FHA, it is now privately owned, but subject to considerable governmental regulation and control. FNMA buys and sells FHA, VA, and conventional mortgages in order to improve the nationwide distribution of investment capital available for residential mortgage financing. FNMA is active in issuing mortgage-backed securities.

GNMA, a 1968 spinoff from FNMA, is a government owned entity within the Department of Housing and Urban Development. GNMA engages in a variety of special assistance activities. It also is involved in the secondary mortgage market via special mortgage investment programs such as the "pass-through" mortgage-backed securities program discussed earlier in this chapter. *See* pp. 27–28 (discussing mortgage-backed securities).

FHLMC is a privately owned corporation heavily regulated by the federal government. It was created in 1970 to establish a viable secondary mortgage market for conventional residential mortgages. FHLMC performs this function in good part by assembling pools of conventional mortgages and selling securities backed by these pooled mortgages. It also may acquire FHA and VA mortgages.

D. OTHER GOVERNMENT INVOLVEMENT

Over the years Congress has enacted laws on a variety of other real estate finance subjects. The following legislative measures have had an impact on the mortgage market.

1. Truth in Lending Act of 1968

The Truth in Lending Act (15 U.S.C.A. § 1601 *et seq.*) requires lenders to disclose financing costs and terms to prospective borrowers. As a general rule, Truth in Lending applies only to consumer credit transactions involving $25,000 or less. Business or commercial loans for any amount are not covered.

Many real estate credit transactions are governed by Truth in Lending. Although business or commercial real estate loans are, of course, exempt, the Act applies to consumer real estate loans regardless of amount. The $25,000 ceiling was removed from this type of transaction so that the average home-buyer is protected when embarking upon the only large-scale financing arrangement that person may ever enter.

As a general matter, the creditor in a standard real estate credit transaction must make the usual disclosure for closed-end transactions including a statement of the amount financed, the finance charge, and the annual percentage rate. Significant differences exist, however, between its disclosure obligations and those of a creditor in a non-real estate transaction. First, the items to be included in computing the finance charge differ. Second, the real estate creditor must state whether the mortgage loan may be assumed. Third, in certain real estate credit transactions the borrower has a right to rescind that must be disclosed. If the transaction creates a lien on the debtor's principal dwelling that secures a non-acquisition or non-construction loan, the consumer may rescind the transaction within three business days after closing or after the rescission right and other material matters are disclosed, whichever is later.

The Truth in Lending Act was amended in 1994 to address problems associated with closed-end home equity loans that bear a high interest rate. *See* pp. 29–30 (discussing home equity loans). These amendments added special disclosure requirements and substantive prohibitions designed to protect borrowers who enter such loan transactions.

2. Interstate Land Sales Full Disclosure Act of 1968

Congress enacted the Interstate Land Sales Full Disclosure Act (15 U.S.C.A. § 1701 *et seq.*) to eliminate the use of fraudulent or misleading practices in the marketing of certain types of raw land. The Act applies to developers who sell or lease unimproved subdivision lots as part of a common promotional plan in interstate commerce or through the mails. Numerous exemptions, both full and partial, are available. For example, developers of subdivisions that include less than twenty-five lots are totally exempt from the Act. Developers of subdivisions containing less than one hundred lots are exempt from the Act's registration and disclosure provisions described below, but are still subject to the Act's antifraud provisions.

Nonexempt subdivision developers must disclose the material facts about the land being offered for sale. Disclosure is accomplished by filing a statement of record with the Office of Interstate Land Sales Registration in the Department of Housing and Urban Development and by delivering a property report to prospective purchasers. The statement of record must include certain specific information about the subdivision, the surrounding area, and the developer. The property report is a condensed more readable version of the statement of record.

The Act gives the purchaser certain remedies for the developer's failure to make proper disclosure. Rescission is available in two general instances. First, if the developer fails to give the purchaser a property report prior to the execution of a sales contract, the purchaser may rescind the contract within two years of its execution. Second, even if the purchaser is furnished with a property report before signing a sales contract, the purchaser may rescind the contract within seven days of its execution. (Frequently, the contract is an installment land contract. *See* Ch. 3, pp. 54–61 (analyzing installment land contract). If so, additional disclosure and rescission provisions of the Act apply.)

The purchaser also has the right to obtain specific performance, damages, or other appropriate relief from the developer for violations of the Act. Although the Act does not apply to lending institutions engaging in the normal course of their real estate financing activities, a lender may be liable for damages if it actively participates in a plan to sell or lease property covered by the Act.

3. National Flood Insurance Program

Over the years large amounts of federal disaster relief funds have been paid to flood victims. Unfortunately, a substantial portion of this money has been used to rebuild structures in the same high-risk location. This situation, coupled with the general unavailability of private flood insurance, led Congress to establish the National Flood Insurance Program in 1968 (42 U.S.C.A. § 4001 *et seq.*). The Program made federally subsidized flood insurance available to property owners in communities which established approved land use ordinances limiting construction in flood hazard areas.

Few communities responded voluntarily. Thus, the Flood Disaster Protection Act of 1973 was enacted. It made participation in the Program virtually mandatory by prohibiting federally regulated lending institutions from making loans secured by mortgages on structures in flood-prone areas unless the borrower obtained flood insurance. Because such insurance is available only in communities participating in the Program, cities and towns began to enact the required land use regulation. Soon flood insurance became available to property owners in most communities with flood-prone areas.

In the late 1970s, the Program was amended to eliminate the prohibition against making mortgage loans on flood plain property in a nonparticipating community. But by that time, the Program had taken hold throughout the country. Moreover, federally regulated lending institutions must still require mortgagors to obtain flood insurance on mortgaged structures in flood-prone areas when such insurance is available.

Due to deficiencies in the Program's structure and implementation, Congress enacted the National Flood Insurance Reform Act of 1994 to broaden and strengthen the Program in various ways. Pub. L. 103–325, Title 5 (1994). This measure obligates mortgage lenders to take certain steps to insure that flood insurance is obtained and maintained in appropriate cases.

The Program is administered by the Federal Insurance Administration. Formerly part of the Department of Housing and Urban Development, this regulatory body now operates within the Federal Emergency Management Agency.

4. Real Estate Settlement Procedures Act of 1974

The Real Estate Settlement Procedures Act (12 U.S.C.A. § 2601 *et seq.*), known as RESPA, is basically a disclosure statute designed to protect homebuyers or homeowners from the imposition of unanticipated, unwarranted, or excessive loan closing costs. RESPA covers all "federally related mortgage loans." Most residential mortgage loans fall within this category. As a general rule, RESPA applies when an institutional lender makes a loan that is secured by a mortgage, first or junior, on one-to-four-family residential real estate.

When a lending institution receives an application for a federally related mortgage loan it must provide the prospective borrower with: (1) a copy of "Settlement Costs," a booklet prepared by the Department of Housing and Urban Development (HUD) and (2) a good faith estimate of all loan closing costs. Then, at or before the closing, the lender or whoever else conducts the closing must provide both the borrower and the seller with a completed HUD–1 Uniform Settlement Statement setting forth the precise amount of all closing costs. The lender may not impose any fee or charge for the preparation or submission of any of the documents required by the Act.

RESPA also requires that lenders disclose to applicants for federally related mortgage loans whether the servicing of the loan may be transferred. Further, the borrower must be notified of any transfer of servicing. *See* pp. 17–18 (analyzing differences among originating/servicing/holding and discussing transfer of servicing rights).

In addition to these disclosure requirements, RESPA includes significant substantive provisions. One portion of the Act is designed to eliminate kickbacks and unearned fees. Another section limits the amount that a lender may require a borrower to place in an escrow account for the payment of casualty insurance premiums and property taxes. *See* Ch. 4, pp. 92–93 (discussing escrow accounts).

5. Home Mortgage Disclosure Act of 1975

As noted earlier in this chapter, one aspect of the mortgage lender's risk is whether the land offered as security is of sufficient market value to satisfy the debt in the event the borrower defaults. *See* pp. 24–25 (discussing application and commitment process). Some lending institutions may consider all property located in a designated area of the community they serve as inadequate or high-risk collateral and, hence, unacceptable as security for a standard mortgage loan. This form of lending discrimination is known as "redlining" because of the manner in which the designated areas may have been identified on a map of the community. Typically, the alleged redlined areas are older, integrated, middle-class or lower middle-class neighborhoods.

The Home Mortgage Disclosure Act (12 U.S.C.A. § 2801 *et seq.*) is designed to identify and help eliminate redlining. The Act requires financial institutions located in metropolitan areas to disclose detailed information about their residential mortgage loans by reference to census tract. Such lenders also must report about their loan applications. Although the Act makes redlining more visible, it does not provide a penalty for such activity. Congress apparently decided to rely on community pressure to force lenders to act responsibly in this regard. However, the Community Reinvestment Act of 1977 (12 U.S.C.A. § 2901 *et seq.*) does place an obligation on regulatory agencies to determine whether a financial institution adequately serves its community and to take this factor into consideration when examining the institution or reviewing an application for a merger, a new branch, or other special action.

6. Comprehensive Environmental Response, Compensation, and Liability Act of 1980

Congress enacted the Comprehensive Environmental Response, Compensation, and Liability Act of 1980 (42 U.S.C.A. § 9601 *et seq.*) (CERCLA) in an attempt to remedy environmental damage caused by hazardous waste sites. CERCLA, commonly called "Superfund", makes owners and operators of hazardous waste facilities liable for cleanup costs. CERCLA expressly excludes from this obligation anyone "who, without participating in the management of a ... facility, holds indicia of ownership primarily to protect his security interest in the ... facility." 42 U.S.C.A. § 9601(20)(A). Notwithstanding this provision, mortgagees, particularly those who take possession of a hazardous waste site upon default or acquire such a site at foreclosure or by deed-in-lieu of foreclosure, face potential liability for cleanup costs as an owner or operator under CERCLA.

In 1996, Congress amended CERCLA to clarify and restrict the meaning of "participating in the management of a ... facility" and to limit the risk of liability for foreclosing mortgagees. Moreover, Congress provided that an Environmental Protection Agency final rule circumscribing lender liability, previously invalidated by court decision, "shall be deemed to have been validly issued...." Pub. L. No. 104–208 §§ 2502, 2504.

CHAPTER 3

REAL ESTATE FINANCING DEVICES

I. MORTGAGE

The mortgage is the most common means of real estate financing. It is both relatively uncomplicated and flexible; most states have a statutory mortgage form that may be expanded as the parties desire. In addition, because the mortgage is a time-tested financing device, the rights and obligations of the parties are generally well established within each state. *See* Ch. 1, pp. 1–10 (discussing mortgage concept, historical development of mortgage, and mortgage theories); Appendices A, B, and C (presenting sample mortgage forms).

A. PURCHASE MONEY MORTGAGE

The purchase money mortgage is an important mortgage species. It has been traditionally defined as a mortgage taken by the seller of real estate to secure payment of part of the purchase price. A mortgage given a third party lender as security for a loan used to acquire the mortgaged property is now also generally considered to be a purchase money mortgage.

47

Illustration: O contracts to sell O's house to MR for $100,000. O conveys the house to MR. MR pays O $10,000 in cash and gives O a promissory note for $90,000 secured by a mortgage on the house. The mortgage is a traditional purchase money mortgage.

Illustration: O contracts to sell O's farm to MR for $80,000. MR has only $20,000 cash so MR obtains a $60,000 loan from ME. MR uses the cash and the loan proceeds to pay O for the farm. O conveys the farm to MR who immediately executes a mortgage on the farm to ME to secure repayment of the loan. The mortgage is generally considered a purchase money mortgage.

It is necessary to identify the purchase money mortgage for two reasons: (1) it is the type of mortgage transaction with which the home buying public is most familiar; and (2) it receives a preferred lien priority position. *See* Ch. 9, pp. 177–179 (analyzing priority of purchase money mortgage).

B.   TAX CONSIDERATIONS

A thorough examination of the tax consequences of a mortgage transaction is beyond the scope of this book. However, the significance of federal income tax considerations in real estate finance at least must be mentioned. As a general rule, the mortgagor may take an income tax deduction for interest paid on the mortgage loan, and the mortgagee must report the interest received as ordinary income. That is about as far as it goes in most residential mortgage transactions. In commercial situations, however, tax matters are often of paramount importance. In fact, some of the financing devices discussed in this chapter were developed in large part as vehicles for tax planning. It is, therefore, imperative that one entering any real estate financing transaction ascertain its tax consequences at the outset, particularly in this era of constant tax reform.

II. DEED OF TRUST

The deed of trust is a real estate financing device used in many jurisdictions. It is a tripartite arrangement in which a landowner-borrower conveys realty to a trustee as security for the payment of an obligation owed a lender. The chief practical distinction between the deed of trust and the mortgage is the manner of enforcement available if the borrower fails to repay the underlying obligation. The deed of trust provides for foreclosure by power of sale; the mortgage usually does not. Consequently, the deed of trust is popular in those states in which out of court sale is the prevalent method of foreclosure. *See* Ch. 10, pp. 206–211 (discussing foreclosure by power of sale).

The deed of trust is generally treated as a mortgage with a power of sale provision. The principles of mortgage law discussed in this book, therefore, are for the most part applicable to the deed of trust.

III. EQUITABLE MORTGAGES

An equitable mortgage arises whenever a court finds that an apparent nonsecurity transaction is in reality a security arrangement. There are many situations in which this may occur. Thus the maxim: "If a transaction resolves itself into a security, whatever may be its form and whatever name the parties may choose to give it, it is, in equity, a mortgage." Those transactions that commonly spawn equitable mortgages are treated in this section.

A. ABSOLUTE DEED GIVEN AS SECURITY

A lender occasionally will require a borrower to convey property to the lender upon the understanding that the lender will hold title as security for the debt. This type of transaction is used by some lenders in an attempt to eliminate the debtor's equity of redemption and thereby avoid foreclosure. *See* Ch. 1, p. 5 (discussing preservation/clogging equity of redemption). If, however, the debtor can prove that a deed absolute on its face was intended as a security device, courts will find that an equitable mortgage was created and give the debtor an equity of redemption. Because of the strong public policy against irredeemable mortgages, courts generally do not consider the parol evidence rule and the Statute of Frauds to be obstacles to this result.

The problem of proof is, however, a difficult matter. The key is the intention of the parties, a question upon which direct testimony is invariably at odds. The courts, therefore, look to several objective factors that include: the parties' prior negotiations, their relative bargaining positions, the adequacy of consideration, and who is in possession of the property. Courts usually require clear and convincing evidence of intent to create a security arrangement.

Illustration: O, a landowner who desperately needs money, asks L for a mortgage loan. L offers to give O $30,000 if O will deed O's property worth $50,000 to L. O agrees upon the condition O can continue to live on the property without paying rent. The transaction is consummated. One year later O tenders $30,000 plus interest to L and requests a deed to the property. L refuses, claiming complete ownership. O's financial difficulty, O's request for a loan, the amount O received compared to the value of the property, and O's continued possession indicate that the parties intended the absolute deed as security for a loan. The transaction, therefore, constitutes an equitable mortgage, and O can redeem the land by paying the debt.

B. CONDITIONAL SALE

The conditional sale consists of an absolute deed coupled with an option or contract to repurchase. Again the issue is whether the transaction was intended as a security device. The same evidentiary factors considered in conjunction with the absolute deed are relevant here.

Illustration: O, owner of a house worth $100,-000, asks L for a mortgage loan. L requires and receives a deed to the house. L gives O $60,000, and the parties enter a contract in which O agrees to repurchase the house for $70,000 within one year. The inadequacy of consideration and O's obligation to repurchase indicate that this conditional sale was intended as a security transaction. Even if O fails to repurchase within the time period specified, courts will grant O an equity of redemption that L can cut off only by foreclosure.

C. NEGATIVE PLEDGE

A lender may require a borrower to agree not to encumber or convey certain of the borrower's realty until a specified loan is repaid. This type of transaction is called a negative pledge. It has been employed when the property in question is already encumbered and the lender either legally cannot take a second mortgage or chooses not to do so as a matter of customer relations. A negative pledge also has been utilized by lenders who, for local procedural reasons, wish to have the alternative of selecting between secured and unsecured creditor status depending upon which position is more advantageous from a debt collection standpoint.

The generally accepted view is that a negative pledge does not create an equitable mortgage. The affirmative intent to create a security interest cannot reasonably be inferred from a negative promise. There is, however, some authority to the contrary.

Illustration: O owns a house. O obtains a loan from Bank. Bank does not take a mortgage on O's house, but wants O to retain the house free from other liens so that O's general financial position is not weakened. Consequently, Bank makes the loan upon the condition that O not convey or further encumber the house until the loan is repaid. If O conveys or further encumbers the house, Bank may have the right to declare its entire loan due, but it has no lien to foreclose. Courts generally refuse to impose an equitable mortgage in Bank's favor on the ground there was no intent to create a security device. *But see* Coast Bank v. Minderhout (Cal.1964) (holding that under circumstances equitable mortgage arose from negative pledge).

D. VENDOR'S AND VENDEE'S LIENS

Breach of a real estate contract may give rise to a lien in favor of either the vendor or the vendee as equity requires. An equitable lien generally may be imposed for the benefit of a vendor who passed legal title to the vendee, but did not receive the entire purchase price. In some states, however, the vendor's lien is not recognized unless it was expressly reserved. An equitable lien also may be imposed in favor of a vendee who paid part of the purchase price, but did not receive title because the vendor breached the contract. In either case, the lien is unlike the other types of equitable mortgages discussed in this section in that it arises by operation of law to prevent injustice, not by virtue of the judicially determined intent of the parties.

Illustration: S owns a parcel of land. S enters a binding real estate contract to convey the land to P for consideration of $10,000 in cash and a $5,000 promissory note payable thirty days after closing. P gives S the cash and the note, and S deeds the land to P. At the end of thirty days, P fails to pay the note. In most states, S receives a $5,000 equitable vendor's lien on the land. In some jurisdictions, however, S does not receive a lien unless it was expressly reserved.

Illustration: S owns a parcel of land. S enters a binding real estate contract to convey the land to P. P makes a $3,000 down payment. S breaches the contract by not having a marketable title as agreed. P has a $3,000 equitable vendee's lien on the property.

IV. INSTALLMENT LAND CONTRACT
A. TRADITIONAL CONTRACT APPROACH

In a country where buying on credit is a way of life, it is to be expected that a financing device providing for the long term installment purchase of land would be developed. The installment land contract, referred to in some states as a contract for deed, fits the bill. It gives the purchaser possession of the land immediately, but allows the purchaser to pay the sale price in monthly installments over a number of years. The seller, on the other hand, is not obligated to convey legal title until all payments have been made. Moreover, the installment land contract features a forfeiture provision to the effect that upon default the seller may recover possession, keep payments received as liquidated damages, and retain title free from any rights the purchaser had under the contract. This type of agreement for the sale of land differs from the standard real estate contract that establishes the rights of the parties pending a relatively expeditious transfer of title.

Because the parties to an installment land contract stand in the same relative position occupied by a mortgagor and a mortgagee, one might logically conclude that the forfeiture provision is really an illegal attempt to clog the purchaser's equity of redemption. *See* Ch. 1, p. 5 (discussing preservation/clogging equity of redemption). This conclusion would be correct if courts applied mortgage law to this financing device. The installment land contract, however, developed under contract law in which freedom of contract was the guiding principle. For this reason, the installment land contract was enforced as written, forfeiture and all.

Treatment of the installment land contract as a contract, not a mortgage, caused it to become a popular means of real estate financing. It remains so today in part because most jurisdictions still recognize the traditional contract approach, at least in limited circumstances.

Under the traditional view, the installment land contract seller enjoys the right to recover the land upon default and keep all payments made. Foreclosure of the purchaser's interest is not required. In addition, the seller obtains a tax advantage by spreading the capital gain over the number of years covered by the contract. (The seller generally may receive the same tax treatment by taking back a promissory note for part of the sale price secured by a purchase money mortgage.) Purchasers are not deterred from entering installment land contracts primarily because a low down-payment is required and many costs associated with mortgage financing are avoided.

Illustration: S owns land that P desires to purchase. Because mortgage financing funds are scarce and P cannot make a large down payment, P is unable to obtain a purchase money mortgage loan from an institutional lender. S and P, therefore, enter an installment land contract that provides for a twenty-year term with equal monthly payments of $100. P takes possession and makes payments for fifteen years. Because P is ill and out of work, P misses the first two payments in the sixteenth year. S declares a forfeiture. Under the traditional contract approach, S can terminate P's interest, retake possession, and retain all money payments made ($18,000 out of the total $24,000 purchase price).

B. PROTECTING THE PURCHASER

There is a strong judicial and legislative trend to devise methods of protecting the purchaser from the harsh results produced by the traditional contract approach to installment land contracts. The protection afforded has taken a variety of forms. In some jurisdictions more than one protective method is employed.

1. Period of Grace Statutes

In some states, statutes give the purchaser a period of grace to cure default before forfeiture can occur. Under these statutes, the seller is often required to follow certain procedures for notifying the purchaser and terminating the purchaser's interest.

2. Compelling Equities View

The courts in a growing number of states have demonstrated a willingness to examine individual installment land contracts to determine whether forfeiture is appropriate under the circumstances. This approach has been labeled the compelling equities view because forfeiture will be enforced unless the purchaser can establish reasons why it would be unjust to do so. In order to determine the appropriateness of the forfeiture in question, courts following the compelling equities view inquire into the extent of the default, the reason for default, and the forfeiture involved in comparison to the purchase price.

Illustration: Assume the same facts as in the immediately preceding illustration. The default was slight, of recent origin, and not willful. Further, the amount to be forfeited was apparently unrelated to S's actual damages. Courts in states following the compelling equities view, therefore, would not enforce the forfeiture as written. The form of relief may vary; reinstating the contract upon the payment of the overdue installments, imposing a period of grace before forfeiture, or requiring foreclosure of P's interest are three likely possibilities.

3. Equitable Mortgage View

A few states recognize the installment land contract as a disguised mortgage and give purchasers an equity of redemption after default. This equitable mortgage view is significantly different from the compelling equities approach. All defaulting purchasers, not just those with substantial equities, are entitled to a foreclosure sale of their interest in the property.

4. Restitution

In some jurisdictions the courts give defaulting purchasers restitution, the right to recover payments made under the installment land contract to the extent the payments exceed the seller's actual damages.

5. Waiver

Courts everywhere may employ the doctrine of waiver to grant the purchaser relief. A seller who has accepted late payments may be estopped to declare a forfeiture unless the seller gives reasonable notice of the intent to assert the seller's contract rights in future cases of default.

C. ENCUMBERING PURCHASER'S
INTEREST

The purchaser under an installment land contract holds an interest in the land that may be encumbered. *See* Ch. 5, pp. 97–98 (discussing mortgageable interests). If the installment land contract purchaser mortgages the purchaser's interest and then defaults on the underlying installment land contract, controversy often arises between the seller and the mortgagee. The conflict centers on two issues. First, must the seller notify the mortgagee before terminating the purchaser's interest? Second, what are the mortgagee's rights after the purchaser's default?

With respect to the first issue, the general rule is that the mortgagee is entitled to notice of the impending termination of the purchaser's interest only if the seller has received notice of the mortgagee's encumbrance. There is, however, a split of authority as to when the seller is on notice of the mortgagee's interest. Some courts hold that the seller must have actual notice of the mortgage. These courts reason that recordation of the mortgage is not sufficient notice to the seller because recording statutes are designed to impart notice to subsequent purchasers, not prior interest holders. Other courts hold that the seller need only have constructive notice of the mortgage. These courts conclude that recordation of the mortgage imparts such notice to the seller because the seller should check the records before extinguishing another's interest. This latter approach is closely analogous to the requirements imposed on a senior mortgagee who seeks to foreclose junior interest holders. *See* Ch. 10, pp. 200–202 (discussing parties defendant in judicial foreclosure).

Assuming that the mortgagee is entitled to notice of the impending termination of the purchaser's interest, a question arises concerning its rights in the land. In a few states the mortgagee apparently is permitted to pay the seller the balance of the contract price and take title to the property. This approach, however, unjustly enriches the mortgagee to the extent the value of the land exceeds the total amount remaining unpaid on the installment land contract and the mortgage. Courts in other jurisdictions treat the mortgagee as a second lienor of the fee and the seller as a first lienor. In these states, the mortgagee, therefore, may either: (1) pay off the seller and be subrogated to the seller's rights, thus becoming the holder of both the first and second liens on the property, or (2) force a sale of the property and satisfy the mortgage lien out of the sale proceeds that remain after the vendor's lien is satisfied. *See* Ch. 8, pp. 169–172 (discussing equity of redemption); Ch. 10, p. 205 (treating disbursement of sale proceeds). Under either alternative, the mortgagee is entitled to recover the value of its lien, but no more. This treatment of the seller and mortgagee as first and second lienors is consistent with the overall movement toward treating installment land contracts as mortgages and, hence, can be expected to gain support.

D. ENCUMBERING SELLER'S INTEREST

The installment land contract seller also holds an interest in the property that may be encumbered. *See* Ch. 5, pp. 97–98 (discussing mortgageable interests). This is commonly accomplished by the seller executing both an assignment of the right to receive payments under the contract and a conveyance of, or a mortgage on, the legal title the seller retains. Controversy exists regarding the means by which the holder of such security may insure lien priority over subsequent creditors of the seller. Some courts require the security interest holder to file a financing statement under Article 9 of the Uniform Commercial Code (UCC) to perfect the holder's security interest in personalty (right to receive payments) and also to make an appropriate recording in the land records to impart notice of the holder's security interest in realty. Other courts, however, require only a recording in the land records. Conversely, some authorities argue that filing a UCC financing statement should be enough.

Sometimes an installment land contract seller pledges as security just the right to receive contract payments. There is general agreement that a UCC filing is all that is necessary in such cases.

V. LEASE

A. VARIETIES

The lease plays an important part in real estate finance, particularly in the area of commercial development. Leases may be used in a variety of ways, frequently in conjunction with another financing device.

1. Ground Lease

A ground lease is a long-term lease employed to acquire raw land for commercial development. Its principal advantages to the lessee over outright purchase are that little or no "up-front" capital is needed and rental payments are tax deductible. The ground lease and the improvements to be constructed on the property are then mortgaged to finance development. The concept of the leasehold mortgage is discussed later in this chapter.

Illustration: D desires to develop a shopping center on O's unimproved land. D and O enter a ground lease for a ninety-nine year term. Other lease provisions are as follows: D will complete the shopping center within a certain time period; ground rent is not payable until the center is completed; D must pay all taxes, utilities, insurance, and maintenance on the property; and all improvements belong to D until the term of the ground lease expires when they go with the land to O. D then obtains mortgage financing for the project. As indicated in this illustration, the tenant under a typical ground lease is responsible for taxes, insurance, and maintenance. When a lease contains a provision of this type it is said to be a "net" lease because the rental income to the lessor is not reduced by payment of operating expenses.

2. Space Lease

The financial success of many developments depends upon the developer's ability to rent the store, apartment, or office space in the project. Space leases play such a significant role in the success of shopping centers and office buildings that permanent mortgage lenders generally require the developer to obtain space lease commitments from a number of substantial tenants before construction begins.

3. Acquisition Lease

In many instances a business will utilize a long-term lease to acquire improved commercial property for expansion of its operations. Because this type of lease is employed as an alternative to the purchase or construction of new facilities, it is called an acquisition lease in this book.

The attractions of the acquisition lease to the lessee are much the same as that of the ground lease: small front-end cash outlay and tax deductible rental payments. These attractions, however, are somewhat stronger in the case of the acquisition lease because of the generally higher value of the leasehold being acquired.

The acquisition lease is usually a "net" lease and also often contains an escalator clause that adjusts the amount of rent to keep pace with inflation. The Consumer Price Index maintained by the Department of Labor is an economic indicator frequently used to accomplish this result. The acquisition lease, of course, is not the only type of lease in which escalator clauses are found.

B. LEASEHOLD MORTGAGE

A lessee may mortgage the leasehold estate. *See* Ch. 5, pp. 97–98 (discussing mortgageable interests). Although the discussion of mortgage law in this book concerns fee mortgages, it is generally applicable to leasehold mortgages. However, additional issues arise when a mortgagee accepts a leasehold as security.

1. Nature of Security

Leasehold mortgage financing involves an inherent drawback; the mortgagee's security interest is subject to the rights of the lessor-owner. Consequently, many mortgagees will not make a leasehold mortgage loan unless the lessor subordinates the fee to the mortgage. *See* Ch. 9, p. 184 (discussing subordination of fee to leasehold mortgage). The lessor may be hesitant to do so because subordination impairs the lessor's ability to borrow on the reversion and subjects the fee to sale upon the lessee's default. Nevertheless, important financial factors may cause the lessor to take this step. Subordination of the fee usually enables the lessee to obtain financing that is otherwise unavailable. Hence, the lessor may demand higher rent and receive property of greater value at the end of the lease term.

2. Lease Provisions

When the lease and leasehold mortgage are successive steps in one financing package, the lease is drafted to meet the requirements of the proposed mortgagee. If, however, the lease predates the mortgage negotiations, it usually is amended as specified by the mortgagee. In either case, leasehold mortgage financing presents unique problems. The areas of greatest concern to the mortgagee are treated in the following subsections of this chapter. A discussion of many other matters important to the mortgagee is outside the purview of this work.

a. Term

The lease term should be at least as long as the mortgage term, otherwise the security will cease to exist before the mortgage debt is paid.

b. Transfer

As a general rule, the lessee may encumber, assign, and sublet the leasehold unless the lease or a statute provides otherwise. The lessee's ability to encumber the estate is obviously essential to the creation of a leasehold mortgage. The lease, therefore, should not limit the lessee's rights in this regard and preferably should specifically permit the lessee to mortgage the leasehold. Also, because the mortgagee may acquire the leasehold upon foreclosure, the lease should not impose restrictions on assignment or subleasing, at least as against the mortgagee.

c. Default

Termination of the lease extinguishes the lease-hold mortgage. Thus, the mortgagee usually requires that it receive notice of and the right to cure the tenant's defaults under the lease.

C. SALE AND LEASEBACK

The lease also constitutes part of an important financing vehicle known as the sale and leaseback. This financing technique is enormously complex in its many variations. The scope of this book permits presentation of only the basic concept.

A typical sale and leaseback is structured as follows: the owner of improved commercial property sells the property to an investor who simultaneously leases it back to the seller on a long-term, "net" basis. The reasons behind this rather puzzling transaction lie in the intricacies of business finance and federal income tax law.

The basic business finance factors are not difficult to comprehend. The owner of the property is able to obtain more capital from the sale and lease-back arrangement than from mortgage financing. Although mortgage loans usually are subject to loan-to-value limits, the sale aspect of the sale and leaseback may produce almost 100% of the current fair market value of the property. Investors are willing to provide such financing because they generally receive a higher rate of return from a sale and leaseback than from a mortgage loan. Furthermore, the return is not limited by usury statutes that apply only to loan transactions.

The general tax ramifications of a sale and leaseback are also easily understood. The seller-lessee realizes a capital gain or loss on the sale of the property and may deduct all rental payments. (Recall that only the interest portion of mortgage loan payments may be deducted.) The investor-lessor receives ordinary income in the form of rental payments, but may claim depreciation deductions on the property.

The elaborate plans of the parties, however, will collapse if the transaction is found to be a security arrangement rather than a genuine sale and leaseback. Factors that tend to indicate that the transaction is really a disguised mortgage are similar to those mentioned in the section of this chapter on equitable mortgages. *See* pp. 50–52 (discussing absolute deed given as security and conditional sale). They include the following: the seller-lessee is financially embarrassed; the parties have not dealt at arm's length; the sale price is inadequate; the transaction, if a mortgage loan, would be usurious; and the seller-lessee is given an option to purchase for a nominal amount.

In the event the transaction is found to be a hidden security arrangement rather than a genuine sale and leaseback, disastrous consequences may result. First, the parties must readjust their tax positions to reflect reality and pay any resulting tax deficiencies. Second, a question of usury may arise.

Third, upon default the investor must terminate the "lessee's" interest in the property by utilizing foreclosure procedures rather than by declaring a forfeiture under the lease.

CHAPTER 4

UNDERLYING OBLIGATION

I. NECESSITY FOR UNDERLYING OBLIGATION

A mortgage is only security. It cannot exist without an underlying obligation. There is, however, no requirement that the mortgagor or anyone else be personally liable on the obligation. A mortgage transaction in which no person or institution has liability is known as a "nonrecourse" or "in rem" mortgage loan.

Illustration: MR executes a promissory note and a mortgage to ME. The note contains a provision that MR shall have no personal responsibility to pay the note and that ME's only remedy in event of default is to foreclose. The mortgage is valid because there is a "real" obligation that supports it.

Illustration: MR–1 executes a promissory note and a mortgage to ME. MR–1 conveys the mortgaged property to MR–2 "subject to" the mortgage. MR–2 does not assume personal responsibility to pay the note. ME then releases MR–1 from liability, but retains its rights under the mortgage. The mortgage continues unaffected by this transaction even though no one is personally liable on the note.

II. FORM OF OBLIGATION

A mortgage may secure any obligation that has an ascertainable monetary value. A court upon foreclosure must be able to determine the amount of the lien in order to properly disburse the sale proceeds.

> *Illustration*: ME owns ten acres of land and agrees to sell two acres to MR upon the condition that MR build a sewer to service the entire original tract. MR pays the full purchase price and executes a mortgage to ME to secure the required promise. The mortgage properly secures the promise to build the sewer. The obligation is one that can be reduced to a money equivalent. *See* Jeffrey Towers, Inc. v. Straus (N.Y.App.Div.1969).

Notwithstanding the generally accepted view stated above, some authority exists for the proposition that the underlying obligation need not be quantifiable in monetary terms. *See id.* This approach has been adopted primarily with respect to mortgages given as security for a promise to provide support for an elderly grantor-mortgagee.

The underlying obligation may be embodied in the mortgage itself, but is usually evidenced by a separate promissory note. The promissory note may be negotiable. *See* UCC § 3–104(a). A statement in the instrument that it is secured by a mortgage does not destroy its negotiability. *See* UCC § 3–

106(a). The note's negotiability is likewise unimpaired by its reference to the mortgage for rights as to prepayment or acceleration. *See* UCC § 3–106(b). If, however, the note incorporates terms of the mortgage for other purposes, it becomes a conditional promise and is thereby rendered nonnegotiable.

III. DESCRIPTION OF OBLIGATION

As between the mortgagor and the mortgagee, it is prudent, but not necessary, to describe the underlying obligation in the mortgage. A description of the obligation, however, is necessary to protect the mortgagee against subsequent purchasers and lienors. Although authorities disagree regarding what information is required to impart adequate notice of the obligation to third parties, the description should specify the obligation's form, amount, interest rate, execution date, and maturity date. The mortgagee, of course, must also record the mortgage to preserve its priority. *See* Ch. 9, pp. 175–176 (discussing recording statutes).

IV. FUTURE ADVANCES
A. THE BASIC CONCEPT

A mortgage may secure the repayment of funds that the mortgagee advances to the mortgagor in the future. In fact, many commonly used mortgage forms contain a future advances clause. Home equity loans, for example, frequently include such a provision. *See* Ch. 2, pp. 29–30 (discussing mortgagor's "equity" and home equity loan concept). The future advances clause also is an integral part of construction loan mortgages under which the lender advances funds as construction on the mortgaged property progresses.

A mortgage that covers future advances constitutes an executory agreement by the mortgagor that the mortgaged property stands as security for all funds advanced by the mortgagee. The arrangement is one transaction, not a series of independent loans. It is specifically so designed for the convenience and economic advantage of the parties. Thus, the lien of a mortgage for future advances arises as at the date of the execution of the mortgage, not when advances are made.

B. METHODS OF SECURING FUTURE ADVANCES

The parties generally provide for coverage of future advances by drafting the mortgage in either of two ways. One technique is to specify a present loan amount in excess of funds actually advanced. A second approach is to state the amount of the current debt and then provide that the mortgage secures future advances, with or without limit on the total amount secured. Both methods have been upheld by the courts, but the second alternative is more common.

C. OBLIGATORY/OPTIONAL DISTINCTION

A mortgagee who holds a properly recorded mortgage for future advances receives priority over parties who subsequently acquire an interest in the mortgaged property. *See* Ch. 9, pp. 175–176 (discussing recording statutes). Courts, however, sometimes limit the priority of a mortgage for future advances in order to preserve the marketability of the mortgaged property for subsequent encumbrance or sale. The necessity for limitation depends in large part upon whether the future advance is obligatory or optional.

1. Obligatory Future Advances

If a mortgagee is contractually obligated to make future advances, the lien for each advance has priority over any encumbrance that attaches to the property subsequent to the execution of the mortgage. This rule applies even when the mortgagee makes an advance with knowledge of an encumbrance that arose in the interim between the execution of the mortgage and the advance. No policy reason exists to change the principle that priority for future advances dates from the day the mortgage was executed. Because the mortgagor has the right to additional future advances, the mortgagor is not prejudiced by the fact that secondary financing on the property is probably unavailable from another lender.

Illustration: MR and ME enter a construction loan agreement that ME will advance funds up to a total of $1,000,000 as construction on the mortgaged property progresses. MR executes a $1,000,000 promissory note and a mortgage to ME who records the mortgage. ME advances $500,000 as construction progresses in accordance with the agreement. At that point MR borrows $200,000 from X and gives X a $200,000 promissory note secured by a mortgage on the same property. X records. ME knows of this lien, but because MR fully complies with the construction loan agreement, ME advances the remaining $500,000. ME has a first lien for $1,000,000 because it was obligated to advance the entire loan amount. X has a second lien for $200,000.

2. Optional Future Advances

Many mortgages for future advances provide that future advances are optional with the mortgagee. Mortgages for optional future advances are sometimes referred to as open-end mortgages.

a. *Priority Problems*

Controversy often arises regarding the priority of optional advances over encumbrances that attach to the mortgaged property subsequent to the execution of the mortgage. The outcome depends upon which of three possible fact patterns is presented: (1) The lien for optional future advances made *before* the attachment of a subsequent encumbrance clearly has priority under the fundamental principle of "prior in time, prior in right." *See* Ch. 9, pp. 175–176 (discussing recording statutes). (2) The lien for optional future advances made *after* the attachment of a subsequent encumbrance and *without notice* of that encumbrance also has priority on the theory that it arose at the date that the mortgage for future advances was executed. (3) The lien for optional future advances made *with notice* of the attachment of a subsequent encumbrance is generally postponed to the lien of the intervening encumbrance on the ground that the marketability of the mortgagor's land for subsequent encumbrance or sale would otherwise be virtually destroyed. If other lenders were unable to ensure the priority of their encumbrances over the lien of later optional future advances, they certainly would not make mortgage loans on the property. The mortgagor then would be left to the whim of the original mortgagee for additional financing. Likewise, it is improbable that potential purchasers would be willing to acquire the property subject to a mortgage arrangement that put the original mortgagee in such a dominant position.

b. *Notice Issue*

The "notice" limitation on the priority of optional future advances is clouded by disagreement over the type of notice required. There are two views on the subject. The generally accepted view is that the lien of an optional future advance loses priority to the lien of an intervening encumbrance only if the mortgagee has actual notice of the encumbrance when it makes the advance. Some states, however, postpone the lien of an optional future advance to the lien of an intervening encumbrance when the mortgagee has either actual or constructive notice of the encumbrance. In these jurisdictions recording the encumbrance imparts constructive notice of its existence to the mortgagee. This approach, however, is inconsistent with established legal principles. Recording systems are designed to work prospectively only; subsequent purchasers, not prior interest holders, receive constructive notice of a recorded document. A mortgagee who makes optional future advances after an intervening encumbrance is recorded can be considered a subsequent purchaser only if the future advance is viewed as a separate loan. This is, of course, contrary to the fundamental notion that the lien for future advances arises at the date of the execution of the mortgage, not when the advance is made.

Illustration: MR borrows $20,000 from ME and gives ME a $20,000 promissory note and a mortgage. The mortgage contains an optional future advances clause and provides for a maximum total indebtedness of $30,000. ME records. MR then borrows $5,000 from X and gives X a $5,000 promissory note secured by a mortgage on the same property. X records. MR next borrows an additional $10,000 from ME under the optional future advances clause in the original mortgage. The generally accepted view is that ME has a first lien for $30,000 unless it had actual notice of X's lien at the time it made the future advance. In some jurisdictions, however, ME's lien for the future advance is postponed in priority to X's lien on the ground that ME was on constructive notice of X's encumbrance. In these states, ME has a first lien for $20,000, X has a second lien for $5,000, and ME has a third lien for $10,000.

D. OBLIGATORY/OPTIONAL DISTINCTION REJECTED BY STATUTE

Several state legislatures have enacted statutes eliminating the distinction between obligatory and optional future advances. In these jurisdictions the lien of all future advances dates from the execution of the mortgage even if the mortgagee makes the advance with actual knowledge of an intervening encumbrance. In other words, obligatory and optional advances are treated the same; each takes priority over intervening encumbrances. Almost all of the statutes that produce this result, however, require that the mortgage specify the total amount to be secured. Moreover, some of these legislative measures allow the mortgagor to restrict the operation of a future advances clause to funds already disbursed by filing a prescribed notice.

E. CONSTRUCTION LENDER'S DILEMMA

The distinction between obligatory and optional future advances for priority purposes has been severely criticized by construction lenders on the ground that its application to advances made under a construction loan mortgage often produces inequitable results. Because the construction lender is obligated to make advances as construction progresses, it receives first lien priority for all advances when the project is completed according to plan. Problems arise, however, when construction does not progress smoothly and the borrower-developer defaults. Construction loan documents typically give the lender the right to stop advancing funds upon the mortgagor's default. Hence, any advances made thereafter are optional and may lose priority to intervening liens. If, however, the construction lender does not make additional advances, the incomplete project will probably not be of sufficient value even to cover the amount of the lien for obligatory advances made before default.

Courts often struggle with the optional/obligatory future advance rule in this situation because completion of the project enhances the value of the security for both the construction lender and any intervening lienor. Although the hazy line dividing optional and obligatory advances gives the judiciary ample opportunity to exercise discretion, many judges mechanistically apply the optional/obligatory rule and conclude that advances made after default are optional. A few courts, however, apparently will award the construction lender complete lien priority if the lender makes post default advances in good faith and under economic compulsion. This result has long been favored by commentators and is reached by statute in those states in which the legislature has eliminated the distinction between obligatory and optional future advances.

F. DRAGNET CLAUSE

The dragnet clause is related to the future advances clause, but is broader in scope. The typical dragnet clause, sometimes referred to as an anaconda, cross-security, or omnibus clause, provides that the mortgage secures all indebtedness owed by the mortgagor to the mortgagee. Every obligation is included regardless of whether it arose before or after the execution of the mortgage or whether it was originated or acquired by the mortgagee.

Illustration: MR executes a $2,000 unsecured promissory note to X. MR then borrows $5,000 from ME and executes a $5,000 promissory note and a mortgage to ME. The mortgage contains a dragnet clause. ME purchases the unsecured note from X at a discount for $1,500. ME now has a $7,000 lien on the mortgage property because both notes are fully secured by the mortgage.

Because a dragnet clause can be used to expand the amount of a lien far beyond the mortgagor's expectations, its scope has been limited by both judicial decision and state legislative action. Numerous forms of limitation exist. Judicially crafted restrictions confine application of the dragnet clause to certain obligations, such as those created directly between the original parties to the mortgage, those arising after execution of the mortgage, or those consistent with the objective of the initial loan. The extent to which courts employ any of these restrictions varies among the states.

V. INTEREST

A. THE NORM

The underlying obligation usually bears interest at a fixed percentage rate per annum. The precise interest rate charged is usually dictated by the money market conditions existing at the time the mortgage loan is made. But regardless of what the rate may be, it remains constant over the entire term of the loan.

A lender may increase its yield beyond the stated fixed interest rate by requiring the borrower to pay discount points at the time the loan is made. One discount point equals one percent of the loan amount.

Illustration: ME agrees to make a $100,000 thirty-year mortgage loan to MR at a 10% fixed interest rate plus two points. MR must pay $2,000 to ME at the time the loan is made. This payment increases the loan's effective yield to above 10%. The amount of the increase depends upon when the loan is paid off. The earlier the payoff, the greater the increase.

B. VARIATIONS FROM THE NORM

During periods of rampant inflation, a fixed rate of interest provides the lender with less yield than originally projected. Consequently, mortgagees have devised other methods to insure a satisfactory return on their investments. Lenders who employ these variations from the norm also may charge discount points for making the loan.

1. Alternative Mortgage Instruments

In the 1970s and early 1980s, the Comptroller of the Currency, the Federal Home Loan Bank Board (today the Office of Thrift Supervision), and the National Credit Union Administration authorized the federally-chartered lending institutions under their control to develop alternatives to the traditional mortgage. Moreover, the Alternative Mortgage Transaction Parity Act of 1982, 12 U.S.C.A. § 3801 *et seq.*, preempted state law on the subject so as to permit nonfederally-chartered institutions to compete effectively in the residential real estate financing marketplace by authorizing them to offer the same alternative residential mortgage instruments available from similar federally-chartered institutions. The states had three years from the passage of the Act to override this preemption. Some states reinstituted local law by doing so.

As a consequence of these regulatory and legislative measures, several significant alternatives to the traditional mortgage have been developed by institutional lenders. Those innovative instruments which alter the standard fixed-interest-rate approach are discussed in this section. Newly developed mortgage formats that provide payment alternatives are treated later in this chapter. Neither analysis is intended to be exhaustive. Some existing alternative mortgage instruments are not mentioned, and additional variations constantly are being introduced.

a. *Adjustable Rate Mortgage*

Mortgage lenders now offer adjustable rate mortgages (ARMs) in which the interest rate rises and falls over the term of the loan in accordance with prevailing market conditions. *See* Appendix B for an Adjustable Rate Note and an Adjustable Rate Rider to a standard mortgage. The market rate of interest is gauged by a predetermined index—some recognized economic indicator reflecting changes in the cost of obtaining mortgage money in the local, regional, or national market. The parties may guard against extreme interest rate fluctuations by establishing floor and ceiling limits.

ARMs, sometimes referred to as variable rate mortgages (VRMs), may be structured in an almost infinite number of ways. Variations exist not only with respect to the index and the use of floors and ceilings, but also as to the frequency and amount of each interest rate adjustment and the way in which interest increases are paid. Moreover, an ARM may be drafted to include other flexibility features such as a graduated payment provision.

There is another noteworthy feature of some ARMs. If increases in the interest rate are added to the principal obligation rather than reflected in increased monthly payments or extended maturity, the phenomenon of negative amortization may occur. That is, over time the principal balance of the loan may increase instead of decrease.

A study conducted by the Federal Home Loan Mortgage Corporation revealed that ARMs had achieved a prominent position in the mortgage financing marketplace by the early 1980s. According to that study, ARMs constituted almost one-half of all home mortgage loans made by surveyed lenders during the first six months of 1983. The study also found that interest rate adjustments usually were on a one-year, three-year, or five-year basis and that indices geared to the rate of Treasury instruments were most common.

The ARMs share of the residential mortgage market has varied over the years depending upon inflation and the volatility of interest rates. During periods of moderate inflation and relative interest rate stability, ARMs tend to become less popular with borrowers.

For a time, an unsettling development in the case law made ARMs less attractive to purchasers of mortgage loans on the secondary mortgage market. Several courts concluded that ARM notes were nonnegotiable on the ground the notes did not contain an obligation to pay a "sum certain." *See* UCC §§ 3–104(1)(b), 3–106 (pre–1990). Assignees of such nonnegotiable instruments do not receive the favorable status accorded holders in due course of negotiable instruments. *See* Ch. 7, pp. 129–138 (discussing defenses available against assignees and payment problems after assignment). Experts in the field, therefore, called for amendment of the UCC to include ARM notes within the definition of negotiable instruments. The widely-adopted 1990 version of the UCC so provides. *See* § 3–112(b).

Consequently, the ARM-negotiability issue has been largely resolved.

b. *Price Level Adjusted Mortgage*

A mortgage format often used in other parts of the world to insulate lenders against inflation is the price level adjusted mortgage (PLAM), also known as an indexed mortgage (IM). This instrument deals with the problem of inflation by tying the outstanding principal to an economic index. Thus, the interest rate remains constant over the term of the loan, but the loan principal varies. In this sense, a PLAM is the opposite of an ARM.

An advantage of the PLAM to the mortgagor is that it bears a low interest rate because inflation need not be factored into the rate of return required by the lender. On the other hand, the PLAM's primary drawback for the borrower is that it produces negative amortization which is usually covered by increased monthly payments.

c. *Shared Appreciation Mortgage*

Shared appreciation mortgages (SAMs) are designed to insure mortgagees of an adequate return during inflationary times and to provide an alternative form of financing for individuals who otherwise might be unable to obtain a mortgage loan. SAMs combine aspects of the standard fixed-interest-rate mortgage with a novel type of return to the lender. Typically SAMs bear a fixed-interest-rate well below current market rates thereby enabling a greater number of individuals to qualify for this form of financing than for standard fixed-interest-rate mortgages or ARMs. The SAM instrument also provides that the mortgagee will receive a portion (e.g., one-third) of the amount the mortgaged property appreciates in value. The lender's fractional share of the appreciation is paid when the property is sold or at the end of a certain period (e.g., ten years), whichever comes first. This share is often called contingent interest.

Although the SAM has appeal to both mortgagees and mortgagors, its use raises a myriad of issues: How does one determine the amount of appreciation? How are improvements made by the mortgagor factored into the calculation of appreciation? If the mortgagor does not sell the property before the lender's share of appreciation must be paid, will satisfactory refinancing be available? These and other questions cloud the SAM picture and lead authorities to draw differing conclusions regarding its future in the residential mortgage marketplace.

2. Buy–Down Mortgage

Mortgagees generally are willing to make below market-interest-rate loans if they receive sufficient upfront money to offset the reduced interest rate of return. A mortgage loan made on this basis is called a "buy-down." Some residential real estate developers have used the buy-down technique to make their properties more marketable by paying an institutional lender to offer low-interest-rate financing to purchasers. In such case, the interest buy-down is typically for only a year or two; thereafter the interest rate returns to the market level.

3. Revenue/Equity Participation

As a hedge against inflation, mortgage lenders sometimes demand a portion of the revenue generated by the project being financed. When this occurs, the lender is said to receive contingent interest or an "equity kicker." Under such an arrangement, the lender typically is entitled to a percentage of gross income or net profits in addition to the specified interest.

Mortgagees may go even further and obtain an ownership interest in the project. Several types of such equity participations exist. The lender may become directly involved by entering a joint venture with the developer or by taking an ownership interest in the entity that controls the project. Equity participation should be distinguished from loan participation discussed earlier. *See,* Ch. 2, p. 26 (discussing loan participation).

4. Due–on–Sale Clause

The due-on-sale clause is commonly used by mortgagees to avoid being tied to low yield mortgages during periods of rising interest rates. A mortgage provision of this type gives the lender the option to accelerate the underlying obligation when the mortgagor conveys the mortgaged property. As a practical matter this enables the mortgagee either to recover its capital for reinvestment at a higher return or to obtain an additional return on the original loan by conditioning its consent to the conveyance on the payment of a transfer fee or an increased interest rate. *See* Ch. 6, pp. 118–125 (discussing due-on-sale clause).

C. USURY

The amount of interest a lender may receive is limited by state usury statutes. The provisions of these statutes vary considerably with regard to: (1) the maximum legal interest rate (2) statutory exemptions, and (3) penalties for violation.

1. Rate

The maximum allowable interest rate on loans varies dramatically from state to state. In many states there are different maximum rates for different types of borrowers. For example, there may be one rate for individuals and another higher rate for corporations.

2. Exemptions

Most usury statutes exempt certain borrowers, lenders, transactions, or a combination of the three.

a. Borrowers

Corporate borrowers are commonly exempt from usury statutes. Moreover, as previously indicated, where corporate borrowers are not exempt, they are usually permitted to pay a higher rate of interest than other borrowers. Authority is divided on the issue of whether the lender may avoid usury laws by requiring the borrower to incorporate.

b. Lenders

Banks and savings and loan associations are exempt from usury statutes in several states.

c. Transactions

FHA insured loans are often excluded from the application of usury laws. In addition, a purchase money mortgage loan taken by a seller of real estate is exempt in many jurisdictions on the theory that a buyer and seller are in substantially equal bargaining positions. Various other transactions, such as loans for business purposes, are sometimes given exempt status.

3. Penalties

In some states the penalty for usury is merely forfeiture of interest in excess of the legal rate. In many jurisdictions the lender forfeits all interest. In other states the lender not only forfeits all interest but also loses the right to recover the principal. Still other penalties exist.

4. Federal Preemption

The Depository Institutions Deregulation and Monetary Control Act of 1980 preempted several aspects of state usury law. The most significant provision for real estate financing purposes is that portion of the Act which exempts most residential first mortgage loans made after March 31, 1980 from state interest rate limits. 12 U.S.C.A. § 1735f–7a. The Act gave the states the option to override this federal preemption before April 1, 1983. Several states did so. Thus, although the Act provides some uniformity in this area of usury law, there is still considerable diversity among the states.

VI. MODIFICATION OF OBLIGATION (EXTENSION AND RENEWAL)

A mortgage secures an obligation, not the instrument which evidences it. A change in the form of the obligation by substitution, extension, or renewal, therefore, generally does not affect the mortgage lien. If, however, either the principal amount or interest rate is increased by modification, the mortgage lien may lose priority to junior encumbrances to the extent of the increase.

VII. DISCHARGE OF OBLIGATION AND MORTGAGE
A. PAYMENT

As discussed previously, a mortgage merely secures an underlying obligation. *See* Ch. 1, pp. 1–2 (discussing mortgage concept). Thus, once the obligation is discharged, usually by payment, the mortgage is extinguished.

The typical modern mortgage loan is amortized over fifteen to thirty years with provision for repayment in monthly installments of principal and interest. The amount of the mortgage lien is reduced proportionately as each monthly payment is made. When the debt is paid in full, the mortgage is discharged.

Illustration: MR executes a $25,000 promissory note and a mortgage to ME. MR pays ME $15,000 on the principal of the note. The amount of the mortgage lien is reduced automatically to $10,000 notwithstanding the fact the mortgage states that it secures a $25,000 debt.

1. New Payment Alternatives

Lending institutions have been authorized to offer alternatives to the traditional payment format.

a. Graduated Payment Mortgage

Under the graduated payment mortgage (GPM), the interest rate usually remains constant throughout the life of the loan, but monthly mortgage payments increase over several years to a specified level. Initial payments are lower than normally required, whereas later payments are abnormally high. Thus, younger homebuyers may make smaller mortgage payments in their early years of employment and larger ones as their income presumably increases. This graduated payment feature may be coupled with an adjustable interest rate.

b. Reverse Annuity Mortgage

The reverse annuity mortgage (RAM) allows older homeowners to borrow money on the equity in their homes. RAMs may take various forms. Under one approach, the loan proceeds are advanced to the mortgagor in monthly installments and are repaid in a lump sum at the end of a set term or when the home is sold.

c. Growing Equity Mortgage

One alternative mortgage instrument includes a fixed-interest-rate, but provides for increasing monthly principal payments so that the loan is repaid in fifteen years or so. It is from this feature that the instrument takes its name—growing equity mortgage (GEM).

Initial payments under a GEM are based on a twenty-five or thirty year amortization. The rate of increased principal payments is specified in the document and may be fixed at a certain percentage or tied to an economic index.

2. Balloon Loans

Many residential mortgage loans executed before the Depression were short-term "balloon" loans upon which the borrower paid only interest until maturity. If the borrower lacked sufficient funds to satisfy the debt when it fell due, the borrower was forced to refinance. This arrangement worked well as long as mortgage loans were readily available. During the Depression, however, money was in short supply, and many borrowers were unable to refinance. Consequently, numerous mortgagors lost their land through foreclosure. This situation caused the federal government to develop programs, notably FHA mortgage insurance, to encourage the use of the long-term fully-amortized mortgage.

Today, a balloon mortgage loan may be defined as one that requires a substantial payment at the end of the term to cover the unamortized loan principal.

Disclosure and other aspects of balloon payment terms may be governed by regulation or statute.

3. Escrow Accounts

The mortgagor frequently is required to make monthly payments that cover not only principal and interest but also build an escrow account from which the mortgagee may pay real estate taxes and insurance on the mortgaged property as they come due. *See* ¶ 2 of Mortgage in Appendix A. The escrow account system originated during the Depression when many mortgagors were unable to pay real estate taxes or insurance premiums and lenders were forced to pay these obligations in order to protect their security.

The handling of escrow account funds traditionally has been left to the mortgagee's discretion. Mortgagees commonly invest escrowed monies with their other funds and retain the resulting returns.

Mortgagors in numerous jurisdictions have instituted lawsuits, often class actions, contesting the legality of a mortgagee's decision not to pay interest on funds held in escrow. Mortgagors have sought relief on various grounds, including express trust and constructive trust theories. These suits generally have been unsuccessful. Although mortgagors occasionally have prevailed, *see, e.g.,* Buchanan v. Century Federal Savings and Loan Association of Pittsburgh (Pa.Super.1988), courts usually have been unwilling to require mortgagees to account for earnings received from the investment of escrowed funds.

The mortgagors' attack on interest free escrow accounts has achieved greater success outside the courtroom. The controversy fueled by their lawsuits has precipitated federal and state legislative action. The federal Real Estate Settlement Procedures Act limits the amount of funds that may be placed in escrow (*See* Ch. 2, p. 44), and statutes in some states require the payment of interest on these accounts.

4. Late Charges

The mortgagor is often required to pay a late charge when tardy in making monthly payments. *See* ¶ 6(A) of Note in Appendix A. There is considerable division of opinion regarding whether to treat late charges as liquidated damages or as additional interest. Nonetheless, courts generally uphold late charges calculated on a reasonable basis as nonusurious compensation to the lender for the administrative expense of handling overdue payments. In many states, late charges are limited in amount or otherwise regulated by statute.

B. PREPAYMENT

The mortgagee contracts to receive interest over the agreed term of the loan. The mortgagor, therefore, has no right to pay the underlying obligation prior to maturity unless the mortgage, the note, a local statute, or a court opinion specifically authorizes the mortgagor to do so.

Illustration: MR borrows $5,000 from ME and executes a $5,000 promissory note and a mortgage to ME. The note is due five years from the date of execution and bears interest at 12% per annum. The instruments are silent regarding prepayment. The next day MR's parents give MR $5,000. MR immediately tenders ME $5,000 to satisfy the loan. In most jurisdictions, ME may reject MR's tender and collect interest as specified in the mortgage note. In a few states, however, a statute or a court opinion gives MR the right to prepay even though MR does not have a contractual right to do so.

Residential mortgage loan documents frequently authorize prepayment without charge. *See* ¶ 4 of Note in Appendix A. Commercial mortgage documents commonly contain a provision giving the mortgagor the privilege to prepay for a fee. The fee is called a prepayment penalty and may be specified in various ways, such as a percentage of the unpaid balance of the loan or interest for a certain number of months. Prepayment penalties are not usually included in residential mortgage loans.

Prepayment penalties generally are enforceable as reasonable compensation for lost interest and other costs. This broad proposition is, however, subject to certain caveats. First, statutes in many states limit the use of prepayment penalties in residential mortgage financing. Second, some bankruptcy decisions have curtailed or invalidated prepayment penalty provisions. Third, courts are reluctant to permit the lender to collect a prepayment penalty when the mortgagor is forced to pay off the loan because the lender accelerated under a general default provision or a due-on-sale clause. Involuntary payment required under such circumstances generally is not viewed as *pre*payment triggering a penalty unless the mortgage specifically so provides. In this regard, Office of Thrift Supervision regulations issued under the Garn–St. Germain Depository Institutions Act of 1982 prohibit mortgagees from charging a prepayment penalty in connection with the enforcement of a due-on-sale clause in a mortgage on a borrower-occupied residence. 12 C.F.R. § 591.5(b)(2) (1996). *See* Ch. 6, pp. 124–125 (discussing practical considerations of enforcing due-on-sale clause).

C. RELEASE OF MORTGAGE

Although the mortgage lien is automatically extinguished when the underlying obligation is satisfied, the recorded mortgage continues to cloud the mortgagor's title. The mortgagor, therefore, is entitled to a recordable mortgage release upon final payment. *See* ¶ 22 of Mortgage in Appendix A. Mortgagees who wrongfully refuse to execute a release may be subject to common law remedies or statutory penalties.

D. STATUTE OF LIMITATIONS

In some states the statute of limitations on the obligation is shorter than the statute of limitations on the mortgage. *See* Ch. 10, p. 196 (discussing statute of limitations on mortgage). When the statute runs on the obligation but not the mortgage, controversy arises regarding the enforceability of the mortgage. The generally accepted view is that the mortgage is still enforceable and may be foreclosed if the obligation is not paid. The running of the statute of limitations renders the obligation unenforceable, but does not discharge it. Because the obligation continues to exist, so does its security. A second view is that the remedy on the mortgage is barred with the remedy on the obligation because the mortgage is dependent on the obligation for its existence and thus, also for its enforceability.

CHAPTER 5

MORTGAGED PROPERTY

I. MORTGAGEABLE INTERESTS

A. GENERAL

Any transferable interest in realty may be mortgaged. Thus, a fee simple, a leasehold, a life estate, a reversion, and a remainder are all mortgageable interests. Although a fee simple is the subject of most mortgages, the leasehold mortgage has become a popular financing vehicle. *See* Ch. 3, pp. 64–66 (analyzing leasehold mortgage). The discussion in this book presumes a fee mortgage unless otherwise indicated.

B. MORTGAGING SEPARATE INTERESTS IN SAME LAND

Two or more interests in the same parcel of real estate may be mortgaged independently.

Illustration: L leases a farm to T for a twenty-year term. L mortgages the reversion in fee to A Bank. T mortgages the leasehold to B Bank. Each mortgage is a valid lien on a separate interest in the farm.

C. DESCRIPTION

The mortgagee usually does not take possession of the mortgaged property, at least not before default. *See* Ch. 8, pp. 159–165 (discussing significance of mortgage theories and mortgagee in possession). Thus, the mortgagee generally may impart notice of its lien only by recording the mortgage. It is, therefore, imperative that the mortgaged realty be described accurately in the mortgage. *See* Ch. 9, pp. 175–176 (treating recording statutes).

II. EXTENT OF MORTGAGE COVERAGE

The mortgage lien may attach to certain property not specifically described in the mortgage.

A. AFTER–ACQUIRED PROPERTY

The mortgagee may seek to extend the mortgage lien to land the mortgagor subsequently obtains by inserting an after-acquired property clause in the mortgage. As a general rule, the clause creates an equitable lien on all real estate the mortgagor acquires after the execution of the mortgage.

Illustration: MR owns Blackacre. MR borrows funds from ME. MR executes a note and a mortgage on Blackacre to ME. The mortgage contains an after-acquired property clause. MR purchases Whiteacre. An equitable lien in favor of ME generally attaches to Whiteacre upon its acquisition by MR.

The predominant theory underlying the enforcement of after-acquired property clauses is that the mortgagee is entitled to specific performance of the parties' contractual arrangement. Some states, however, apparently restrict the application of after-acquired property clauses to property functionally related to that initially encumbered.

After-acquired property clauses may be included in corporate mortgages in an attempt to make all of the company's ever-changing real and personal property collateral for the loan. Subject to certain qualifications, personal property as well as realty is covered by an after-acquired property clause. However, the coverage of personalty under such a clause, and related personal property issues, are beyond the scope of this work.

Because a mortgage containing an after-acquired property clause is outside the chain of title of real estate subsequently obtained by the mortgagor, purchasers or lienors of such realty from the mortgagor generally will not be on record notice of the mortgagee's equitable lien. The mortgagee, therefore, must take further action to preserve the priority of its lien. It may by mortgage provision require the mortgagor to execute recordable mortgage amendments specifically describing after-acquired land as it is obtained.

B. EASEMENTS

Easements appurtenant to the mortgaged land are part of the property and, thus, are automatically subject to the mortgage lien irrespective of whether they arise before or after the execution of the mortgage.

C. FIXTURES

A fixture is an item of tangible personal property that becomes realty by virtue of its attachment to land with the intent it remain permanently affixed. The fixture concept presents two real estate finance problems.

The first issue is whether the item in controversy is a fixture. If it is a fixture, the item constitutes part of the mortgaged land and is subject to the mortgage lien without additional description, regardless of whether it became part of the realty before or after the execution of the mortgage. If the item is not a fixture, it is not part of the mortgaged land and, hence, not subject to the mortgage lien unless specifically covered in the mortgage. Most mortgage transactions involve no controversy with respect to identifying fixtures. For example, the parties generally agree that a building on the property is covered by the mortgage. Moveable articles, however, present troublesome questions that should be resolved by the parties at the time the mortgage is negotiated.

Even if the item in question is found to be a fixture subject to the mortgage, a second problem arises. The mortgagee must insure that the mortgage constitutes a first lien on the fixture. This issue is treated in the portion of these materials dealing with lien priorities. *See* Ch. 9, pp. 184–185 (discussing liens on fixtures).

D. CONDEMNATION AWARDS

If all or part of the mortgaged property is taken by eminent domain, the mortgagee's lien attaches to the condemnation award on the theory that the award is a substitute for the land. When all the mortgaged property is taken, the mortgagee is immediately entitled to satisfy the underlying obligation out of the award. When only part of the mortgaged property is taken, authorities differ regarding how much of the award the mortgagee should receive. Thus, the issue of condemnation is often the subject of extensive negotiation and mortgage provision. *See* ¶ 10 of Mortgage in Appendix A.

E. INSURANCE PROCEEDS

A casualty insurance policy is a personal indemnification contract. Insurance proceeds generally are not considered to be a substitute for the destroyed property. The mortgagee, therefore, has no interest in the proceeds of a policy obtained by the mortgagor unless the policy specifically insures the interests of both parties.

Mortgages commonly provide that the mortgagor must insure the mortgaged property for the benefit of both the mortgagor and the mortgagee. *See* ¶ 5 of Mortgage in Appendix A. The mortgagee's interest may be covered by the addition of a clause to the mortgagor's policy. Two types of clauses are used to accomplish this result—the standard mortgage clause and the loss payable or open mortgage clause. The standard mortgagee clause is preferred by lenders because the mortgagee thereby receives an independent right of recovery against the insurer. This right continues even if the mortgagor voids the mortgagor's coverage by violating the terms of the policy. On the other hand, the mortgagee's rights under a loss payable clause are derived from the mortgagor and are lost if the mortgagor negates the mortgagor's coverage by breaching the policy.

When the parties are both insured and loss occurs, controversy may arise regarding whether the insurance proceeds should be applied to reconstruction of the premises or to payment of the mortgage debt. When the mortgage is silent on this issue, the generally accepted view is that the mortgagee may choose between these alternatives. There is, however, some authority to the contrary, which holds that under certain circumstances insurance proceeds must be used to rebuild. *See* Starkman v. Sigmond (N.J.Super.1982).

The application of insurance proceeds often is specifically covered in the mortgage. Sometimes the mortgage provides for rebuilding if certain conditions are met. *See* ¶ 5 of Mortgage in Appendix A. On other occasions, the mortgage gives the mortgagee the option to use the proceeds for rebuilding or for payment of the debt. Courts generally enforce these clauses as written. However, one court refused to recognize a lender's right to apply proceeds to the debt under an "option" clause where the security was not impaired and the loan payments were current. It found that "good faith" and "fair dealing" required use of the funds for reconstruction. Schoolcraft v. Ross (Cal.App.1978).

F. RENTS AND PROFITS

The mortgagee may have the right to collect rents and profits from the mortgaged property and apply them to the mortgage debt. *See* Ch. 8, pp. 159–168 (discussing right to possession and rents).

III. WASTE OF MORTGAGED PROPERTY
A. DOCTRINE OF WASTE

Once the mortgagee has accepted the land as adequate security for the debt, it is concerned, of course, that the mortgagor maintain the mortgaged premises so that the property does not decrease in value. The mortgagor's duties in this regard are generally governed by the doctrine of waste, the principle that prohibits a lawful possessor from physically damaging or destroying the property occupied.

B. MORTGAGEE'S REMEDIES FOR WASTE

When the mortgagor commits waste, the mortgagee generally may pursue one or more of the following courses of action: seek damages, request an injunction, commence foreclosure proceedings.

1. Damages

In title theory states, the mortgagor is treated as a tenant liable for common law waste and the mortgagee is viewed as fictional title holder who can recover actual damages to the land either before or at foreclosure. In lien theory states, the mortgagor is the owner of the mortgaged property, so the mortgagor cannot commit common law waste. That doctrine applies only to acts committed by rightful possessors such as life tenants, lessees, and concurrent owners. Although in lien theory jurisdictions the mortgagee may not recover damages to the land, it may recover damages for the impairment of its security interest. Authorities, however, differ as to what constitutes impairment and whether an action for damages may be brought before foreclosure.

2. Injunction

In all jurisdictions a mortgagee may obtain an injunction against equitable waste when the mortgagor causes the property to diminish in value to the extent that the mortgagee's security is impaired. It is generally agreed that impairment in this case occurs when the property depreciates in value to a point at which the margin between the value of the land and the amount of the mortgage debt is less than prudent lenders normally require.

Illustration: MR owns property worth $11,000. MR mortgages the property to ME to secure an $8,000 promissory note. MR cuts timber on the land that reduces it in value to $10,000. Assuming that mortgage lenders generally will not make loans in excess of 80% of the value of the mortgaged property, ME may enjoin MR from cutting more timber.

3. Foreclosure

Mortgages commonly provide that waste is an event of default and, therefore, a basis for acceleration and foreclosure. *See* ¶ 6 of Mortgage in Appendix A.

CHAPTER 6

TRANSFER OF MORTGAGOR'S INTEREST

I. MORTGAGOR'S INTEREST

The precise nature of the mortgagor's interest in the mortgaged property varies among the states depending upon the prevailing mortgage theory. *See* Ch. 1, pp. 8–10 (discussing mortgage theories). Nonetheless, the mortgagor is viewed everywhere as owner of the property for transfer purposes. This is true even in title theory states where the mortgagee holds legal "title" as security. *See* Ch. 1, p. 9 (analyzing title theory). As owner of the mortgaged premises, the mortgagor may transfer the property by deed or will or further encumber it by mortgage. Moreover, the mortgaged property may be transferred by forced sale or by intestate succession. This chapter deals primarily with issues that arise when the mortgagor transfers the mortgaged property by deed of conveyance.

II. CONVEYANCE OF MORTGAGED PROPERTY

A. MORTGAGOR'S POWER TO CONVEY

The mortgagor may freely convey the mortgaged property. A mortgage provision purporting to prevent conveyance is void as an illegal disabling restraint on alienation. However, as discussed later in this chapter, the mortgage may authorize the mortgagee to accelerate the debt if the mortgagor conveys the mortgaged property without the mortgagee's consent. *See* pp. 118–125 (analyzing due-on-sale clause).

B. EFFECT OF CONVEYANCE ON MORTGAGE

When the mortgagor conveys the mortgaged property, it is important to determine whether the mortgage is discharged before title passes or survives the conveyance. The answer depends upon the contract between the mortgagor/grantor and the grantee.

1. Mortgage Is Discharged/Refinancing

The parties frequently agree that the mortgagor will pay off the mortgage debt at closing and transfer the property free from the mortgage lien. (It is assumed that the mortgage documents permit prepayment. *See* Ch. 4, pp. 93–95 (discussing prepayment).) In this case, the purchase price is set at an amount sufficient to pay the mortgagor for the mortgagor's equity in the property and also to satisfy the mortgage debt. If the grantee does not have enough money on hand to pay the purchase price, and the grantee usually does not, the grantee must obtain a new mortgage loan to make up the deficit. This method of acquiring mortgaged property is termed refinancing because the existing mortgage is discharged and replaced by a new mortgage.

Illustration: MR owns a house encumbered by a $30,000 mortgage held by ME. GE agrees to purchase the property for $90,000. GE has $20,000 cash and obtains a $70,000 loan from Bank. GE pays $60,000 to MR for MR's equity and $30,000 to ME to satisfy the mortgage debt. ME releases its mortgage, and MR deeds the property to GE. GE then executes a new $70,000 mortgage to Bank. This is an example of refinancing the purchase of mortgaged property.

2. Mortgage Survives

The parties may agree that the existing mortgage will survive the conveyance. In this event, the grantee pays the mortgagor the value of the mortgagor's equity and takes title subject to the mortgage lien. Even absent such an agreement, a properly recorded mortgage will survive unless it is satisfied at or before closing. *See* Ch. 9, pp. 175–176 (discussing recording statutes).

C. RIGHTS AND OBLIGATIONS OF PARTIES WHEN MORTGAGE SURVIVES CONVEYANCE

When the mortgage survives the conveyance, the legal relationship among the mortgagee, the mortgagor, and the grantee depends upon whether the grantee assumes personal responsibility for the underlying obligation.

1. "Subject to" Conveyance

a. Grantee's Rights and Obligations

If the grantee does not assume the mortgage debt, the conveyance is merely "subject to" the mortgage. Upon default, the mortgagee may foreclose and have the property sold, but as a general rule the mortgagee may not proceed against the "subject to" grantee personally.

Illustration: MR conveys mortgaged property to GE by deed that provides that the conveyance is "subject to" a prior recorded mortgage. This means that GE takes the property subject to the mortgage lien, but generally has no personal responsibility to pay the underlying obligation. The term "subject to" is not a promise from GE to pay the mortgage debt.

As indicated in the immediately preceding illustration, the deed from the mortgagor to the "subject to" grantee usually provides that the grantee takes title subject to the mortgage. Although a provision of this type is not necessary for the survival of a properly recorded mortgage, it is utilized by the mortgagor to limit the mortgagor's liability on the deed's covenants of title by excluding the mortgage from their coverage.

Illustration: MR conveys mortgaged property to GE by general warranty deed that does not mention a prior recorded mortgage. GE takes the property subject to the mortgage because GE is on constructive notice of the recorded instrument. GE, however, may have a cause of action against

MR for breach of the deed's present covenant against encumbrances.

Although the "subject to" grantee is not personally liable on the mortgage debt, the grantee generally pays the obligation to avoid losing the property by foreclosure.

b. Mortgagor's Rights and Obligations

The mortgagor remains personally liable on the debt following a "subject to" conveyance unless released by the mortgagee. When not released, the mortgagor becomes a surety, liable to the extent the land proves to be of insufficient value to satisfy the debt. As a surety, the mortgagor generally is still subject to suit by the mortgagee directly on the underlying obligation and is liable for any deficiency resulting from a foreclosure sale. If, however, the mortgagor is forced to pay the entire debt, the mortgagor generally is subrogated to the mortgagee's rights and can foreclose in order to be reimbursed to the extent of the value of the land.

Illustration: MR executes a $10,000 promissory note and a mortgage to ME. MR then conveys the mortgaged property to GE by deed which provides that title is "subject to" the mortgage. The parties make no agreement regarding payment of the note. GE fails to pay the note. ME generally may either (1) foreclose and seek a deficiency judgment against MR if the sale proceeds are insufficient to satisfy the debt or (2) bring suit against MR on the note without foreclosing. ME chooses the second alternative. MR pays ME $10,000 and is subrogated to ME's right to foreclose. MR forecloses and the property brings $8,000 at sale. MR is entitled to the $8,000, but MR generally must absorb a $2,000 loss because GE had no personal liability on the note.

2. "Assumption" Conveyance

a. *Grantee's Rights and Obligations*

A grantee taking land encumbered by a mortgage may personally assume liability for the mortgage debt. When this occurs, the transaction is termed an "assumption" conveyance. Although the assumption may be accomplished outside the conveyance, it is usually based on a clause in the deed to the effect that the grantee "assumes and agrees to pay" the mortgage debt. When the grantee accepts a deed containing a clause of this type, the grantee also accepts personal responsibility for the debt.

The mortgagor, as one of the contracting parties, may, of course, enforce the assumption contract. The mortgagee may also enforce the contract against the grantee under either of two theories. (1) The generally accepted view is that the mortgagee is a third party beneficiary of the assumption contract. (2) Some courts consider the mortgagee's rights against the grantee as "derived" under equitable principles from the mortgagor's rights in the assumption contract. In either case, the consequence of an "assumption" conveyance is that, upon default, the mortgagee may foreclose and also obtain a deficiency judgment against the grantee.

Furthermore, in most jurisdictions the mortgagee may obtain judgment against the grantee on the obligation without foreclosing the mortgage. Some derivative theory states, however, refuse the mortgagee this right on the ground that the grantee is not liable on the assumption contract until the mortgagor suffers actual loss.

b. Mortgagor's Rights and Obligations

The grantee's assumption of personal responsibility for the mortgage debt does not relieve the mortgagor of liability. (*But see* pp. 124–125 for federal regulations apparently requiring the mortgagee to release the mortgagor in certain situations.) Again the mortgagor becomes a surety, liable for any deficiency resulting from a foreclosure sale and in most jurisdictions subject to direct suit on the debt. The mortgagor is, however, in a much better position in an "assumption" conveyance than in a "subject to" transfer. First, because the assuming grantee is personally liable on the underlying obligation, the grantee has greater incentive to pay than when the grantee only risks loss of the land on default. Second, if the mortgagor pays the debt, the mortgagor is subrogated to the mortgagee's rights and may look to both the land and the grantee personally for reimbursement. Third, the generally accepted view is that the mortgagor may sue the defaulting grantee for breach of the assumption contract without first having paid the mortgage debt and apply monies recovered toward satisfaction of the debt.

Illustration: MR executes a $30,000 promissory note and a mortgage to ME. MR then conveys the mortgaged property to GE by deed that provides that GE assumes and agrees to pay the mortgage debt. GE fails to pay. In most states ME may either (1) foreclose and seek a deficiency judgment against MR and GE if the sale proceeds are insufficient to satisfy the note, (2) bring suit against MR on the note without foreclosing, or (3) bring suit against GE on the note without foreclosing. ME chooses the second alternative. MR pays ME $30,000 and is subrogated to ME's rights against GE. MR may now either (1) foreclose and recover any deficiency from GE or (2) sue GE directly on the note and the assumption contract without foreclosing.

c. *Successive "Assumption" Conveyances/Break in Chain of Assumptions*

When successive "assumption" conveyances are made, each grantee is personally liable on the mortgage debt. The last assuming grantee, however, bears primary responsibility.

Illustration: MR executes a $20,000 note and a mortgage to ME. MR makes an "assumption" conveyance to GE–1 who in turn makes an "assumption" conveyance to GE–2 who defaults. ME forecloses and receives $18,000 from the foreclosure sale. ME obtains a $2,000 deficiency judgment against GE–1. If GE–1 pays, GE–1 has the right to obtain reimbursement from GE–2.

If the chain of assumptions is broken by a "subject to" conveyance, authorities are divided on whether grantees who assume after the break are personally liable on the mortgage debt. In jurisdictions that view the mortgagee as a third party beneficiary of the assumption contract, a subsequent assuming grantee generally is liable. Some courts, however, have found the grantee free from liability on the ground that the parties did not intend the mortgagee to benefit from the assumption. In derivative theory states, a grantee who assumes after a break is not liable because the mortgagee has no claim against the "subject to" grantee and, therefore, cannot derive rights from that individual's assumption contract with a subsequent grantee.

d. *Termination or Modification of Assumption Contract*

Authorities also disagree as to whether the mortgagee's rights against an assuming grantee are affected when the grantee is released from the assumption contract by the grantor. In most third party beneficiary theory states, the mortgagee's rights survive the release if the mortgagee accepted, adopted, or relied on the assumption agreement prior to the release. In a few third party beneficiary jurisdictions, the mortgagee's rights survive the release in all cases on the theory that the mortgagee's rights vested immediately upon the execution of the assumption contract. In derivative theory states, the mortgagee's rights are destroyed by the release unless the mortgagee has previously filed a foreclosure suit or it would be inequitable to enforce the release.

A similar diversity of opinion exists on the question of whether the mortgagee's rights are affected by modification of the assumption contract.

3. Extension Problem

The grantee normally pays the mortgage debt in both the "subject to" and the "assumption" conveyance situations. If the grantee has difficulty doing so, the mortgagee may extend the time for payment. Serious collateral consequences may result. The extension may operate to discharge the mortgagor in whole or in part on the theory that it impairs the mortgagor's right as a surety to pay the debt at maturity and to be subrogated to the mortgagee's position at that time.

An extension granted an assuming grantee operates to completely discharge the mortgagor. This is because the extension denies the mortgagor subrogation rights against the grantee for the entire debt. The rule, however, operates to discharge the mortgagor only if the mortgagee had knowledge of the assumption when it granted the extension.

Authorities disagree as to the effect of an extension granted a "subject to" grantee. The generally accepted view is that the mortgagor is discharged to the extent of the value of the land at the time the extension was granted. This is because the extension costs the mortgagor the opportunity to be subrogated to the mortgagee's right to foreclose. Some states go further and completely discharge the mortgagor in this situation. Other jurisdictions consider the mortgagor's liability to be unaffected by the extension.

These rules on discharge are subject to two important qualifications. First, the mortgagor is discharged only by an extension agreement that is legally binding on the mortgagee. Mere inaction by the mortgagee after default does not constitute such an extension. Second, even when the grantee obtains a binding extension, the mortgagor is not discharged if the mortgagor consents to the arrangement. Consequently, most modern mortgages provide that the mortgagee may grant extensions to subsequent grantees without affecting the mortgagor's liability. *See* ¶ 11 of Mortgage in Appendix A.

D. ACQUISITION BY MORTGAGEE

A mortgagee may acquire the mortgaged property from the mortgagor by a transaction separate and distinct from the mortgage agreement. Acquisitions of this type do not violate the rule that prohibits contemporaneous clogs of the mortgagor's equity of redemption. *See* Ch. 1, p. 5 (discussing clogging). Such transactions, however, are subject to strict judicial scrutiny so that the mortgagor is protected from the generally superior bargaining power of the mortgagee. If the acquisition is made in bad faith or for inadequate consideration, it will not be recognized by the courts, and the mortgagor will continue to hold an equity of redemption.

1. Deed in Lieu of Foreclosure

The most common type of acquisition by the mortgagee is the deed in lieu of foreclosure. Upon default the mortgagee frequently is willing to cancel the mortgage debt and accept a deed to the mortgaged property in lieu of foreclosing the mortgagor's equity of redemption. The transaction generally is advantageous to both parties. The mortgagee avoids the expensive and protracted foreclosure process, and the mortgagor avoids a potential deficiency judgment. *See* Ch. 8, pp. 172–174 (discussing alternatives to foreclosure).

2. Merger

The doctrine of merger provides that when successive real property interests come into the same hands, the lesser interest merges into the greater interest and is thereby extinguished. Thus, when the mortgagee acquires the mortgaged property, the mortgage normally merges into the fee. However, because merger is predicated on the actual or presumed intention of the individual in whom the interests unite, the mortgage is preserved if merger would be detrimental to the mortgagee.

Illustration: MR owns Blackacre subject to a first mortgage to ME–1 and a second mortgage to ME–2. MR conveys Blackacre to ME–1. Merger does not occur unless ME–1, with knowledge of the mortgage held by ME–2, expresses an intent for it to do so. It is presumed that ME–1 does not intend to gratuitously benefit ME–2 by giving ME–2's mortgage first lien priority.

III. DUE–ON–SALE CLAUSE

A. GENERAL

Although the mortgagee cannot prohibit the mortgagor from transferring the mortgaged property, the mortgagee may include a provision in the mortgage giving it the right to accelerate the debt if the mortgaged property is conveyed without its consent. *See* ¶ 17 of Mortgage in Appendix A. A mortgage provision of this type is known as a due-on-sale clause. Such clauses are often broadly worded to cover the transfer of any interest in the property. Transfer by land contract, lease, or junior encumbrance, as well as by outright conveyance, are therefore acts that may trigger acceleration of the debt.

Mortgagees today may freely enforce due-on-sale clauses in most cases. A federal statute, discussed later in this section, so mandates. The current situation, however, is a product of years of litigation, regulation, and legislation on the subject. This historical background is traced below.

B. STATE LAW BACKGROUND

At one time considerable controversy existed regarding the enforceability of due-on-sale clauses. At the beginning of the 1980s, the states were divided into two camps: those following the "automatic enforcement" approach and those subscribing to the "impairment of security" view. This split of authority was primarily the result of differing judicial attitudes as to whether the enforcement of a due-on-sale clause constituted an unreasonable restraint on alienation.

Courts adopting the automatic enforcement approach generally reasoned as follows: To the extent enforcement of a due-on-sale clause directly or indirectly limits the mortgagor's ability to convey the mortgaged property, such restraint on alienation is reasonable. Mortgagees are justified in using a contractual provision to get rid of low-interest-rate loans in order to maintain their lending portfolios at or near the current market interest rate. Moreover, mortgagors in general benefit from a rule permitting mortgagees to enforce due-on-sale clauses at their discretion. The acceleration of low-interest-rate loans creates additional funds for new borrowers. It also tends to reduce the overall mortgage interest rate by alleviating the mortgagees' need to charge exceptionally high rates on new mortgage loans in order to compensate for low returns on outstanding loans.

Some state courts that adopted the automatic enforcement approach used markedly different analysis in doing so. They determined that due-on-sale clauses are not restraints on alienation in any sense and, therefore, are enforceable contract provisions. *See, e.g.*, Occidental Savings and Loan Association v. Venco Partnership (Neb.1980).

Courts in a number of states found due-on-sale clauses enforceable only if the mortgagee established that the conveyance in question would impair the security or enhance the likelihood of default. These courts concluded that it is unreasonable for a mortgagee to exercise a due-on-sale clause merely to improve its financial condition. Additional justification is necessary to tip the balance to the reasonable side of the scale. The grantee's present financial situation, credit history, and background respecting property use and maintenance are factors relevant to this determination.

Some courts espousing the impairment of security point of view concluded that automatic enforcement of a due-on-sale clause constitutes an unreasonable restraint on alienation. *See, e.g.,* Wellenkamp v. Bank of America (Cal.1978). Other courts adopted the impairment of security view on another theory. They reasoned that it is inequitable for a mortgagee to accelerate the debt under a due-on-sale clause solely for economic reasons. The results of this approach were essentially the same as produced by the restraint on alienation analysis. In addition, some state legislatures enacted statutes incorporating the impairment of security approach.

As state law became increasingly fractured along the lines discussed above, pressure mounted for a solution to the due-on-sale clause conflict. The federal government became involved, and in the end,

Congress settled the matter by statute. Following is an overview of significant federal activity in the due-on-sale clause area.

C.   FEDERAL HOME LOAN BANK BOARD REGULATIONS

The Federal Home Loan Bank Board (today the Office of Thrift Supervision) in 1976 authorized federal savings and loan associations to freely enforce due-on-sale clauses in most cases. 12 C.F.R. § 545.8–3(f) & (g) (1982). There was some question, however, as to whether this regulation preempted restrictive state laws on the subject. The Supreme Court answered the preemption question in the affirmative in Fidelity Federal Savings and Loan Association v. de la Cuesta (S.Ct.1982), thereby eliminating any doubt about the authority of federal savings and loan associations in this area.

D.   GARN—ST. GERMAIN DEPOSITORY INSTITUTIONS ACT OF 1982

1. General

Because of the fragmented law on the enforceability of due-on-sale clauses and the adverse economic impact of due-on-sale restrictions on lending institutions, Congress included provisions in the Garn—St. Germain Depository Institutions Act of 1982 preempting state due-on-sale law and establishing a national standard for the enforcement of due-on-sale clauses. 12 U.S.C.A. § 1701j–3. As a general proposition, the Act permits mortgagees to freely enforce due-on-sale clauses. There are, however, exceptions to this basic rule—one for "window period" loans and another for certain transfers of residential mortgaged property.

2. Window Period Loan Exception

A window period loan is one made or assumed before the effective date of the Act (October 15, 1982) in a jurisdiction that had a statewide restriction on the enforcement of due-on-sale clauses in place at the time the loan was executed or assumed. Window period loans remained subject to the restrictive state law for three years (until October 15, 1985) unless the appropriate regulatory body for the originating lender provided otherwise. Under this scheme, 12 U.S.C.A. § 1701j–3(c), state legislatures were given the power to "otherwise regulate" window period loans made by lenders that are not federally chartered. Lawmakers in a few window period jurisdictions extended state law restrictions on such window period loans for various periods beyond October 15, 1985.

Mortgage loans made by federal savings and loan associations were specifically excluded from the window period exception. This is, of course, consistent with the *de la Cuesta* decision discussed above.

3. Exempt Transfers

The Act permanently exempts certain transfers of residential mortgaged property "containing less than five dwelling units." Mortgagees are prohibited from enforcing a due-on-sale clause in the following residential transfer situations: "(1) the creation of a lien or other encumbrance subordinate to the lender's security instrument which does not relate to a transfer of rights of occupancy in the property; (2) the creation of a purchase money security interest for household appliances; (3) a transfer by devise, descent, or operation of law on the death of a joint tenant or tenant by the entirety; (4) the granting of a leasehold interest of three years or less not containing an option to purchase; (5) a transfer to a relative resulting from the death of a borrower; (6) a transfer where the spouse or children of the borrower become an owner of the property; (7) a transfer resulting from a decree of a dissolution of marriage, legal separation agreement, or from an incidental property settlement agreement, by which the spouse of the borrower becomes an owner of the property; (8) a transfer into an inter vivos trust in which the borrower is and remains a beneficiary and which does not relate to a transfer of rights of occupancy in the property; or (9) any other transfer or disposition described in regulations prescribed by the Federal Home Loan Bank Board." 12 U.S.C.A. § 1701j–3(d).

4. Role of Office of Thrift Supervision

A final note of caution is in order. The Office of Thrift Supervision (OTS) (formerly the Federal Home Loan Bank Board) is empowered to issue rules, regulations, and interpretations of the Act that apply to all lenders. 12 U.S.C.A. § 1701j–3(e)(1). OTS activity in this area should be consulted because the Act raises, but does not answer, numerous practical questions. *See* 12 C.F.R. §§ 591.1–591.6 (1996) for OTS regulations.

E. PRACTICAL CONSIDERATIONS

When the mortgage contains an enforceable due-on-sale clause and the mortgagor desires to transfer the mortgaged property, the mortgagee has at least three alternatives.

(1) The mortgagee may withhold consent to the transfer, accelerate the debt upon transfer, and then reinvest the funds at the current market interest rate. Some lenders also have sought a prepayment penalty under these circumstances, but such attempts generally have been rejected by the courts on the ground that once the lender accelerates the debt there can no longer be any *pre*payment. Moreover, Office of Thrift Supervision regulations issued under the Garn—St. Germain Depository Institutions Act of 1982 prohibit mortgagees from charging a prepayment penalty in connection with the enforcement of a due-on-sale clause in a mortgage on a borrower-occupied residence. 12 C.F.R. § 591.5(b)(2) (1996). *See* Ch. 4, pp. 94–95 (discussing prepayment penalties).

(2) The mortgagee may consent to the transfer conditioned upon the grantee's assumption of the mortgage and the payment of a transfer fee or increased interest rate. The Garn—St. Germain Depository Institutions Act of 1982 contains an unusual provision which "encourage[s]" the lender to consent to transfer upon the grantee's assumption of the mortgage at a blended interest rate not more than the average of the original rate and the current market rate. 12 U.S.C.A. § 1701j–3(b)(3). If the

lender consents to an assumption of a loan on a borrower-occupied residence, it apparently must by regulation release the mortgagor from personal liability. 12 C.F.R. § 591.5(b)(4) (1996). This regulation, however, has been interpreted in various ways.

(3) The mortgagee may promote customer relations by consenting to the transfer without imposing any conditions.

IV. FURTHER ENCUMBRANCE OF MORTGAGED PROPERTY

A mortgagor may place a junior mortgage on the mortgaged property. *See* Ch. 2, pp. 28–29 (discussing creation of junior mortgages). Such further encumbrance, however, may permit the mortgagee to accelerate the debt under a due-on-sale clause.

V. TRANSFER AT MORTGAGOR'S DEATH

On the mortgagor's death, the mortgaged property passes to the mortgagor's heirs or devisees. Because the mortgage debt is a personal obligation, the heir or devisee generally may compel the decedent's personal representative to pay the debt. In some states, however, statutes relieve the personal estate of this burden. In addition, specific testamentary directions regarding the payment of mortgage debts may render the general rule inapplicable in individual cases.

CHAPTER 7

TRANSFER OF MORTGAGEE'S INTEREST

I. MORTGAGEE'S INTEREST

The legal problems that arise from the transfer of the mortgagee's interest are some of the most complicated and confusing ones in real estate finance. This is primarily because the mortgagee's interest in the mortgage loan consists of two types of property, the obligation which is personalty and the mortgage which is realty. The material in this chapter is more easily understood if the reader remains constantly aware of this duality.

II. ASSIGNMENT OF MORTGAGE LOAN

A. BASIC CONCEPT

A mortgage cannot be transferred except in connection with the transfer of the obligation it secures. *See* Ch. 1, p. 2 (discussing obligation/security distinction). This principle has two facets. First, when the mortgagee assigns only the underlying debt, the mortgage is automatically carried to the assignee as an inseparable incident of the debt. The assignee then may require the mortgagee to execute a formal mortgage assignment. Second, when the mortgagee assigns only the mortgage, the transaction is invalid, and the assignee acquires no interest in either the mortgage or the debt. If, however, the mortgagee intends the separate mortgage assignment to operate also as an assignment of the secured indebtedness, the transfer is valid, and the assignee receives an equitable right to the debt.

Illustration: MR executes a promissory note and a mortgage to ME. ME assigns the note to A who purchases it without knowledge that it is secured by the mortgage. Nonetheless, A has an equitable right to the mortgage. ME holds the mortgage in trust for A and must transfer it to A upon request.

Illustration: MR executes a promissory note and a mortgage to ME. ME assigns the mortgage to A, but keeps the note under the mistaken belief that both parties (ME and A) have rights against MR. The attempted transfer is ineffective. A acquires no interest in the mortgage loan.

Illustration: MR executes a promissory note and a mortgage to ME. ME gives the note to ME's attorney X for safekeeping. Later ME requests X to return the note so that ME can transfer it to A. X refuses on the ground that ME has failed to pay for legal services rendered. ME is undeterred and assigns the mortgage to A with the express intention that the assignment also operate as an assignment of the note. The assignment is effective. A may enforce both the note and the mortgage subject to X's lien rights, if any. *See* Beaty v. Inlet Beach, Inc. (Fla.1942).

The usual transfer of a mortgage loan involves separate assignments of the obligation and the mortgage. The validity of the assignment of the underlying obligation is determined by reference to contract and commercial paper law. The formal assignment of the mortgage must comply with the legal requirements for the conveyance of an interest in land.

B. RIGHTS OF ASSIGNEE

The assignee of a properly transferred note and mortgage is entitled to collect payment of the debt from the mortgagor and, in the event of default, is empowered to foreclose the mortgage. The assignee's rights, however, are subject to the limitations discussed in the following sections on defenses that may be available against the assignee and on payment problems that may arise after the assignment.

C. RECORDING ASSIGNMENT

The assignee must record the mortgage assignment in order to preserve its interest against subsequent purchasers or encumbrancers of the mortgaged property. *See* Ch. 9, pp. 175–176 (discussing recording statutes).

Illustration: MR owns land worth $20,000. MR executes a $10,000 promissory note and a mortgage on the property to ME. ME assigns and delivers the instruments to A, but A does not record. ME and MR enter into a scheme to defraud A. ME executes a release of the mortgage to MR who records it. MR then conveys the land to X, an innocent purchaser, for $20,000, an amount that is twice as much as MR normally could have obtained. *See* Ch. 6, pp. 107–108 (analyzing effect of conveyance on mortgage). X owns the land free from the mortgage because the land records did not reflect A's current lien on the property. A's only recourse is against MR and ME.

D. SECONDARY MORTGAGE MARKET

The assignment process occurs thousands of times each day. Many mortgagees originate mortgage loans and then sell and assign them to permanent investors. The aggregate of these assignment transactions constitutes the secondary mortgage market. *See* Ch. 2, pp. 36–38 (describing secondary mortgage market support institutions).

III. DEFENSES AVAILABLE AGAINST ASSIGNEE

As a general rule, the right of an assignee of a mortgage loan to foreclosure the mortgage upon default depends on its ability to enforce the underlying obligation. This doctrine rests on the basic concept that the obligation is the essential aspect of the transaction, while the mortgage is just an appendage. The form of the underlying obligation (negotiable/nonnegotiable), therefore, is of primary importance in determining what defenses the mortgagor may assert against an assignee of the mortgage loan.

A. NONNEGOTIABLE OBLIGATION

If the underlying obligation is nonnegotiable, the assignee takes the note and the mortgage subject to all defenses the mortgagor had against the mortgagee.

Illustration: ME agrees to loan $3,000 to MR. MR executes a $3,000 nonnegotiable note and a mortgage to ME. ME, however, does not actually advance any money to MR. ME immediately assigns the documents to A, who is a bona fide purchaser for value without notice of ME's failure to advance funds. MR refuses to pay A. A cannot recover on the note nor can A foreclose the mortgage; A took the documents subject to MR's defense of failure of consideration.

B. NEGOTIABLE OBLIGATION

It is more difficult to determine what defenses the mortgagor may assert against an assignee when the underlying obligation is negotiable. The answer depends upon whether the assignee qualifies as a holder in due course. An assignee may become a holder in due course only if certain requirements are met. First, the obligation, of course, must be negotiable. *See* UCC § 3–104(a). Second, it must have been transferred to the assignee by negotiation. *See* UCC § 3–201. Third, the assignee must have obtained the instrument for value, in good faith, and without notice of any defect, such as an alteration, claim, or defense. *See* UCC § 3–302(a).

If the underlying obligation is negotiable and the assignee is a holder in due course, the assignee takes the note *and* the mortgage free from "personal" defenses the mortgagor had against the mortgagee. Personal defenses include failure of consideration, payment, and fraud in the inducement. *See* UCC § 3–305.

The negotiable mortgage concept rests on the theory that negotiable notes should be freely transferable and that the mortgage, as mere security, should travel with the note. A handful of jurisdictions, however, apparently reject this principle on the ground that a mortgage is a property interest for all purposes and thus, cannot assume the characteristics of commercial paper. Under this minority approach, even a holder in due course takes the mortgage subject to personal defenses the mortgagor had against the mortgagee.

Illustration: ME agrees to loan $3,000 to MR. MR executes a $3,000 negotiable note and a mortgage to ME. However, ME does not actually advance any money to MR. ME immediately negotiates the note and assigns the mortgage to A, a holder in due course. As a holder in due course, A takes the note free from any personal defenses MR had against ME. The defense of failure of consideration is a personal defense. A, therefore, may recover $3,000 on the note from MR. In the vast majority of states, A also may foreclose on the theory that the mortgage is clothed with the negotiable characteristics of the note and thus, A also takes the mortgage free from personal defenses. In a handful of jurisdictions, however, A apparently cannot foreclose on the ground that a mortgage can never become negotiable and therefore, MR can assert MR's personal defense in a foreclosure suit.

Even if the assignee qualifies as a holder in due course, it still takes subject to "real" defenses the mortgagor has on the negotiable obligation. Real defenses include incapacity, duress, infancy, and fraud in the fact. *See* UCC § 3–305(a)(1) & (b).

Illustration: Assume the same fact situation as in the immediately preceding illustration except MR was mentally incompetent at the time MR executed the note and mortgage. Even though the note is negotiable and A is a holder in due course, A takes the note subject to the real defense of incapacity. Because MR has a valid defense against enforcement of the negotiable note, MR also has a defense against enforcement of the mortgage. Thus, A can neither recover on the note nor foreclose.

Of course, if the assignee does not qualify as a holder in due course, it takes the note and the mortgage subject to both real and personal defenses the mortgagor had against the mortgagee. *See* UCC § 3–305(a).

C.   ESTOPPEL CERTIFICATE

Many assignees will not accept an assignment of a mortgage loan unless they receive an estoppel certificate from the mortgagor specifying the unpaid balance of the obligation and stating that the mortgagor claims no defenses against its enforcement. The assignee may thereby protect itself from all defenses, whether real or personal.

IV.   PAYMENT PROBLEMS AFTER ASSIGNMENT

The assignee of a mortgage loan is entitled to receive all payments made after the assignment. Nonetheless, the mortgagor or a grantee may continue to pay the original mortgagee through inadvertence or ignorance. In most instances, the original mortgagee merely forwards the payment to the assignee, and the parties eventually work out the administrative details. Problems arise, however, when the original mortgagee absconds with the funds or becomes insolvent. Who bears the loss, the payor or the assignee? In order to answer this question, one must ascertain who made the payment (the mortgagor or a grantee), the form of obligation involved (negotiable or nonnegotiable), and the type of payment made (part or final). Because the mortgage is a mere incident of the obligation, commercial paper law generally dictates the outcome. The result is not always consistent with the policy underlying the recording statutes.

A. PAYMENT BY MORTGAGOR

1. Negotiable Obligation

If the underlying obligation is negotiable, the generally accepted view is that the mortgagor pays the original mortgagee at the mortgagor's peril. Proper payment, whether part or full, can be made only to the holder of a negotiable instrument. *See* UCC § 3–602(a). The mortgagor is protected by the right to demand production of the instrument and its surrender if the payment is final, or an endorsement thereon of part payment if that is the case. If, however, the holder is not a holder in due course and the mortgagor paid the original mortgagee without notice of the prior assignment, the mortgagor may be able to successfully assert the contract defense of payment against the holder. *See* UCC § 3–305(a)(2). (The issue of notice is discussed in the following subsection on nonnegotiable obligations.)

In a handful of states, statutes authorize the mortgagor to pay the mortgagee until an assignment of the mortgage is recorded. Such statutes, of course, run contrary to basic commercial paper policy stated above.

The severity of the general rule that the mortgagor must pay the holder of a negotiable instrument is softened by the realities of mortgage financing. Often the assignee of the negotiable note and mortgage will authorize the mortgagee to "service" the loan. *See* Ch. 2, pp. 17–18 (analyzing differences among originating/servicing/holding and discussing transfer of servicing rights). The mortgagee thereby continues to collect payments, but now as agent for the assignee. Naturally, such payments are good against the servicing agent's principal—the holder of the negotiable note.

2. Nonnegotiable Obligation: Notice Problem

If the underlying obligation is nonnegotiable, the mortgagor may safely pay the mortgagee until receiving notice of an assignment. The mortgagor may obtain notice in various ways.

a. Actual Notice

The mortgagor may receive actual notice of the assignment from the assignor, the assignee, or otherwise. Most assignees notify the mortgagor of the assignment as a matter of routine.

b. Record Notice

The recordation of a mortgage assignment generally is not considered constructive notice to the mortgagor because recording imparts notice only to subsequent purchasers, not to prior interest holders. There is, however, some authority that recording the assignment puts the mortgagor on notice.

c. Inquiry Notice

By weight of authority, the mortgagor receives inquiry notice of an assignment if upon final payment the mortgagee does not produce and surrender the note or give a reasonable excuse for its inability to do so. This view is based on the belief that it is prudent business practice for the mortgagor to demand production of a nonnegotiable note when paying it off. In some jurisdictions, however, the mortgagor is not on inquiry notice of an assignment when the mortgagee fails to produce the note upon final payment. This view is supported by the fact that the assignee could have easily protected itself by notifying the mortgagor of the assignment.

The mortgagor's part payment of a nonnegotiable obligation is viewed in a different light. It is not common business practice to require production of a nonnegotiable note upon part payment. The mortgagor, therefore, is generally not on inquiry notice of an assignment just because the mortgagee fails to produce the note each time an installment payment is made.

B. PAYMENT BY GRANTEE

When the mortgagor transfers the mortgaged property to another party, additional payment problems arise.

1. Negotiable Obligation

If the underlying obligation is negotiable, the grantee must pay the holder of the note. The grantee cannot safely pay the mortgage owner of record because commercial paper law makes a negotiable instrument freely transferable. The grantee, therefore, must demand production of the note before making either part or full payment. However, the defenses discussed above in connection with payment by the mortgagor also may be available to the grantee.

2.   Nonnegotiable Obligation: Notice Problem

If the underlying obligation is nonnegotiable, the grantee may pay the mortgagee until the grantee receives notice of an assignment. Again notice may come from several sources.

a.   *Actual Notice*

The grantee may receive actual notice of the assignment from the mortgagor, the assignor, the assignee, or otherwise.

b.   *Record Notice*

The grantee also may receive notice from the public records. A properly recorded mortgage assignment is constructive notice to a subsequent grantee.

Illustration: MR executes a nonnegotiable note and a mortgage to ME. ME assigns the documents to A who records the mortgage assignment. MR then sells and conveys the mortgaged property to GE subject to the mortgage. GE has no actual knowledge of the assignment, so GE makes part payment to ME. The payment is not good against A. GE was on constructive notice of A's interest because the records reflected the assignment at the time GE purchased the mortgaged property.

c. Inquiry Notice

The grantee generally may receive inquiry notice of an assignment in the same fashion as the mortgagor. Thus the discussion of inquiry notice found in the subsection on payment by the mortgagor is applicable here.

V. CONFLICTING ASSIGNMENTS

An unscrupulous mortgagee may sell and assign the mortgage loan to two or more parties. The conflict among these assignees is not easily resolved.

A. NONNEGOTIABLE OBLIGATION

If the underlying obligation is nonnegotiable, priority among assignees is governed by applicable recording statutes. This means that the first assignee prevails unless a subsequent assignee fits within the protection afforded by the statutes. *See* Ch. 9, pp. 175–176 (discussing recording statutes).

Illustration: MR executes a nonnegotiable note and a mortgage to ME. ME sells, assigns, and delivers the documents to A–1 who records the mortgage assignment. ME then sells and assigns to A–2, but, of course, cannot deliver the documents. A–1 and A–2 each claim ownership of the mortgage documents. A–1 prevails over A–2, because A–2 received constructive notice of A–1's prior assignment from the record. A–2 also received inquiry notice from ME's failure to deliver the documents.

B. NEGOTIABLE OBLIGATION

If the underlying obligation is negotiable, the generally accepted view is that commercial paper law, not the recording statutes, determines the rights of competing assignees. Hence, the assignee who takes possession of the note and the mortgage generally prevails.

Illustration: MR executes a negotiable note and a mortgage to ME who records. ME sells and assigns the loan to A–1, but retains possession of the documents. A–1 records the mortgage assignment. ME then sells the loan to A–2. ME negotiates the note, assigns the mortgage, and delivers the documents to A–2 who takes in good faith without actual notice of the prior assignment. A–1 and A–2 each claim ownership of the note and the mortgage. Under the generally accepted view, A–2 prevails over A–1 because constructive notice from the land records does not prevent A–2 from becoming a holder in due course. There is, however, authority to the contrary.

Illustration: MR executes a negotiable note and a mortgage to ME. ME sells the loan to A–1. ME negotiates the note and assigns the mortgage to A–1 who takes possession of the documents, but does not record the mortgage assignment. ME then sells and assigns the documents to A–2 who relies on the record, but, of course, does not receive the documents. A–1 and A–2 each claim ownership of the note and the mortgage. Under the generally accepted view, A–1 prevails because

A–2 is not a *holder* in due course and, therefore, takes subject to A–1's claim of legal title.

VI. FRACTIONAL ASSIGNMENTS (LOAN PARTICIPATION)

A. FORMS OF LOAN PARTICIPATION

Mortgagees commonly assign fractional interests in large mortgage loans to other investors. This technique is referred to as loan participation. *See* Ch. 2, p. 26 (discussing loan participation). A loan participation is generally structured in either of two ways. (1) The mortgagee takes a single mortgage note from the mortgagor, holds it, and issues participation certificates to the investors. (2) The mortgagee takes a series of notes from the mortgagor, each note for a fraction of the mortgage debt. The mortgagee then assigns some of the notes to the investors.

The series-of-notes method of participation was formerly quite common, but today the certificate approach is used almost exclusively. In either case, priority problems arise when the foreclosure sale proceeds are insufficient to pay all the investors.

B. AGREEMENT ESTABLISHING PRIORITY

Most modern participations are governed by a separate participation agreement that establishes priority among the parties. (An agreement regarding priority, of course, could be included in the mortgage.) The agreement usually provides that all investors, including the mortgagee, have equal priority and share ratably in the foreclosure sale proceeds.

C. PRIORITY ABSENT AGREEMENT— SERIES OF NOTES

Participations originally involved the assignment of a series of notes. The parties to these participations often failed to make provision in the mortgage for priority among the holders of the notes. Absent such an agreement, the courts were forced to develop principles governing the allocation of foreclosure sale proceeds. A tangle of conflicting rules and exceptions resulted.

1. Pro Rata Rule

The general rule is that, absent agreement fixing priority, the mortgage is enforced on a pro rata basis in favor of the mortgagee and all assignees. This rule is predicated on the theory that equality is equity.

Illustration: MR executes five $1,000 promissory notes and a mortgage to ME. ME sells and assigns one note to each A, B, C, and D. ME retains one note. The parties make no agreement regarding the priority of their interests. MR defaults, and a foreclosure sale produces $2,000. Under the pro rata rule each ME, A, B, C, and D is entitled to ⅕ of the $2,000 proceeds ($400).

a. Guaranty Exception

Courts in most pro rata states make an exception to the general rule when the mortgagee assigns a note by unqualified endorsement or with a guaranty of payment. In those cases, the assignee is generally awarded priority over the mortgagee on the theory that the assignee has the greater equity.

b. Priority–for–Assignees Exception

In a few pro rata jurisdictions, the general rule is not available to the mortgagee. The note or notes the mortgagee retains are postponed in priority to those held by the assignees.

Illustration: Assume the same fact situation as in the immediately preceding illustration. In a state that applies the pro rata rule only to assignees, A, B, C, and D have a $4,000 first lien as a group, and ME has a $1,000 second lien. Each assignee receives ¼ of the $2,000 proceeds obtained at foreclosure ($500). ME recovers nothing because the proceeds are not sufficient to pay off the assignees' $4,000 first lien.

Priority for assignees is justified on a variety of equitable grounds that have a common source, the theory that assignment of part of the debt operates also as a pro tanto assignment of the mortgage lien. Thus, the priority-for-assignees exception to the pro rata rule is sometimes inaccurately referred to as the pro tanto rule. The label is misleading because the pro tanto assignment concept is applied only between the mortgagee and the assignees. The assignees themselves share pro rata. The priority-for-assignees exception is, therefore, at most a severely limited pro tanto approach. As discussed later in this chapter, the true pro tanto rule establishes priority among assignees in the order they acquire their notes.

c. Order of Maturity Exception

Some pro rata states do not apply the general rule if the mortgage debt is represented by a series of notes having different dates of maturity. In these states priority is awarded the parties in the order of maturity of their notes.

Illustration: MR executes to ME a series of three $1,000 promissory notes: # 1 matures in one year, # 2 matures in two years, and # 3 matures in three years. The notes are all secured by a single mortgage. ME sells and assigns note # 1 to A and note # 2 to B. The parties make no agreement regarding the priority of their interests. MR defaults, and a foreclosure sale produces $1,500. Under the order of maturity exception, A receives $1,000, B receives $500, and ME receives nothing.

2. Priority of Assignment Rule (Pro Tanto Rule)

A few jurisdictions reject the pro rata rule with its various exceptions in favor of the principle that, absent agreement to the contrary, assignees have priority in the order the assignments were made. This approach, known as the priority of assignment rule or the pro tanto rule, is based on the theory that each assignee receives that portion of the mortgage necessary to secure the interest assigned. Under this approach, subsequent participants take subject to the rights of prior assignees, and the mortgagee takes subject to all.

Illustration: MR executes to ME a series of three $1,000 promissory notes maturing in three successive years. The notes are secured by a single mortgage. ME assigns one of the notes to A and then assigns another note to B. ME retains one note. The parties make no agreement regarding the priority of their notes. MR defaults, and foreclosure sale produces $1,500. Under the pro tanto rule, A receives $1,000, B gets $500, and ME receives nothing. The maturity dates of the notes are irrelevant.

D. PRIORITY ABSENT AGREEMENT—PARTICIPATION CERTIFICATES

The interest of each loan participant is usually represented by a participation certificate. Priority among the investors is almost invariably covered by a participation agreement. In the rare instances where no agreement exists, the pro rata rule applies because the certificates do not purport to assign any specific part of the mortgage loan. Thus, absent an agreement to the contrary, all investors, including the mortgagee, hold undivided interests having equal priority.

There is one exception to this rule. If the mortgagor guarantees payment of a certificate, the certificate holder is given priority over the mortgagee on the ground the guaranty indicates an intent to grant the certificate holder a superior claim.

VII. ASSIGNMENT BY OPERATION OF LAW (SUBROGATION)

Courts may imply an assignment of the mortgage by operation of law under the equitable doctrine of subrogation. In real estate finance law, subrogation is the substitution of one who pays the mortgage debt to the position of the mortgagee.

A. INDIVIDUALS FOR WHOM SUBROGATION IS AVAILABLE

A payor who is neither the primary obligor nor a mere volunteer may be subrogated to the rights of the mortgagee. (The primary obligor and the volunteer are not eligible for subrogation because they have no compelling equities in their favor.) Following are four situations in which the payor commonly qualifies for this form of equitable relief.

1. Mortgagor as Surety After Conveyance

Upon conveying away the mortgaged property subject to the mortgage, the mortgagor becomes a surety. *See* Ch. 6, pp. 108–116 (discussing rights and obligations of parties when mortgage survives conveyance). If the grantee fails to pay the obligation and the mortgagor is forced to do so, justice demands that the mortgagor be subrogated to the rights of the mortgagee.

Illustration: MR executes a promissory note and a mortgage to ME. MR sells and conveys the mortgaged property to GE subject to the mortgage. GE fails to pay the obligation, so MR as surety pays ME. MR is thereby subrogated to ME's right to foreclose. If GE assumed the obligation, MR also receives ME's right to recover a deficiency judgment against GE.

2. Junior Mortgagee

When a junior mortgagee pays off a prior lien for the protection of its own security interest, it is subrogated to the rights of the mortgagee receiving payment.

Illustration: MR executes a $10,000 promissory note and a mortgage to ME–1. MR then executes a $5,000 note and a second mortgage on the same property to ME–2. MR becomes insolvent and defaults on both obligations. Property values have recently slumped, and it is projected that a foreclosure sale will produce only $10,000. Because ME–2 will receive nothing in that case, ME–2 desires to postpone foreclosure. ME–2, therefore, pays ME–1 and is subrogated to ME–1's rights. The land remains subject to two liens, both in favor of ME–2 who can wait until property values rise to foreclose.

3. Lender of Pay Off Funds

One who loans funds to pay off an existing mortgage may be subrogated to the rights of the mortgagee receiving payment.

Illustration: MR executes a promissory note and a mortgage to ME. MR obtains a loan from L to pay off ME and executes a new promissory note and mortgage to L. MR uses the loan proceeds to pay ME. L's mortgage, however, is defective for some reason. L is subrogated to ME's lien rights in order to cure the defect and give L the security for which L bargained.

Illustration: ME–1 holds a first mortgage on MR's land, and ME–2 holds a second mortgage. MR borrows money from L to pay off ME–1. L is ignorant of ME–2's mortgage even though it is recorded. MR executes a promissory note and a mortgage to L. MR uses the loan proceeds to pay ME–1. L then discovers ME–2's mortgage lien. Courts following the generally accepted view subrogate L to ME–1's priority position on the theory that equity demands it and ME–2 is not prejudiced. Some courts, however, refuse to apply the doctrine of subrogation because L's loss was the result of L's own negligence in failing to check the records. Sometimes a line is drawn between ordinary negligence and unjustifiable negligence.

4. Purchaser of Mortgaged Property

When a purchaser of the mortgaged property assumes and pays the mortgage debt under the mistaken belief that no junior encumbrances exist, the purchaser may be subrogated to the rights of the mortgagee. There is, however, a division of opinion on the question.

Illustration: MR owns land subject to a first mortgage to ME–1 and a second mortgage to ME–2. MR sells and conveys the land to GE who assumes the obligation to ME–1. GE is ignorant of ME–2's mortgage even though it is recorded. If GE pays ME–1, many courts will subrogate GE to ME–1's priority position in order to prevent the gratuitous advancement of ME–2's lien priority. Other courts, however, deny subrogation for various reasons, including the notion that GE is now the primary obligor, a party for whom subrogation is unavailable.

B.   CONVENTIONAL SUBROGATION

The mortgagor and the payor sometimes enter an agreement that subrogation should occur in the payor's favor. Although subrogation consistent with this agreement is called conventional subrogation, the actual legal effect of the agreement is subject to dispute. Some courts treat conventional subrogation as solely contractual in nature and, therefore, separate from equitable subrogation. (Equitable subrogation is sometimes referred to as legal subrogation.) Many courts, however, view the agreement calling for subrogation as merely an important factor that often influences equity to act to prevent injustice in individual cases.

Illustration: MR obtains a construction loan from ME and executes a promissory note and a mortgage to ME. During the course of construction, M performs work on the project, but is not paid. Under state law, M may file a mechanics' lien on the property within ninety days after completion of the project. The lien will relate back to the date of commencement of construction. *See* Ch. 9, pp. 185–189 (analyzing mechanics' lien statutes). ME's construction loan mortgage was recorded prior to commencement of construction and thus, under state law has priority over all mechanics' liens. Sixty days after completion of construction, P makes a permanent mortgage loan to MR to "take-out" ME's construction mortgage loan. *See* Ch. 2, pp. 13–14 (discussing relationship between construction lenders and permanent lenders). MR executes a new promissory note and mortgage to P who is justifiably ignorant of M's claim. The mortgage contains a provision that P is subrogated to any lien discharged by proceeds of P's loan. Eighty days after completion of construction, M records a mechanics' lien that relates back to the date of construction and, therefore, is prior to the lien of P's mortgage. P, however, is subrogated to ME's priority position. This conclusion may be reached on various grounds. One approach is that subrogation is enforced as a contractual right. Another view is that subrogation occurs by operation of law and that the existence of the agreement merely indicates P is entitled to equitable relief.

C.   RIGHT TO FORMAL ASSIGNMENT

A subrogee usually may compel the mortgagee to formally assign the obligation and the mortgage.

VIII.   ASSIGNMENT AS SECURITY

The mortgagee may assign the note and the mortgage as security. *See* Ch. 5, pp. 97–98 (discussing mortgageable interests). Such collateral assignments are common practice, notably among mortgage bankers who frequently employ this technique to obtain financing. *See* Ch. 2, pp. 21–22 (discussing mortgage banking companies and mortgage warehousing).

An institution that takes a collateral assignment must perfect its security interest against other creditors of the mortgagor by taking possession of the note pursuant to the requirements of UCC Article 9. *See* UCC § 9–304(1). Recording in the land records generally is considered unnecessary to protect the assignee's security rights in the mortgage on the theory the mortgage travels with the note. There, however, is some authority to the contrary. In any event, the prudent assignee will record the assignment for purposes addressed elsewhere in this chapter, particularly to protect itself against subsequent purchasers of the mortgaged property.

IX. TRANSFER AT MORTGAGEE'S DEATH

The mortgagee's interest in the mortgage loan passes as personal property at the mortgagee's death on the theory that the mortgage, the realty aspect of the mortgage loan, is merely an incident of the obligation, the personalty aspect. This rule is, however, of waning significance. Two reasons exist for its decline in importance. First, most mortgagees are institutions that may last in perpetuity. Second, even when the mortgagee is an individual, modern intestacy statutes generally provide that personalty and realty descend in the same way.

CHAPTER 8

AFTER DEFAULT AND BEFORE FORECLOSURE

I. DEFAULT

A. DEFINITION AND SIGNIFICANCE OF DEFAULT

Default occurs when the mortgagor fails to pay the underlying debt or to perform some other obligation secured by the mortgage. What constitutes default in each case, therefore, can be determined only by examining the mortgage documents in question.

Default activates a set of mortgage law principles that determine the rights and obligations of the mortgagor and the mortgagee until foreclosure occurs. This chapter is devoted to an analysis of these principles.

B. COMMON TYPES OF DEFAULT

1. Failure to Pay Principal and Interest

Most defaults occur as a result of the mortgagor's failure to pay monthly installments of principal and interest.

2. Failure to Pay Taxes or Insurance

The mortgagor's failure to pay taxes or insurance premiums once were common types of default. The use of escrow accounts, however, has reduced the frequency of default in these areas. *See* Ch. 4, pp. 92–93 (discussing escrow accounts).

3. Waste

Mortgages commonly provide that the commission of waste on the mortgaged property constitutes default. *See* ¶ 6 of Mortgage in Appendix A. *See also* Ch. 5, pp. 103–105 (discussing waste of mortgaged property).

4. Construction Difficulties

Construction mortgages present additional possibilities for breach. Default often occurs because the mortgagor is unable to complete the contemplated improvements in accordance with the terms of the construction loan agreement. *See* Ch. 2, pp. 14–16 (analyzing construction lender's special risks).

C. WAIVER OF DEFAULT

The mortgagee may waive default by accepting late payment or other tardy performance. Lenders usually are willing to make some allowance for the borrower's financial difficulties because a modicum of tolerance often reaps greater monetary return than hasty invocation of expensive and protracted foreclosure procedures. *See* Ch. 10, pp. 199–212 (discussing foreclosure process).

Waiver of one late performance traditionally has not been viewed as constituting waiver of subsequent late performances. Some courts, however, may require a mortgagee who has regularly accepted late performance to give the mortgagor notice of its intention to require timely performance in the future. Many modern mortgages address this subject by providing that forbearance does not constitute waiver. *See* ¶ 11 of Mortgage in Appendix A. Clauses permitting the mortgagee to assess a charge for late payment also are common. *See* ¶ 6(A) of Note in Appendix A; Ch. 4, p. 93 (considering late charges).

II. ACCELERATION

A. THE ACCELERATION CLAUSE

One of the most significant provisions in the modern amortized mortgage is that clause authorizing the mortgagee to accelerate the entire debt when the mortgagor defaults in the payment of a single monthly installment or in the performance of any other obligation secured by the mortgage. *See* ¶ 21 of Mortgage in Appendix A. Without an acceleration clause, the mortgagee can institute foreclosure proceedings to recover only the amount in default. *See* Ch. 10, pp. 199–212 (discussing foreclosure process). Further, if the mortgagee does foreclose in such a situation, authorities are in conflict as to whether the lien for the amount not in default survives foreclosure.

Illustration: MR executes a $40,000 promissory note and a mortgage to ME. The documents provide for equal monthly payments of $300 over a thirty-year term, but do not include an acceleration clause. MR misses two payments. ME may institute foreclosure proceedings, but is only entitled to that part of the proceeds sufficient to satisfy the partial default ($600). In some states, the mortgage lien continues on the property to secure the unpaid balance of the debt. Any surplus goes to the mortgagor. In other jurisdictions, however, the property is sold free from the mortgage lien. In such case, the surplus is usually either applied immediately to the unpaid balance of the loan or placed in trust to cover the debt as it matures.

An acceleration clause should be included in both the note and the mortgage. These clauses should coincide in all respects. In this regard, the note may refer to the mortgage for acceleration rights. *See* ¶ 10 of Note in Appendix A. The note's negotiability is not affected by such reference. *See* UCC § 3–106(b). *See also* Ch. 4, pp. 70–71 (discussing form of obligation).

If an acceleration clause is included only in the mortgage, the mortgagee may experience difficulty in accelerating the loan. Authorities are divided concerning the significance of its omission from the note. One view is that the mortgagee can accelerate under both documents on the ground the note and the mortgage are integral parts of one contract. The other view is that the mortgagee can only accelerate under the mortgage.

Illustration: MR executes a promissory note and a mortgage to ME. An acceleration clause is included in the mortgage, but is omitted from the note. MR defaults by failing to make two monthly payments. ME can accelerate under the mortgage, foreclose, and apply the foreclosure sale proceeds to the entire debt. In some states ME also can obtain a deficiency judgment against MR on the note. In others, ME cannot.

B. CURING DEFAULT BEFORE ACCELERATION

The mortgagor may reinstate the mortgage loan by curing default before the mortgagee accelerates.

Illustration: MR executes a promissory note and a mortgage to ME. The documents contain identical acceleration clauses. MR defaults by missing one monthly payment. If MR makes late payment to ME before ME accelerates, the loan is reinstated. ME may not use the cured default as a basis for acceleration. ME, of course, may accelerate after a later default.

Today, residential mortgages often provide that, with certain exceptions, the mortgagee must give the mortgagor notice of impending acceleration and the opportunity to avoid it by curing default. *See* ¶ 21 of Mortgage in Appendix A.

C. TRIGGERING ACCELERATION

Acceleration clauses are usually activated at the mortgagee's option. A self-operating clause could result in acceleration contrary to the mortgagee's best interest. Optional acceleration is triggered by the mortgagee's performance of an act that clearly evidences the intent to treat the entire debt due. In most states, formal notice of acceleration is unnecessary. The filing of a foreclosure complaint is generally sufficient to indicate an election to accelerate.

D. CURING DEFAULT AFTER ACCELERATION

1. General Rule

The general rule is that after the mortgagee accelerates, the mortgagor cannot reinstate the loan by curing the original default. The mortgagor must pay the entire debt or face foreclosure. However, several state legislatures have enacted statutes that permit mortgagors to nullify acceleration by just paying the amount originally in default. Moreover, some commonly used mortgage forms now give the mortgagor a similar contract right. *See* ¶ 18 of Mortgage in Appendix A.

2. Equitable Relief

Mortgagors occasionally seek to have an acceleration set aside on the ground the default which triggered it resulted from misunderstanding or excusable neglect. Equitable relief is commonly unavailable in such cases. Many courts view an acceleration clause as an agreement regarding the time for payment whose enforcement does not exact a penalty or involve a forfeiture. Thus, the mortgagee may enforce the clause as written unless it has acted fraudulently, unconscionably, or in bad faith. There is, however, a contrary view. In an increasing number of jurisdictions, courts refuse to recognize an acceleration that would produce an inequitable or unjust result.

Illustration: MR executes a promissory note and a mortgage to ME. The documents contain identical optional acceleration clauses. MR goes to Europe on business, but advises an assistant to make the next required payment to ME. MR's assistant uses the wrong mathematical formula to compute the interest and, therefore, pays a little less than is due. ME elects to accelerate and foreclose because of this minor default. MR returns from Europe, makes late tender of the unpaid interest, and requests the court to set aside the acceleration. In many states, courts will not grant relief for breach of contract resulting from MR's negligence. *See* Graf v. Hope Building Corporation (N.Y.1930). The trend, however, is to grant MR relief when acceleration is inequitable or unjust under the circumstances. Although MR's willingness to cure the default is not sufficient reason to grant equitable relief under this modern view, other factors, such as MR's good faith and the unusual situation, indicate that the acceleration should be set aside. *See* Federal

Home Loan Mortgage Corporation v. Taylor (Fla. App.1975).

F. DUE–ON–SALE CLAUSES

Mortgages often provide for acceleration if the mortgagor transfers any interest in the mortgaged property without the mortgagee's consent. *See* ¶ 17 of Mortgage in Appendix A. These due-on-sale clauses present special legal problems that are discussed in an earlier chapter. *See* Ch. 6, pp. 118–125 (analyzing due-on-sale clauses).

III. RIGHT TO POSSESSION AND RENTS
A. SIGNIFICANCE OF MORTGAGE THEORIES

Title, intermediate, and lien mortgage theories are significant today primarily as they relate to possession of the mortgaged property. *See* Ch. 1, pp. 8–10 (discussing mortgage theories). Possession is important because with it comes the right to rents and profits produced by the property.

A basic tenet of common law is that possession is an attribute of legal title. Thus, in title theory states, the mortgagee receives the right to possession when the mortgage is executed. In intermediate theory jurisdictions, the mortgagee ostensibly receives title, but is allowed by law to take possession only upon default. In lien theory states, the mortgagee does not receive title and, therefore, cannot take possession at any time, even after default.

The confusion created by these conflicting theories has been somewhat alleviated by the common practice of dealing with the issue of possession in the mortgage contract itself. The modern mortgage often provides that the mortgagor has the right to possession until default and the mortgagee has the right thereafter. Courts in some lien theory states, however, refuse to enforce mortgage agreements of this type for public policy reasons. But even in these jurisdictions, the mortgagor may give possession to the mortgagee after default.

Hence, as a practical matter, default frequently gives the mortgagee the right to possession either by operation of law or by mortgage provision. The consequences of this right are explored in the next section.

B. MORTGAGEE IN POSSESSION

1. Definition

When the mortgagee lawfully exercises dominion and control over the property under the mortgage, it is known as a mortgagee in possession. A mortgagee may take possession without physically entering or occupying the mortgaged property so long as it exercises substantially the same control over the property as the mortgagor normally would exert.

Illustration: MR executes a mortgage on a vacant farm to ME. The mortgage authorizes ME to take possession upon default. MR defaults. ME need not actually occupy the farm to become a mortgagee in possession. Maintaining the property and seeking tenants would be sufficient.

2. Rights

A mortgagee in possession may control the property until either redemption or foreclosure occurs and collect all rents and profits arising from the land during that time. The mortgagee, of course, does not acquire title to the mortgaged property merely by taking possession of it under the mortgage.

3. Obligations

All states impose trustee-like obligations on a mortgagee in possession.

a. *Management*

A mortgagee in possession must manage and maintain the property in a prudent manner and apply receipts in excess of costs to the mortgage debt. The obligation of prudent management requires that a mortgagee in possession use reasonable efforts to make the property productive. The mortgagee is, therefore, chargeable for rent it could have secured but for lack of reasonable diligence. And, if the mortgagee occupies the property for its own use, it is generally accountable for the fair rental value of its occupancy without regard to whether the property produces more or less than that amount.

b. Accounting

A mortgagee in possession does not act free from judicial scrutiny. The mortgagor can require the mortgagee to make a detailed accounting of receipts and expenses, but only in a foreclosure action or upon redemption.

c. Liability to Third Parties

A mortgagee in possession may incur liabilities to third parties. The mortgagee is responsible in tort for its negligence in managing the mortgaged property and in contract for goods and services properly supplied to the property during the mortgagee's possession.

4. Problem of Leases Existing at Default

When mortgaged property is subject to a lease at the time of default, a mortgagee who has the right to take possession either by law or by agreement can ascertain its rights and duties vis-à-vis the lessee only by determining whether the lease was made before or after the execution of the mortgage. It is assumed in the following discussion that all instruments were promptly recorded, so that the order of their execution is also the order of their priority under applicable recording statutes. *See* Ch. 9, pp. 175–176 (discussing recording statutes).

a. Prior Leases

If the lease was executed before the mortgage, the mortgagee in possession is bound by the lease because the mortgagee's security extends only to the interest the mortgagor owned at the time the mortgage was created. The lessee under a prior lease is also bound because the mortgagee in possession succeeds to the mortgagor's reversion and thereby establishes privity of estate. Hence, the lessee may remain on the property, but must pay rent to the mortgagee in possession.

b. *Junior Leases*

If the lease was executed after the mortgage, the mortgagee may take possession and thereby terminate the lease on the theory that the lessee can have no greater right to possession than the lessor. Although the mortgagee appears to be in a generally favorable position in this situation, it is really at an advantage only if it desires to terminate the junior lease. If the mortgagee wants to continue the junior lease and collect rent from the junior lessee, difficulty arises because the lessee is liable only to one with whom the lessee is in either privity of contract or privity of estate. The junior lessee clearly has no contractual obligation to the mortgagee. In addition, no privity of estate exists between the junior lessee and the mortgagee because the mortgage could not transfer the mortgagor's reversion against a lessee not then in existence. The mortgagee, therefore, faces "Catch 22" of real estate finance law. Because the mortgagee cannot force the junior lessee to enter a contract, the mortgagee is entitled to receive rent only if it can establish privity of estate with the lessee. If, however, the mortgagee attempts to do so by taking possession, the junior lease and the lessee's obligations thereunder are destroyed on the ground that the mortgagee's possession relates back to the date the mortgage was executed.

The mortgagee in possession may avoid this dilemma by persuading the junior lessee to enter an attornment agreement recognizing the mortgagee as lessor. This arrangement establishes the privity of contract necessary for the mortgagee to enforce the lease. The attornment agreement is in reality a new lease. Hence, the lessee and the mortgagee in possession may choose to set entirely new terms.

Although many junior lessees attorn to a mortgagee in possession, others take advantage of the situation to rid themselves of what they consider to be an undesirable lease. This may be disastrous to the mortgagee who was depending upon their rents to pay the mortgage debt.

The mortgagee, therefore, should take steps to insure that it can preserve and enforce junior leases after default. Four options are available. First, the mortgagee could subordinate the mortgage to junior leases so that they would be treated as prior leases and, therefore, survive the mortgagee's possession. *See* Ch. 9, pp. 179–184 (discussing subordination agreements). Second, the mortgagee could require the mortgagor to negotiate an attornment provision in each valuable junior lease whereby the junior lessee agrees to recognize the mortgagee as landlord if the lessor/mortgagor defaults on the mortgage. The lessee, of course, may seek to have the mortgagee execute a non-disturbance agreement in return. Such a combination of attornment and non-disturbance agreements is the rough functional equivalent of a subordination. Third, the mortgagee could require that the mortgagor assign rents generated by the mortgaged property as additional security. This alternative is explored in the following subsection. Fourth, at default the mortgagee could seek the appointment of a receiver of rents, a course of action that is discussed later in this chapter.

C. ASSIGNMENT OF RENTS

The mortgagee may require the mortgagor to execute an assignment of rents giving the mortgagee an interest in all present and future leases and in all rents issuing from the mortgaged property independent of any right the mortgagee may have to take possession of the property. The practical effect of an assignment of rents is that upon default the mortgagee, as assignee of the mortgagor's rights, may collect rents without taking possession under the mortgage. Thus, the mortgagee can preserve and enforce junior leases until foreclosure.

A division of opinion exists as to how an assignment of rents may be activated. The precise language of the assignment may be determinative. There is considerable authority that an assignment of rents is an "absolute" assignment triggered automatically upon default. However, the generally accepted view is that an assignment of rents constitutes a security interest that the mortgagee must trigger by taking some affirmative step after default. The type of action required varies among the states. Depending upon the jurisdiction, the mortgagee may activate the assignment of rents by making formal demand of the mortgagor, by giving notice to the lessees, by filing a foreclosure suit seeking the appointment of a receiver, by taking possession of the property, or by obtaining the appointment of a receiver.

An assignment of rents also protects the mortgagee from being bound by agreements for advance rental payment, rent reduction, or lease cancellation commonly used by mortgagors in distress to milk the mortgaged property of all potential revenue. If the mortgagee obtains an assignment of rents, records it, and gives notice to existing lessees, all lessees enter advance payment, rent reduction, and cancellation agreements with the mortgagor at their peril.

D. RECEIVER

1. Background

The mortgagee may seek to have a receiver for rents and profits appointed in an action for foreclosure. This is a particularly valuable option in lien theory states where the mortgagee cannot obtain possession and reach rents and profits absent the mortgagor's agreement that the mortgagee may do so.

Even when the mortgagee has the right to possession of the property upon default, the mortgagee may prefer to have a receiver appointed rather than take possession itself. Three reasons support this preference. First, the stringent accounting duties imposed on a mortgagee in possession are avoided. Second, the potential tort and contract liabilities of a mortgagee in possession are eliminated. Third, junior leases are preserved and rents may be collected under those leases even when there is no assignment of rents.

2. Grounds for Appointment

A receivership is an equitable remedy designed to preserve the mortgaged property pending foreclosure. The appointment of a receiver is generally within the sound discretion of the court bounded only by the traditional requirement that the court give due consideration to the financial position of the mortgagor, the adequacy of the security, and the danger of waste, destruction, or loss of the property. Judicial authority in this area has been further broadened by the common use of a mortgage clause authorizing the mortgagee to obtain the appointment of a receiver.

Courts have exercised their virtually unbridled discretion in markedly different ways. In many jurisdictions, the appointment of a receiver is almost automatic upon request. In others, a receiver is appointed only in the most compelling circumstances.

3. Receiver's Powers

Once appointed, the receiver generally is empowered to preserve the mortgagee's security by taking possession of the mortgaged property and collecting rents and profits. Although an exhaustive analysis of a receiver's authority is beyond the scope of these materials, three areas of receiver action deserve additional discussion.

a. Collecting Rent From Junior Lessees

A mortgagee may utilize a receiver to reach rent payable under a lease entered after the execution of the mortgage even when there is no assignment of rents. The receiver's action is that of the court, not the mortgagee, so it does not automatically destroy the junior lease.

b. Collecting Rent From Mortgagor

A vexing rent collection problem arises when the mortgagor occupies the mortgaged property as a residence. There is authority that a receiver may collect rent from the mortgagor in such cases. However, courts may be hesitant to permit a receiver to do so. *See* Holmes v. Gravenhorst (N.Y.1933).

c. Operating Mortgagor's Business

Mortgagees may request the appointment of a receiver to operate the mortgagor's business pending foreclosure. A court generally will grant the request only if the business is either specifically covered by the mortgage or based primarily on the rental value of the mortgaged property, as in the case of an apartment building.

IV. EQUITY OF REDEMPTION

A. AVAILABILITY

Certain qualified individuals may prevent foreclosure by paying off the mortgage debt before the completion of foreclosure proceedings. *See* Ch. 10, pp. 199–212 (discussing foreclosure process). This right of late payment is known as the equity of redemption. *See* Ch. 1, pp. 4–5 (tracing evolution of equity of redemption).

B. INDIVIDUALS WHO MAY REDEEM

The mortgagor, of course, may redeem. In addition, anyone acquiring an interest in, or a lien on, the mortgaged property after the attachment of the mortgage may redeem because their interests will be cut off by foreclosure. Eligible redemptioners include grantees, heirs, devisees, junior lessees, and junior encumbrancers. When several individuals have equitable redemption rights, they may redeem in the order of the priority of their interests, subject to the mortgagor's ultimate right to redeem.

C. AMOUNT REQUIRED FOR REDEMPTION

Equitable redemption generally can be accomplished only by paying the entire mortgage debt. However, in the event that the entire debt is not in default, as in the case of an unaccelerated amortized loan, the mortgagor may reinstate the loan and avoid foreclosure by making late payment of the overdue amount. In the following discussion it is assumed that the entire mortgage debt is in default.

D. EFFECT OF REDEMPTION

1. By Mortgagor or Mortgagor's Successor

Redemption by the mortgagor or the mortgagor's successor discharges the mortgage lien. Junior interests survive unless also paid off.

2. By Junior Interest Holder

Redemption by a junior interest holder does not terminate the mortgage from which the property is redeemed. On the contrary, the mortgage survives, and the one who redeems is subrogated to the rights of the mortgagee. *See* Ch. 7, pp. 145–150 (discussing subrogation).

Illustration: MR executes a $10,000 first mortgage to ME–1, then a $5,000 second mortgage to ME–2, and finally a $2,000 third mortgage to ME–3. MR defaults on all loans, and each mortgagee accelerates. MR may pay ME–1 $10,000 and free the land from the first mortgage. In that case, the second and third mortgage liens would remain. ME–2 also may pay ME–1 $10,000 before MR does so. This would not terminate the first mortgage. All three mortgages would remain, but now ME–2 would hold both the first and second mortgages. ME–3 could then redeem from ME–2 by paying ME–2 the total amount of the first and second liens ($15,000). This would not terminate either the first or second mortgages. All three mortgages would remain, but they now would be held by ME–3. MR has the last right to redeem. MR, however, must pay ME–3 the total of all mortgage liens ($17,000) to redeem the land free from encumbrances.

E. ENFORCEMENT OF RIGHT TO REDEEM

If the parties cannot agree on the question of redemption, the one asserting a right to redeem may file a bill in equity to enforce this right.

F. WAIVER/CLOGGING

Courts will not recognize mortgage clauses that waive or otherwise clog the mortgagor's equity of redemption. *See* Ch. 1, p. 5 (discussing prohibition against clogging).

G. WHEN RIGHT OF REDEMPTION ENDS

1. Foreclosure

The completion of foreclosure terminates the equity of redemption of all parties defendant. If foreclosure is by judicial sale, the right to redeem generally ends when the court confirms the sale. If foreclosure is by power of sale, the right to redeem ends when the sale is final under local law.

A junior interest holder omitted from the foreclosure proceedings retains both the junior interest and an equity of redemption. The omitted junior interest holder, therefore, may seek to assert the right to redeem even after foreclosure. *See* Ch. 10, p. 204 (analyzing rights of omitted junior lienor).

2. Termination by Other Means

A mortgagor's equitable right to redeem may be barred by estoppel, laches, or a statute of limitations. Generally, none of these possibilities will arise if the mortgagor remains on the mortgaged property. It is when the mortgagee takes possession that circumstances are ripe for the development of these bars to redemption.

V. ALTERNATIVES TO FORECLOSURE

Although a mortgagee is entitled to commence foreclosure proceedings after default, it may decide to pursue another course of action initially.

A. WORKOUT ARRANGEMENT

Institutional mortgage lenders desire to avoid foreclosure. Their business is to obtain a reasonable return on their investments, not to engage in litigation. Consequently, they often lower monthly payments, extend the time for payment, waive late charges, or make any other reasonable arrangement that allows the mortgagor to work out of temporary financial difficulty.

B. DEED IN LIEU OF FORECLOSURE

If the mortgagor cannot possibly pay the mortgage obligation, the mortgagee may be willing to accept a deed to the property in lieu of foreclosure. *See* Ch. 6, p. 117 (discussing deed in lieu of foreclosure).

C. RECOVERY ON THE NOTE ALONE/"ONE ACTION" RULE

Even if litigation is necessary, the mortgagee generally may sue on the note without foreclosing the mortgage. This principle is predicated on the notion that because the underlying obligation is the essential element of the transaction, the mortgagee may treat the note as unsecured if it so wishes. In California and a few other states, however, the mortgagee's only remedy on default is to foreclose and obtain a deficiency judgment if appropriate. *See* Ch. 10, pp. 205–206 (discussing deficiency judgment). This "one action" rule is based on the theory that because the mortgaged property is the primary fund for repayment of the debt, the mortgagee must exhaust it before seeking satisfaction from the mortgagor's other assets. The rule also is designed to protect the mortgagor from multiple actions arising from the same loan transaction.

Where suit on the note alone is permitted, the mortgage is not affected by the resulting personal judgment against the mortgagor. The debt merges into the judgment, and the judgment becomes the underlying obligation. Whatever the mortgagee then collects from the mortgagor's other assets is credited against this obligation. The only significant change in the legal relationship of the parties is that enforcement of the underlying obligation is now governed by the statute of limitations on judgments rather than by the statute of limitations on promissory notes.

CHAPTER 9

PRIORITIES

I. GENERAL PRINCIPLES

When foreclosure is imminent, the mortgagee and other parties holding interests in the mortgaged property become particularly concerned about the priority of their respective interests. Their concern is well founded. First, interests acquired before the mortgage survive foreclosure; those acquired after the mortgage are extinguished. Second, the mortgagee and subsequent lienors are paid from the proceeds of the foreclosure sale in the order of their priority, and the proceeds are often insufficient to pay everyone.

II. RECORDING STATUTES

The principle "prior in time, prior in right" determines the order of priority among interest holders in the mortgaged property unless a subsequent purchaser fits within the protection afforded by the local recording statute. Recording statutes vary with regard to the requirements that a subsequent purchaser must meet. Depending on the jurisdiction, a subsequent purchaser must either (1) be without notice of the prior interest (notice statute),

175

(2) be without notice of the prior interest and record first (race-notice statute), or (3) record first (race statute). In all jurisdictions, the prior interest holder may preserve the holder's original priority position by recording the interest immediately after its acquisition.

Illustration: MR executes a mortgage to ME–1 who records immediately. MR then executes a mortgage to ME–2. ME–2 cannot change the order of priority under any type of recording statute because ME–2 is on constructive notice of the prior interest and also has lost the race to record.

III. SELECTED ISSUES

Priority issues are inextricably entwined with the development of certain fundamental mortgage concepts. Thus, several priority problems are discussed in earlier chapters. *See* Ch. 4, pp. 71–79 (future advances and dragnet clause), Ch. 5, pp. 98–99 (after-acquired property clause), Ch. 6, pp. 116–117 (acquisition of mortgaged property by mortgagee), and Ch. 7, pp. 138–145 (conflicting and fractional assignments). Additional selected priority matters are presented here. In this discussion it is assumed, unless otherwise indicated, that all mortgages and other interests were recorded immediately after their acquisition.

A. PURCHASE MONEY MORTGAGE

1. Distinguishing Features

A purchase money mortgage is a mortgage taken by the seller of real estate as security for part of the purchase price or by a third party lender as security for purchase funds advanced. *See* Ch. 3, pp. 47–48 (describing purchase money mortgage). In either situation, purchase money mortgage status is available only when the deed and the mortgage are components of one continuous transaction.

Illustration: MR desires to purchase certain land for sale in another part of the state. MR does not have sufficient cash on hand to do so. Thus, MR asks ME for a $20,000 loan. ME advances MR $20,000 to purchase the land. MR gives ME a $20,000 promissory note and agrees to secure the note with a mortgage on the property when MR acquires it. Later that day MR travels to the land and makes an offer to purchase it. After three days of protracted negotiations the transaction is completed, and MR receives a deed to the property. MR returns home. On the second day following MR's return, MR executes a mortgage on the property to ME. This is a purchase money mortgage. As long as the mortgage is an inseparable aspect of the acquisition of the mortgaged property, it need not be executed at the same time as the deed. *See* Stewart v. Smith (Minn.1886).

2. Preferred Priority Position

A purchase money mortgage has priority over any interest attaching to the property through the purchaser-mortgagor. Underlying this principle is the equitable theory that when the mortgagor receives the property, it is already encumbered with a lien in favor of the purchase money mortgagee whose willingness to extend credit or advance funds made the acquisition possible. Accordingly, a purchase money mortgage takes precedence over judgment liens against the mortgagor, liens arising from after-acquired property clauses in other mortgages executed by the mortgagor, and claims against the mortgagor for dower or homestead.

Illustration: JL obtains a judgment against MR and receives a judgment lien on all real estate owned by MR. Later MR borrows money from ME to purchase a parcel of land. MR executes a mortgage on the land to ME to secure repayment of the loan. Under the purchase money mortgage rule, ME's mortgage lien has priority over JL's judgment lien.

The priority of a lien or other interest existing on the property at the time of its acquisition by the mortgagor is not affected by the purchase money mortgage rule. The rule only postpones the priority of liens and claims that attach to the property through the mortgagor.

Illustration: O owns a parcel of land. JL obtains a judgment against O and receives a judgment lien on all real estate owned by O, including the land in question. The lien is of record. O then conveys the land to MR. The lien is not discharged. MR pays O with funds borrowed from

ME and executes a mortgage on the land to ME to secure repayment of the loan. Although ME's mortgage qualifies as a purchase money mortgage, it does not take precedence over JL's prior lien on the property.

B.　SUBORDINATION AGREEMENTS

Established priorities may be altered by agreement. Such an agreement is called a subordination because it involves a senior interest holder voluntarily subordinating its rights to those of a junior interest holder. Three common subordination situations are treated in this subsection.

1.　Subordination of Purchase Money Mortgage to Construction Loan Mortgage

a.　*Background*

Subordination agreements are often employed as part of the real estate development process. Developers, of course, need raw land upon which to construct shopping centers, apartment houses, office buildings, subdivisions, and other projects. Because developers are typically unable to purchase land outright and because institutional lenders generally are reluctant to make land acquisition loans, sellers often finance the sale themselves. This form of financing is not difficult to implement. The seller conveys the land to the developer in exchange for a small down payment and a note for the balance of the purchase price secured by a purchase money mortgage on the land conveyed. The developer then obtains financing for the actual development. Construction lenders, however, normally demand a first lien on the property as security. In order for the planned development to occur, the seller, therefore, must subordinate the purchase money mortgage to the construction loan mortgage. The seller is usually willing to take this risk on the expectation that the development will enhance the property's value to the extent that the seller will be in a better security position as a second mortgagee of improved land than as a first mortgagee of unimproved land. Moreover, the seller typically is able to demand a higher than normal purchase price for the property as compensation for agreeing to the subordination.

b. Subordination Agreement in General

The subordination is normally part of the original agreement between the seller and the developer and is covered in either the real estate contract, the purchase money mortgage, or a separate document. An advance subordination agreement may take either of two forms: (1) an agreement that subordination occurs automatically when the construction loan mortgage is executed or (2) an agreement to execute a formal subordination upon request once the construction loan is obtained.

c. Describing Construction Loan

The subordination agreement must contain an adequate description of the construction loan. If the subordination agreement does not, courts refuse to enforce the agreement on the ground it is impossible to tell what has been promised.

The question of whether the description of the construction loan is so indefinite as to render the subordination contract unenforceable is often difficult to resolve. Although courts generally agree that the maximum amount of the construction loan must be stated, they disagree as to whether the interest rate, maturity, use of loan proceeds, or other loan details also must be specified. Furthermore, some courts may enforce a less detailed subordination agreement when the missing terms are left for determination to an institutional construction lender. This approach is based on the rationale that institutional lenders are bound by regulation, custom, and usage to impose reasonable loan terms.

In California, the indefinite description issue is further complicated by a decision of the supreme court of that state requiring all subordination agreements to be just and reasonable to the seller. Handy v. Gordon (Cal.1967). What this "fairness" doctrine demands with regard to precision in describing the construction loan remains an open question.

d. *Obtaining Construction Loan Described*

If the developer obtains a construction loan that varies materially from the loan described in the subordination agreement, subordination does not occur.

e. Diversion of Construction Loan Funds

Priority problems may arise even after the specified construction loan is obtained. Occasionally, a mortgagor-developer diverts loan proceeds from the project with the result that the property is not sufficiently enhanced in value to adequately secure the subordinated purchase money mortgage loan. In such case, the purchase money mortgagee is likely to claim that the subordination agreement has been breached and that the original lien priority has been restored. When this issue first arose, the courts generally held that, absent an agreement to the contrary, a construction loan mortgagee acting in good faith has no duty to monitor the application of construction funds. The construction lender, therefore, retains the lien priority granted to it in the subordination agreement unless it advances money to the developer in bad faith.

This principle survives, but its significance has been eroded by three developments. First, purchase money mortgagees commonly condition subordination upon actual use of the construction loan funds for construction purposes. Second, a similar condition may be implied in certain cases. *See* Middlebrook–Anderson Co. v. Southwest Savings and Loan Association (Cal.App.1971). Third, some courts have concluded that construction lenders owe subordinated lienors a duty to exercise reasonable care in disbursing construction loan funds.

When subordination is expressly or impliedly conditioned upon the proper application of loan proceeds and funds are diverted, the purchase money mortgagee is entitled to relief. The purchase money mortgage generally should be restored to priority over the construction loan mortgage to the extent of the diverted funds. Thus, lien priority generally should be established as follows: (1) construction lender for funds properly applied to the project, (2) purchase money mortgagee for the full amount of the purchase money mortgage, and (3) construction lender for diverted funds. There is, however, authority that the purchase money mortgagee should be reinstated to first lien priority when the construction lender breaches an express condition to subordination.

f. Optional Advance Risk

Even if all funds are used for construction, the construction lender may lose priority to the subordinated purchase money mortgage for advances made ahead of schedule or after default on the theory such advances are optional, not obligatory. *See* Ch. 4, pp. 77–78 (considering construction lender's dilemma).

2. Subordination of Lease to Mortgage and Vice Versa

A mortgagee may desire to enhance its security position by switching priorities with a lessee of the mortgaged property. Reversal of priorities may occur in either direction. If an unattractive lease has original priority, the mortgagee might demand subordination of the lease to the mortgage as a condition of making the mortgage loan. The subordination enables the mortgagee to terminate the lease if the mortgagee takes possession after default or forecloses. If an attractive lease is originally junior to the mortgage, the mortgagee might subordinate the mortgage to the lease in order to collect rents from the lessee on default and preserve the lease at foreclosure. *See* Ch. 8, pp. 162–165 (analyzing problem of leases existing at default).

3. Subordination of Fee to Leasehold Mortgage

Leasehold mortgagees frequently require the owner of the leased property to submit the fee simple to the mortgage lien. Although this arrangement is commonly termed subordination of the fee, it obviously does not involve switching lien priorities. *See* Ch. 3, pp. 64–66 (discussing leasehold mortgage).

C. FIXTURES

A mortgage is a lien on all fixtures on the mortgaged property. *See* Ch. 5, pp. 100–101 (treating mortgage coverage of fixtures). These fixtures also may be subject to the lien of a security interest that attached to them before they became fixtures. Controversy often arises between the mortgagee and the holder of the security interest regarding the priority of their respective liens. Section 9–313 of the Uniform Commercial Code (UCC) is designed to resolve this priority issue. Following is a summary of its provisions.

As a general rule of § 9–313, priority between the holder of a security interest in fixtures and the mortgagee goes to the first one to properly file in the public records. A purchase money security interest filed before or within ten days after the goods become fixtures, however, takes priority over existing nonconstruction loan mortgages on the theory that the party who supplies the money used to acquire the fixtures should be favored. But, because a construction lender provides funds for the entire improvement and expects all parts thereof to serve as collateral for its loan, existing construction loan mortgages take priority over purchase money security interests in goods that become fixtures during construction. Finally, with regard to the recordation process, the UCC requires that fixture financing statements be filed and indexed in local real estate records so a person conducting a title search can discover them. *See* UCC §§ 9–401(1), 9–403(7).

D. MECHANICS' LIEN STATUTES

1. General

Mechanics' lien statutes exist in every state to give an individual who has supplied services, labor, or materials to a construction project a lien on the property as security for payment due. These measures vary greatly among the states with regard to persons protected, the lien amount, lien priority, and numerous other factors. Only general amount, priority, and constitutional issues are treated here.

2. Amount

Mechanics' lien statutes generally take one of two markedly different approaches regarding the amount that a lien claimant may recover. Some states, following the New York system, view the rights of lien claimants as derived from the general construction contract and limit recovery to the balance due on the contract at the date the lien is filed. Other jurisdictions, adopting the Pennsylvania system, give lien claimants direct rights and permit recovery for the full value of their goods or services.

3. Priority

Priority problems frequently arise between mechanics' lienors and mortgagees, particularly construction mortgage lenders. In order to resolve these issues, it is necessary to ascertain the priority accorded mechanics' liens under local statutes. The statutes are far from uniform on this subject.

a. Relation Back to Commencement of Construction

In many states, a mechanics' lienor's priority relates back to the date construction began. Under this approach, the construction lender can protect its lien against all mechanics' lienors by recording the construction loan mortgage before construction commences. But, if the lender fails to do so, it loses priority to all mechanics' lienors, not just those who did work before the mortgage was recorded.

Illustration: MR decides to construct a building on MR's property, so MR hires X to clear the land

and do the necessary excavation work. X completes the job and is paid by MR. Six weeks later, MR obtains a construction mortgage loan from ME who promptly records the mortgage. After the mortgage is recorded, Y does work on the building. Y is not paid. Y, therefore, files a mechanics' lien. Y's lien relates back to the date X did the initial construction work and thereby takes priority over ME's mortgage.

Even when the construction loan mortgage is recorded before work begins, controversy may develop as to the priority of future advances made by a construction lender over an intervening mechanics' lien. The issue usually arises when a mechanics' lienor contends that all construction advances made after the attachment of its mechanics' lien are optional, not obligatory, and thereby lose priority to its encumbrance. *See* Ch. 4, pp. 77–78 (considering construction lender's dilemma).

b. Other Approaches

The remaining states take a wide variety of approaches to the mechanics' lien priority issue. Certain jurisdictions grant lien priority from the date the claimant actually began work or supplied materials. In some states, the lien receives priority as of the day the claimant files. Other jurisdictions base lien priority on additional considerations, such as the time the general construction contract was entered.

4. Constitutionality of Mechanics' Lien Statutes

Mechanics' lien statutes generally authorize mechanics and materialmen to perfect their liens without judicial involvement and sometimes without prior notice to the property owner. This procedure has been attacked in several jurisdictions as a denial of the property owner's Fourteenth Amendment due process rights.

Most courts faced with this issue have upheld the mechanics' lien statute in question on the theory that a mechanics' lien does not constitute a taking of property within the meaning of the Fourteenth Amendment. These courts reason that the attachment of the lien does not deprive the owner of possession, use, or enjoyment of the land and any impairment of the owner's ability to sell or encumber the property is merely a de minimus taking that does not trigger the application of procedural due process safeguards. A few courts, however, have concluded that a mechanics' lien affects a Fourteenth Amendment property interest by impairing the property owner's ability to alienate the land and also by reducing the value of the owner's equity. Some of these courts further held that local statutory procedures for perfecting mechanics' liens were constitutionally defective on due process grounds.

5. Other Protection for Mechanics and Materialmen

It is noted earlier in this section that in most states a prudent construction lender may secure priority over a mechanics' lienor by recording the construction loan mortgage before construction commences. Hence, if the project fails and the mortgagee forecloses, mechanics' lienors usually receive nothing from the foreclosure sale. To correct this inequity, some states have given mechanics and materialmen lien rights in addition to those they receive under the traditional mechanics' lien statute.

a. Stop Notice Statutes

In some jurisdictions an individual who has supplied services, labor, or materials to a construction project may obtain a statutory lien on construction loan money not yet disbursed by the lender. Legislation of this type is known as a stop notice statute. These statutes differ in various respects. As a general proposition, a stop notice statute permits an unpaid mechanic or materialman to file a notice of claim with the lender who then must stop advancing funds for construction or, at least, withhold funds to cover the claim.

b. Equitable Liens

A number of courts have used the equitable lien concept to fashion a remedy for mechanics and materialman similar to that available under stop notice statutes. Under the equitable lien approach, an unpaid lien claimant may reach undisbursed construction loan funds if the claimant can show special equities or establish that the lender has been unjustly enriched.

E.   TAX LIENS

1.   State and Local Real Estate Tax Liens

Statutes in most states impose a lien on real estate to secure the payment of taxes or assessments levied on the land. Usually these real estate tax and assessment liens are allowed to leapfrog existing encumbrances to the first lien priority position. In order to minimize the risk of losing priority to subsequent tax liens, mortgagees commonly require the mortgagor to escrow funds for the payment of real property taxes. *See* Ch. 4, pp. 92–93 (discussing escrow accounts).

2.   Federal Income Tax Liens

The federal government may obtain a lien against the real property of a delinquent income taxpayer. The federal tax lien arises upon assessment, but, unlike state and local real estate tax liens, it does not receive priority over existing encumbrances. It also is not valid against subsequent mortgages until notice of its existence is filed in the public records. Even a filed federal tax lien loses priority to certain interests that arise subsequent to its filing, such as real estate tax liens and certain mechanics' liens. *See* 26 U.S.C.A. §§ 6321–6323. Numerous other priority issues arise under federal tax lien law, but they are beyond the scope of this work.

F.   LIS PENDENS

Under the common law doctrine of lis pendens, the pendency of a suit concerning title to or possession of land imparts constructive notice to the world of the claims of the litigants. One who acquires an interest in property involved in litigation, therefore, takes subject to the judgment of the court. Because it is difficult to discover the existence of pending litigation, statutes in most states limit the application of the lis pendens doctrine by requiring that a separate notice of the suit be filed.

Illustration: O conveys land to GE who records. O initiates suit to have the deed set aside and records a lis pendens notice as required by state law. GE executes a mortgage on the land to ME. The court then renders judgment in favor of O and sets aside the deed. Because ME was on lis pendens notice of O's interest, O takes the property free from ME's mortgage. In those states that continue to follow the common law lis pendens doctrine, O would take free from the mortgage even if O had failed to file separate notice of the suit.

G. MARSHALLING

The equitable doctrine of marshalling assets does not deal so much with determining the priority of interests in the mortgaged property as with equitably preserving the value of each interest once priority has been established. The doctrine has two main facets: the two funds rule and the sale in inverse order of alienation rule. These principles of marshalling overlap somewhat; both may be applicable in certain situations. Matters are complicated further by conflict over what particular circumstances call for the application of each rule.

1. Two Funds Rule

The two funds rule is the most familiar principle of marshalling. It provides that when a senior mortgagee has a claim against two funds and a junior mortgagee has a claim against only one of them, the senior mortgagee must enforce its claim so as to best preserve the value of the junior mortgagee's security. Although the senior mortgagee may proceed at law against either or both funds, equity requires it to seek satisfaction first from the fund the junior mortgagee cannot reach. Only when this fund is exhausted may the senior mortgagee proceed against the sole fund to which the junior mortgagee has access.

Illustration: MR owns two parcels of land, lot A worth $10,000 and lot B worth $4,000. MR borrows $12,000 from ME–1 and gives ME–1 a first mortgage on both lots. MR then borrows $5,000 from ME–2 and gives ME–2 a second mortgage on lot A. MR defaults on both mortgages. ME–1 forecloses on lot A only, and the foreclosure sale brings $10,000. ME–1 claims the entire amount as first lienor. Although ME–1's $12,000 mortgage was a first lien on lot A, under the two funds rule ME–1 receives foreclosure sale proceeds as if it had satisfied itself first out of lot B and then out of lot A. Under this principle, ME–1 receives $8,000 (the amount of its lien minus the value of lot B), and ME–2 is entitled to $2,000.

Illustration: Assume the same fact situation as in the immediately preceding illustration except that no default occurs and ME–1 releases its lien on lot B even though it actually knows of ME–2's second mortgage on lot A. Under the two funds rule, ME–1 retains a first lien on lot A for only $8,000 (the amount of the original lien minus the value of lot B), and ME–2 has a second lien for $5,000.

2. Sale in Inverse Order of Alienation Rule

The doctrine of marshalling also applies when a large tract of mortgaged land is subdivided and sold in separate parcels to individuals who pay the full purchase price for their lots without obtaining a partial release of the blanket mortgage. If the blanket mortgage was recorded, its lien follows each lot into the hands of the lot purchaser. (Payment of the full purchase price to the mortgagor does not discharge the mortgagee's lien.) Although the purchaser would not have consummated the deal if the purchaser had searched the title, the purchaser is not completely unprotected. Equity gives the purchaser the right to require that the land retained by the seller be sold at foreclosure before the purchaser's lot is sold. Because this concept favors the purchasers in the order they acquired lots, it is called the sale in inverse order of alienation rule.

Illustration: MR owns a ten-acre tract subject to a recorded mortgage in favor of ME. MR subdivides the tract into ten one-acre lots and sells lots A and B successively to purchasers who each pay the full sale price for their respective lots. MR defaults on the blanket mortgage, and ME forecloses. Under the sale in inverse order of alienation rule, equity requires the court to direct the sheriff to sell first the land retained by MR, next lot B, and finally lot A. The sale process ends whenever the cumulative proceeds are sufficient to satisfy the mortgage debt.

The sale in inverse order of alienation rule is limited in several respects. First, the rule is inapplicable when a purchaser pays a reduced purchase price for taking the property subject to the mortgage. Second, most purchasers making full payment search the record and demand a partial release of the mortgage. Third, the mortgagee may avoid application of the rule by placing an anti-marshalling clause in the mortgage.

3. Anti–Marshalling Clause

Courts generally will not apply marshalling in either of its forms in the face of a contrary agreement. Mortgagees, therefore, often insist on a mortgage provision giving them the right to release or foreclose and sell parcels of the mortgaged property free from any requirement to marshall assets.

CHAPTER 10

FORECLOSURE

The evolution of the foreclosure concept is traced in Chapter 1. This chapter is designed to promote understanding of the procedure as it presently exists.

I. AVAILABILITY AND PURPOSE OF FORECLOSURE

On default, the mortgagee may have the mortgaged property sold to satisfy the unpaid mortgage debt. *See* Ch. 1, pp. 6–8 (discussing development of foreclosure by sale). Although this process is customarily referred to as mortgage foreclosure, it is really the mortgagor's equity of redemption that is foreclosed.

The foreclosure process generally may be commenced by the mortgagee anytime after default. *See* Ch. 8, pp. 152–159 (discussing default and acceleration). Its purpose is to cut off the mortgagor's equity of redemption and the rights of all parties who acquired interests in the land after the mortgage was executed so that whoever purchases the property at foreclosure receives title as it existed in the hands of the mortgagor immediately before the mortgage attached. An important corollary of this

195

principle is that interests acquired by third parties prior to the execution of the mortgage survive foreclosure. In this way, the mortgagee obtains the full benefit of the security for which it bargained, but no more.

II.　STATUTE OF LIMITATIONS

In most states, the mortgagee must foreclose within a certain statutory period after maturity of the mortgage. Because needless controversy arises when the statute of limitations on the mortgage and the underlying debt differ, several jurisdictions have enacted statutes that bar the enforcement of both simultaneously. *See*, Ch. 4, pp. 95–96 (analyzing problem presented when statute of limitations runs on debt, but not on mortgage).

III.　FEDERAL LEGISLATION AFFECTING FORECLOSURE

A.　MORTGAGOR IN BANKRUPTCY

Following is a discussion of two significant ways that proceedings under the federal Bankruptcy Code may intrude on the foreclosure process. Various other aspects of bankruptcy law also may affect foreclosure.

1.　Automatic Stay of Foreclosure Proceedings

The mortgagor's bankruptcy may significantly alter the mortgagee's right to foreclose. The filing of any form of bankruptcy petition automatically stays foreclosure proceedings against the mortgagor. 11 U.S.C.A. § 362(a). The Department of Housing and Urban Development, however, receives a limited exception from this automatic stay rule; it may still foreclose certain multi-living unit mortgages it holds. 11 U.S.C.A. § 362(b)(8).

The bankruptcy court may grant the mortgagee relief from the automatic stay in certain situations. Relief may be granted (1) "for cause, including the lack of adequate protection" of the mortgagee's interest; (2) when the mortgagor does not have any equity in the mortgaged property, and the "property is not necessary to an effective reorganization;" or (3) when provisions covering "single asset real estate" are met. 11 U.S.C.A. § 362(d).

2. Nullification of Prior Foreclosure Sale

Problems may arise even when the mortgagor enters bankruptcy after the foreclosure process has been completed. A bankruptcy trustee may set aside a prior foreclosure sale as a fraudulent transfer if the sale was held within one year of the filing of the bankruptcy petition at a time the mortgagor was insolvent, and the sale price did not constitute "reasonably equivalent value." 11 U.S.C.A. § 548. However, for many years, disagreement existed regarding how to determine "reasonably equivalent value." Ultimately the issue reached the Supreme Court where the justices concluded that the proceeds produced by a properly conducted state foreclosure sale satisfy the "reasonably equivalent value" standard. *See* BFP v. Resolution Trust Corp. (S.Ct.1994).

Although courts are divided on the issue, a bankruptcy trustee may seek to avoid a prior foreclosure sale as a preference when a number of conditions are met. In general terms, a voidable preference may be found when a mortgagee purchases at a sale held within ninety days of bankruptcy at a time the mortgagor was insolvent, and the mortgagee thereby received more than it would have obtained in a straight bankruptcy liquidation. 11 U.S.C.A. § 547.

B. MORTGAGOR IN MILITARY SERVICE

The Soldiers' and Sailors' Civil Relief Act of 1940, 50 U.S.C.A. App. § 501 *et seq.*, grants special protection to mortgagors on active duty in the armed forces. The following discussion treats the default judgment and stay portions of the Act as they relate to mortgage foreclosure proceedings.

The Act provides that a serviceperson may apply to a court to set aside default judgments rendered against the serviceperson on either pre-service or in-service obligations. The mortgagee, therefore, must file an affidavit specifying the military status of a mortgagor who does not answer the foreclosure complaint. Failure to file an affidavit does not affect the validity of the proceedings against a civilian defendant who does not appear. If, however, the mortgagor is in the armed forces, the foreclosure can be properly completed only if the serviceperson appears or is represented at the proceedings.

A serviceperson also may seek relief under the stay provisions of the Act. The serviceperson's ability to stay foreclosure proceedings depends primarily on whether the mortgage obligation was incurred before or after the serviceperson's entry on active duty. If the mortgage is a pre-service obligation and the mortgagor's ability to meet the debt has been materially affected by military service, the court must stay the foreclosure or grant other appropriate equitable relief. If the mortgage is an in-service obligation, the court may stay the foreclosure only if the mortgagor's ability to participate in the foreclosure proceedings is materially affected by the mortgagor's military service.

IV. FORECLOSURE BY JUDICIAL SALE

Foreclosure by judicially approved sale constitutes the backbone of our system of mortgage foreclosure. *See* Ch. 1, pp. 6–8 (discussing development of foreclosure by sale). Such a proceeding is available in all states and the required method of foreclosure in a number of jurisdictions. Although court supervised foreclosure is the best way to ascertain the rights of the parties involved and thereby to produce the most marketable title, it is often a complex, protracted, and expensive procedure. The numerous legal difficulties inherent in this process are analyzed in this section.

A. PARTIES DEFENDANT

A foreclosure decree affects only those persons before the court. The naming of parties defendant, therefore, is a critical step in the foreclosure process.

1. Necessary/Proper Parties

Parties defendant can be placed into two general categories: necessary parties and proper parties. A necessary party defendant to a foreclosure suit is anyone who must be joined in order to accomplish the purpose of foreclosure which, as previously noted, is to sell the mortgagor's interest in the property as it existed immediately before the execution of the mortgage. Thus, the mortgagor and all persons who acquired interests in the property after the execution of the mortgage are necessary parties and may be joined without their consent. The interests of necessary parties omitted from the suit survive foreclosure.

Illustration: MR executes a first mortgage to ME–1. MR then executes a second mortgage to ME–2, leases a part of the mortgage property to L, and grants an easement over another part to X. MR defaults on the first mortgage, and ME–1 commences foreclosure proceedings. MR, ME–2, L, and X are all necessary parties defendant because their interests must be extinguished if the foreclosure sale purchaser is to receive MR's interest as it existed immediately before the first mortgage was executed.

A proper party defendant to a foreclosure suit is one whose joinder is desirable, but not essential to accomplish the purpose of foreclosure. Senior mortgagees and those who hold no interest in the property but are personally liable on the debt are proper parties. Although an individual personally liable on the debt can be involuntarily joined, a senior mortgagee generally cannot be joined without its consent.

2.　Intentional Omission of Junior Lessees

When a junior lease is particularly favorable to the lessor, it is to the mortgagee's advantage to keep the lease alive through foreclosure and thereby enhance the sale value of its security. Because the rights of a junior interest holder not made a party defendant survive foreclosure, it would appear that a mortgagee could preserve a valuable junior lease by intentionally omitting the lessee from the foreclosure suit. In some states, the mortgagee may keep a junior lease alive in this fashion. In other jurisdictions, however, foreclosure extinguishes an intentionally omitted junior lease, at least when the lessee does not want to preserve it. This approach may be justified on the ground that joinder requirements are for the protection of junior interest holders, not the mortgagee.

In view of the uncertainty that exists with regard to preserving intentionally omitted junior leases, a mortgagee sometimes will subordinate the mortgage to a valuable junior lease to insure that the lease will survive foreclosure. *See* Ch. 8, pp. 162–165 (considering problem of junior leases existing at default); Ch. 9, pp. 183–184 (discussing subordination of mortgage to lease).

3. Lis Pendens

Under the doctrine of lis pendens, parties who acquire an interest in the mortgaged property with notice of the foreclosure proceedings are bound by the foreclosure decree just as if they had been named parties defendant. *See* Ch. 9, pp. 190–191 (analyzing doctrine of lis pendens).

B. SALE PROCEDURES

The judicial foreclosure sale procedure is governed by statutory law that varies from state to state. These statutes normally call for a public sale conducted by the sheriff or a court appointed official.

C. CONFIRMATION/ADEQUACY OF SALE PRICE

Foreclosure by judicial sale is not final until the sale is confirmed by the court. Absent fraud or chilled bidding, inadequacy of the foreclosure sale price is generally not a ground upon which courts will refuse to confirm. Statutes in some states require that the sale price be a specified fraction of the appraised value of the property, e.g., two-thirds, but in certain of these jurisdictions, mortgagors commonly waive appraisal as a matter of course. *See* ¶ 23 of the Mortgage in Appendix A.

D. PURCHASER

1. Purchaser's Title

The purchaser at a judicial foreclosure sale receives title to the property as it existed in the hands of the mortgagor immediately before the execution of the mortgage. Although the rights of the mortgagor, the mortgagee, and junior interest holders named parties defendant are extinguished, the rights of individuals who acquired interests prior to the execution of the mortgage survive foreclosure.

Illustration: MR grants an easement over MR's property to X. MR then executes a first mortgage to ME–1, a second mortgage to ME–2, a third mortgage to ME–3, and a lease of part of the property to L. ME–2 forecloses, naming all necessary parties in the suit. *See* pp. 200–201 (discussing necessary/proper parties). P acquires title at the foreclosure sale. Although the interests of MR, ME–2, ME–3, and L end at foreclosure, P takes the property subject to the interests of X and ME–1.

Because the foreclosure sale proceeds are used to satisfy the mortgage debt, the purchaser also is subrogated to the rights of the mortgagee. *See* Ch. 7, pp. 145–150 (analyzing subrogation—assignment by operation of law). This concept is important in determining the purchaser's position vis-à-vis a junior lienor omitted from the original foreclosure proceeding.

2. Purchaser Versus Omitted Junior Lienor

When a junior lienor is not named as a party defendant, the junior lien survives foreclosure. The omitted junior lienor may still either foreclose the junior lien or redeem the senior mortgage. *See* Ch. 8, pp. 170–171 (discussing redemption by junior interest holder). The purchaser at the foreclosure sale, however, may eliminate the omitted junior lien by using any one of three methods—redemption, reforeclosure, or possibly strict foreclosure. Because the purchaser succeeds to the mortgagor's right to redeem junior liens, the purchaser may extinguish the omitted junior lien by simply paying it off. The purchaser also is subrogated to the mortgagee's right to foreclose. The purchaser, therefore, may eliminate the omitted junior lien by reforeclosing the mortgage, or in some jurisdictions, by strictly foreclosing the rights of the junior lienor.

3. Purchase by Mortgagee

The mortgagee may purchase the mortgaged property at the foreclosure sale. Because the mortgagee is entitled to receive as much of the sale proceeds as is necessary to satisfy the mortgage debt, the mortgagee may bid up to that amount without having to produce any cash. As a consequence the mortgagee often is the highest bidder at the foreclosure sale.

4. Purchase by Mortgagor

If the mortgagor or the mortgagor's agent purchases at the foreclosure sale, unpaid junior liens survive on the theory that the purchase was really payment of the senior lien. This is, of course, an exception to the rule that all properly joined junior interests are cut off by foreclosure.

E. DISBURSEMENT OF SALE PROCEEDS

The proceeds of the foreclosure sale are disbursed in the following order: (1) expenses of foreclosure, (2) satisfaction of the mortgage debt, and (3) satisfaction of junior liens in the order of their priority. Any excess belongs to the current owner of the property who in most cases is the mortgagor.

F. DEFICIENCY JUDGMENT

1. General

If the foreclosure sale proceeds are insufficient to satisfy the underlying debt, the mortgagee generally may obtain a deficiency judgment against the mortgagor and anyone else personally liable on the debt.

Illustration: MR executes a $10,000 promissory note and a mortgage to ME. MR conveys the property to GE who assumes and agrees to pay the mortgage debt. GE defaults, and ME forecloses. The foreclosure sale produces $8,000 after expenses. ME receives the $8,000 and generally may obtain a deficiency judgment for $2,000 against each MR and GE. Naturally, ME may recover no more than $2,000 on these judgments.

2. Anti–Deficiency Legislation

Depression era legislation still restricts the recovery of deficiency judgments in many jurisdictions. One statutory approach is to prohibit deficiency judgments in certain situations, such as in the case of purchase money mortgages or when foreclosure is by power of sale. Another approach is to limit deficiency judgments to the amount by which the debt exceeds the fair market value of the property. Waiver of the protection provided by anti-deficiency legislation is generally considered ineffective as against public policy.

V. FORECLOSURE BY POWER OF SALE

Foreclosure by out-of-court sale is recognized in a substantial majority of states. This method of foreclosure usually is termed foreclosure by power of sale because it is based on a mortgage provision authorizing sale of the property without court supervision. Although foreclosure by power of sale represents a relatively expedient and inexpensive means of foreclosure, it is prohibited in a number of jurisdictions and where permitted, it exists as an alternative to foreclosure by judicial sale. See Ch. 12, pp. 225–230 (treating reform measures employing out-of-court foreclosure).

A. COMPARISON TO JUDICIAL SALE

Foreclosure by power of sale serves generally the same purpose as foreclosure by judicial sale. However, some significant differences exist.

1. Form of Security Device

Because the deed of trust is designed to be enforced by an out-of-court sale conducted by the trustee, it is a popular financing device in states where foreclosure by power of sale is permitted. *See* Ch. 3, p. 49 (discussing deed of trust). A regular mortgage, of course, may be drafted to include a power of sale provision.

2. Sale Procedures

The procedure for foreclosure by power of sale generally is regulated by statute. These statutes usually provide for a public sale conducted only after proper notice. Typically, notice by advertisement in a local newspaper for a prescribed period is required. In several states, additional notice by mail or personal service must be given to the mortgagor. Junior interest holders of record are entitled to such added notice in only a few of these jurisdictions.

3. Purchaser's Title

The purchaser at a power of sale foreclosure receives the same rights as a purchaser at a judicial foreclosure. Nonetheless, the title of the purchaser at a power of sale foreclosure generally is less secure because the sale has not been confirmed by a court and is, therefore, more likely to be the subject of future litigation.

4. Purchase by Lender

The form of the financing device authorizing foreclosure by power of sale determines whether the lender may bid at the sale. If a mortgage with a power of sale provision is involved, the mortgagee has a duty to conduct the sale in an impartial manner. Thus, the mortgagee may not purchase the property unless it has contractual or statutory permission to do so. If a deed of trust is used, the lender may freely bid because the trustee conducts the sale.

5. Deficiency or Surplus

Foreclosure by power of sale is extrajudicial. Consequently, the mortgagee must take additional action when either a deficiency or a surplus results. If the proceeds are insufficient to satisfy the mortgage debt, the mortgagee must bring a separate action to recover a deficiency judgment against a party personally liable on the underlying obligation. As discussed earlier in this chapter, in many jurisdictions deficiency judgments are subject to legislative prohibition or limitation. If the proceeds exceed the amount of the mortgage debt, the mortgagee may file an interpleader action to obtain protection against liability for paying the surplus to the wrong parties.

6. Judicial Review

Although the courts do not oversee foreclosure by power of sale, the process is always subject to later judicial scrutiny. This possibility reduces the value of the property to prospective purchasers and may cause the mortgagee to forego foreclosure by power of sale in favor of foreclosure by judicial sale.

B.　CONSTITUTIONAL ISSUES

Foreclosure by power of sale has come under constitutional attack. Some authorities have argued that the notice and hearing procedures used in the typical power of sale foreclosure do not meet the procedural due process requirements of the Fifth and Fourteenth Amendments. This attack really involves several issues.

1.　Governmental Action

The Fifth and Fourteenth Amendments limit governmental action, not private activity. The first issue, therefore, is whether a power of sale foreclosure involves significant federal or state action.

The federal action question usually arises when the foreclosing mortgagee is connected to the federal government in some way. The few courts that have considered the question have tended to find federal action if the mortgagee is a branch of the federal government such as the Department of Veterans Affairs, but not if it is a private entity closely related to the federal government such as the Federal National Mortgage Association. Although there

is some authority that neither the Federal Home
Loan Mortgage Corporation nor the Government
National Mortgage Association is a federal instrumentality bound by due process restrictions, such
hybrid organizations are difficult to categorize.
Thus, the federal action question remains partly
unresolved.

The state action question is relatively well settled. The prevailing view is that power of sale
foreclosure does not involve state action. Courts
generally conclude that this method of foreclosure is
established by private contract even though it may
be recognized and regulated by state statute. Unsuccessful arguments for state action have been
based on encouragement, enforcement, and participation theories.

2. Notice and Hearing

In those instances in which foreclosure by power
of sale is considered to involve governmental action,
procedural due process requires that the mortgagor
and other interested parties receive adequate notice
of the foreclosure and a presale opportunity to be
heard. In order to determine whether these requirements have been met, it is necessary to examine
the mortgage documents in question and the applicable local statutes. Power of sale procedures rarely
satisfy due process standards. The mandated notice
often is not reasonably calculated to reach all interested parties. Moreover, an opportunity for a presale hearing normally is not provided.

3. Waiver

Even assuming that the requisite governmental action is present and that the local procedure violates either the Fifth Amendment or the Fourteenth Amendment, a power of sale foreclosure still may be conducted if the mortgagor knowingly and voluntarily waives the mortgagor's procedural due process rights. The validity of individual waivers, of course, can only be determined on a case by case basis.

VI. STRICT FORECLOSURE

Strict foreclosure was the method originally used to extinguish the mortgagor's equity of redemption. A defaulting mortgagor was given a set period of time to pay the debt or forever lose all interest in the mortgaged property. This means of foreclosure generally was not accepted in this country. *See* Ch. 1, p. 6 (discussing historical development of strict foreclosure). Today, strict foreclosure is available as a principal method of foreclosure in only a handful of states. In several other jurisdictions, however, its use is authorized against necessary parties omitted from a prior judicial foreclosure suit. Such use of strict foreclosure is discussed earlier in this chapter.

Statutes in a few New England states provide for a special form of strict foreclosure that is accomplished by entry plus possession for a specified time period which ranges between one and three years. The effect is the same as the traditional form of strict foreclosure; the mortgagor's equity of redemption is extinguished without sale.

VII. STATUTORY REDEMPTION
A. AVAILABILITY

Although the equitable right of redemption ends at foreclosure, statutes in approximately one-half of the states establish a right to redeem the mortgaged property *after* the foreclosure sale. *See* Ch. 1, p. 8 (discussing statutory redemption). The primary purpose of statutory redemption is to protect the mortgagor and junior interest holders from sale of the property at a price far below its value. An additional objective of these statutes is to give the mortgagor more time to obtain the funds necessary to retain the land. Statutory redemption laws vary considerably, but all specify a certain time period, often one year, within which redemption must be accomplished. In a number of jurisdictions, statutory redemption does not apply to power of sale foreclosure.

As a general rule, the mortgagor may retain possession of the mortgaged property during the statutory redemption period. If redemption is not accomplished by the end of that period, the purchaser at the foreclosure sale receives title to and possession of the property.

B. INDIVIDUALS WHO MAY REDEEM

The mortgagor, the mortgagor's successors, and any junior lienor joined in the foreclosure may exercise a right of redemption under most statutes. The mortgagor and the mortgagor's successors generally are given an exclusive right to redeem for a specified period of time. After the mortgagor's redemption period has elapsed, junior lienors usually have the right to redeem in the order of their priority.

C. AMOUNT REQUIRED FOR REDEMPTION

The amount required for statutory redemption is generally the foreclosure sale price, not the amount of the mortgage debt.

D. EFFECT OF REDEMPTION

1. By Mortgagor or Mortgagor's Successor

Statutory redemption by the mortgagor or the mortgagor's successor annuls the sale and restores title to the redeemer. Authorities differ, however, as to whether unsatisfied pre-existing liens are revived.

2. By Junior Lienor

When a junior lienor redeems, the junior lienor generally receives the rights of the purchaser at the foreclosure sale. Other junior interest holders usually may redeem from the original redemptioner.

E. WAIVER

The states are divided on the question of waiver of the statutory right of redemption. Some states prohibit waiver. At the opposite end of the spectrum, certain jurisdictions allow mortgagors to waive their statutory redemption rights by mortgage provision. Other states permit waiver only in limited situations, such as when the mortgagor is a corporation.

F. COMPARED TO EQUITY OF REDEMPTION

Statutory redemption often is confused with equity of redemption. *See* Ch. 1, pp. 4–5 & Ch. 8, pp. 169–172 (discussing equity of redemption). Although both methods of redemption are designed to protect the mortgagor, they differ significantly. First, equity of redemption developed as a part of our common law and is available in all states. Statutory redemption is a legislative creation that exists in approximately one-half of the states. Second, the mortgagor's equity of redemption is extinguished at foreclosure. The mortgagor's statutory right of redemption arises then. An equity of redemption and a right of statutory redemption, therefore, cannot exist in the same person at the same time. Third, the mortgagor's equity of redemption generally is not extinguished at the end of any specific time. It lasts until terminated by foreclosure. Statutory redemption, however, exists within a precise time frame, running from foreclosure to the end of the period established by statute. Fourth, redemption in equity is from the mortgage. Redemption under statutory provision is from the foreclosure sale. Thus, the amount required for equitable redemption is the amount in default, usually the unpaid balance of the mortgage debt. The amount required for statutory redemption generally is the foreclosure sale price. Fifth, the right of equity of redemption may not be waived. Statutory redemption, however, may be waived by mortgage provision in some states.

G. CRITICISM OF STATUTORY REDEMPTION

Statutory redemption often is criticized on the ground that it does not really accomplish its intended purpose—to produce realistic bids at the foreclosure sale. *See* United States v. Stadium Apartments, Inc. (9th Cir.1970). Many critics go even further and suggest that statutory redemption is counterproductive. The fact that the purchaser must wait for a year or so before receiving the property may dampen bidding by outsiders and thereby depress the sale price. Moreover, this delay and its attendant risks may cause mortgagees to lend less or demand a higher rate of return in states that utilize a statutory redemption period to "protect" mortgagors.

CHAPTER 11

FINANCING COOPERATIVES AND CONDOMINIUMS

I. BACKGROUND

As the population of this country began to crowd our urban centers during the first half of the twentieth century, it became increasingly difficult for many people to realize the American dream of home ownership. Housing cooperatives and condominiums were developed in large part to meet the public's desire in this regard. Both offer the individual the opportunity to acquire a unit in a multi-unit building. Although cooperatives and condominiums are generally residential developments, either form of ownership may be used for a commercial project.

The cooperative and the condominium pose unique real estate finance problems. These issues are explored in this chapter, but first it is necessary to review the general legal principles underlying each form of development.

II. COOPERATIVES

A. COOPERATIVE CONCEPT

Cooperative apartments became popular in New York City during the early 1900s and soon spread to other major metropolitan areas. Title to the cooperative apartment building, and the land upon which it is located, typically is held by a nonprofit corporation. Stock in the corporation is allocated among the cooperative apartment units based upon their relative size or value, usually value. Each cooperative member purchases the stock assigned to a specific apartment and receives a long-term "proprietary" lease to that unit. Rent payable under the lease is the cooperative member's proportionate share of the expenses the corporation incurs in operating the cooperative. Expenses include costs for taxes, insurance, maintenance, management, and, as discussed below, mortgage debt service.

B. FINANCING COOPERATIVES

1. Construction or Acquisition Financing

In order to finance the purchase or construction of the cooperative building, the cooperative corporation places a blanket mortgage on the property. This general financing arrangement presents the individual cooperative members with certain financing problems.

2. Loans on Individual Units

Lending institutions commonly are reluctant or unable to take an individual member's stock and proprietary lease as security for a long-term loan. Although such loans are more readily available today than they were some time ago, cooperative apartment purchasers still face considerable difficulty in obtaining adequate financing in many areas of the country. As a result, the purchaser of a cooperative apartment unit often must have enough ready cash to pay for the stock allocated to the unit or find a seller who is willing to recover the seller's equity in installments over a number of years.

3. Partial Default on Blanket Mortgage

The financial interdependence of the cooperative members is another source of concern. The existence of a single blanket mortgage paid by rent receipts means that if some members fail to pay rent, the cooperative may not have sufficient funds to meet a mortgage loan installment. The entire membership is then faced with foreclosure unless they take action to cure the default. Although reserves and special assessments may be utilized to cover such a contingency, there is always the possibility that available funds will be inadequate and that all cooperative members will be at the mercy of the blanket mortgagee.

III. CONDOMINIUMS

A. CONDOMINIUM CONCEPT

Although cooperative apartment members are more than ordinary tenants, they do not hold title to their units. Condominium owners do. This idea of separate ownership of housing units in a multi-unit building originated long ago and was utilized throughout Europe in the Middle Ages.

Condominium development became popular in the United States only recently. Changes in economic, political, and social conditions precipitated dramatic condominium growth in this country since the early 1960s. The combination of a land shortage in populous regions, legislation in each state establishing guidelines for the creation of condominiums, and the willingness of the federal government to insure mortgages on individual condominium units caused condominium developments to spring up in such number that they now occupy a significant position in the overall housing picture. Commercial condominiums are also quite common. As might be expected, the cooperative dwindled in importance as the condominium rose in popularity.

A condominium is created when a developer records a formal declaration that the developer submits certain property to the local condominium act. The property may consist of various kinds of development, such as a single high-rise structure, a number of garden apartment buildings, or a series of row houses. In every case, each condominium unit is identified in the declaration.

The purchaser of a unit receives the fee simple to that unit and an undivided percentage interest in the common areas of the development as a tenant in common with the other unit owners. The common areas include the land and all the structural aspects of the building not included within the description of individual units. An owners association, usually formed as a nonprofit corporation, manages the common areas and facilities.

The concept of individual ownership of part of a building has generated numerous legal problems. Litigation and legislation in the area is ever increasing. In 1977, the National Conference of Commissioners on Uniform State Laws approved the Uniform Condominium Act as a means to deal with unsettled condominium issues on a consistent basis throughout the country. Three years later the Commissioners amended and reissued the Act. The 1980 version of the Act has been adopted in a number of jurisdictions with modifications that vary from state to state.

This book is designed to present the fundamentals of real estate finance, not an exhaustive analysis of condominium law. Hence, the remainder of this section treats only the narrow area of condominium financing.

B. FINANCING CONDOMINIUMS

1. Construction Financing

Condominium construction lending is in many respects similar to financing subdivision development. In each case, the developer obtains a blanket construction mortgage loan to finance the contemplated improvements. When construction is completed and a unit purchaser located, the purchaser obtains a permanent mortgage loan to pay the purchase price of the unit being acquired. The developer uses the money received from the purchaser to pay a proportionate share of the blanket construction loan. The construction lender in turn executes a partial release of the construction mortgage so that the developer can convey clear title to the unit in question. The end result is that the purchaser holds title to the unit subject only to the lien of the permanent purchase money mortgage. This process is repeated until no units are left in the hands of the developer. Thus, the transition from the construction loan to permanent financing is accomplished in a series of transactions as housing units in the subdivision or condominium are sold.

The condominium construction lender, however, faces a problem the subdivision financer does not. Construction of the condominium building cannot be halted in midstream if the units are not selling well. Further, if the lender executes a partial release as each unit is conveyed, the lender may end up with a lien on only the least valuable portions of its original security. Many condominium construction lenders, therefore, will not execute any partial releases until the developer has obtained sales contracts for a certain percentage of the units. The lender also may require the developer to have a plan for converting the development into a rental project in the event the units do not sell.

2. Conversion Financing

Owners of rental apartment buildings often convert to condominiums as a means to profitably dispose of their property. The condominium conversion process presents some financing problems. The existing mortgagee may be unwilling to cooperate with the conversion and to grant partial releases as the condominium units are sold. In this event, the owner must obtain short-term mortgage financing from another source in order to bridge the conversion period. The proceeds of the new mortgage loan are used to satisfy the original mortgage debt. The owner then organizes the condominium and sells the units. The transition from the interim loan to permanent financing is accomplished in the same fashion as described in the preceding subsection on construction financing.

3. Loans on Individual Units

a. General

The owner of a condominium unit may obtain financing on the unit in the same manner as the owner of a single family dwelling. *See* Appendix C for a Condominium Rider to a standard mortgage. Thus, there is not the same financial interdependence among condominium owners as exists among cooperative apartment members. If one condominium unit owner defaults in the payment of the unit owner's mortgage loan, the unit owner faces foreclosure alone. The lender does not necessarily have a lien on any other unit. This availability of separate financing of individual units is the most striking advantage of condominium ownership over investment in a cooperative apartment.

b. *Priority vis-à-vis Assessment Liens*

Although condominium unit owners are less financially interdependent than are cooperative apartment members, they are far more so than are conventional home owners. This is because unit owners must work together to maintain the condominium common areas. To achieve this objective, the condominium homeowners association makes an assessment against each unit owner for the unit owner's share of the expenses of the condominium project. If a unit owner does not pay the assessment, the association receives a statutory lien against the delinquent owner's condominium unit. Under many condominium statutes, a lien for unpaid assessments is junior to an existing first mortgage on the unit. The Uniform Condominium Act, however, gives an assessment lien priority over an existing first mortgage for up to six months of unpaid assessments on the ground that such a limited preference is crucial to the financial well-being of the development. *See* U.C.A. § 3–116. Mortgage lenders indirectly benefit from fully-funded maintenance programs because the value of their security is thereby preserved. Moreover, lenders may easily protect themselves against loss of lien priority by requiring the unit owner to escrow funds for assessments just as they often require the unit owner to place monies in escrow for taxes and insurance.

CHAPTER 12

REFORM

I. NEED FOR REFORM

The diverse real estate finance law discussed in the first eleven chapters of this book has impeded the free flow of funds for residential and commercial mortgage financing. Because national lenders must vary their procedures to meet a wide variety of state laws, the overall cost of administering mortgage loans is higher than if lenders had but one set of legal principles to follow. In addition, where mortgagees view local law as particularly burdensome, they tend to become more conservative in their lending practices and may even reduce their mortgage investments.

The current judicial foreclosure system is subject to especially heavy criticism. During the protracted, complex, and expensive court-supervised foreclosure process, mortgage money is tied up and the mortgaged property may deteriorate or be destroyed, vandalized, or milked of its value.

II. REFORM MEASURES

In the latter part of the twentieth century, proposals to reform the law of real estate finance have been advanced by various sources.

A.　FEDERAL ACTION

1.　Nationwide Foreclosure System

Federal housing and secondary mortgage market programs are burdened by the absence of uniform state mortgage law. The 93rd Congress, therefore, entertained a bill to establish a standard nationwide procedure for foreclosing mortgages owned, insured, or guaranteed by an instrumentality of the federal government. This proposal, known as the Federal Mortgage Foreclosure Act, provided for nonjudicial foreclosure of all such federally related mortgages by a foreclosure commissioner. H.R. 10688, 93rd Cong., 1st Sess. (1973); S. 2507, 93rd Cong., 1st Sess. (1973). Although the Act was not adopted, it clearly demonstrated Congressional concern about the present fragmented state foreclosure system. Two decades later the 104th Congress indicated a renewed interest in this issue by considering, but not adopting, a measure that would have authorized federal agencies to foreclose their mortgages by nonjudicial sale conducted by a foreclosure trustee. 141 Cong. Rec. H10745–H10748 (1995); 142 Cong. Rec. S3667–S3670 (1996).

Although a broad federal foreclosure system has not been enacted, twice Congress has passed narrow-gauged legislation on the subject. The Multifamily Mortgage Foreclosure Act of 1981, 12 U.S.C.A. § 3701 *et seq.*, establishes an out-of-court foreclosure system for certain multifamily mortgages held by the Department of Housing and Urban Development (HUD). A foreclosure commissioner is designated to conduct the procedure. The Single

Family Mortgage Foreclosure Act of 1994, 12 U.S.C.A. § 3751 *et seq.*, creates a similar extrajudicial foreclosure scheme for certain single-family mortgages held by HUD.

2. Other Federal Statutes Preempting State Mortgage Law

Certain federal statutes preempting state real estate finance law on nonforeclosure matters are addressed elsewhere in this book. Earlier chapters include discussion of qualified preemption of state usury law (*see* Ch. 4, pp. 88–89), of state limitations on the use of alternative mortgage instruments (*see* Ch. 4, p. 81), and of state law regarding due-on-sale clauses (*see* Ch. 6, pp. 121–125).

3. Preemption of State Mortgage Law in Courts

The number of lawsuits brought by federal agencies challenging the applicability of local law to federally owned mortgages is another indication of the federal government's dissatisfaction with current mortgage law. In some of these cases, courts have found various state mortgage laws unenforceable against federal agencies on the ground that federal law or policy preempted the field. State statutes establishing a statutory redemption period and limiting deficiency judgments are just two types of local laws that have met this fate.

4. Standard Mortgage Forms

Secondary mortgage market support institutions have brought a measure of uniformity to mortgage law and practice by standardizing mortgage forms. The Federal National Mortgage Association (FNMA) and the Federal Home Loan Mortgage Corporation (FHLMC) have developed uniform mortgage instruments with appropriate "riders". *See* Appendices A, B, and C. These uniform instruments are used widely.

5. Further Federal Action

Piecemeal federal legislation or sporadic litigation of the preemption issue is not an adequate substitute for a uniform mortgage law. Neither is the widespread use of standard mortgage forms. Consequently, Congress may continue to legislate on real estate finance matters and indeed, someday may adopt a wide-reaching system of out-of-court foreclosure. Whether such measures are ever enacted depends in good part on the states. If they can agree on some uniformity in the real estate finance area, the impetus for further federal action may abate.

B. UNIFORM LAND SECURITY INTEREST ACT

1. General

The tool to achieve a unified real estate finance law among the states is available in the form of the Uniform Land Security Interest Act (ULSIA). Introduced originally in the mid–1970s as Article 3 of the Uniform Land Transactions Act, ULSIA was approved as a separate uniform act by the National Conference of Commissioners on Uniform State Laws in 1985.

ULSIA is designed to reform and unify the law governing real estate security arrangements through the adoption of personal property concepts embodied in the Uniform Commercial Code (UCC). ULSIA § 102. Modeled after Article 9 of the UCC, ULSIA dramatically revises current real estate finance law. Although ULSIA deals in detail with a wide range of land financing problems, the scope of this work permits presentation of only its most significant aspects.

2. Significant Provisions

a. Coverage

With a few minor exceptions, ULSIA applies to every consensual arrangement that creates a security interest in realty. ULSIA §§ 102, 110. Thus, installment land contracts are treated the same as mortgages. See Ch. 3, pp. 54–61 (discussing installment land contract).

b. New Terminology and Concepts

ULSIA employs UCC-like terminology for traditional real estate financing concepts. Under the Act, mortgages are called "security agreements," mortgagors are termed "debtors," and mortgagees are labeled "secured creditors." ULSIA § 111.

ULSIA also establishes "protected party" status for certain persons. A protected party is basically a residential landowner who mortgages the owner's residence. ULSIA § 113. Such individuals receive special treatment in numerous ways. For example, a protected party is given rights at foreclosure not available to mortgagors in general.

c. Rights and Obligations Before Foreclosure

ULSIA attempts to resolve many of the controversies that may arise between the parties before foreclosure. The Act is pro-lender in that it strengthens the mortgagee's security position, but not necessarily to the detriment of mortgagors. Indeed, the changes in the law incorporated in ULSIA are designed to reduce uncertainties that drive up the cost of real estate financing.

The major question in this area concerns the mortgagee's right to take possession and collect rents and profits. *See* Ch. 8, pp. 159–168 (analyzing right to possession and rents). ULSIA adopts the intermediate mortgage theory thereby permitting the mortgagee to take possession upon the mortgagor's default. The rights and obligations of a mortgagee in possession are better defined than under existing law, and the obligations are not as burdensome. Moreover, rules are established regarding the mortgagee's right to collect rents, with or without taking possession. The overall effect is two pronged. First, it is easier for the mortgagee to collect rents, take possession, or both. Second, the need for a costly receiver is thus reduced. ULSIA §§ 503–505.

d. Foreclosure Procedures

ULSIA foreclosure provisions contain the reform of greatest interest to the real estate finance community. ULSIA §§ 506–514. Although foreclosure by judicial sale is still available in all cases, ULSIA recognizes and promotes power of sale foreclosure. Notice requirements for power of sale foreclosure, however, are more stringent than under existing law. *See* Ch. 10, pp. 206–211 (discussing foreclosure by power of sale).

Two other changes in prior foreclosure law deserve note. First, there is no statutory redemption period under ULSIA. Second, the purchaser's title at a power of sale foreclosure conducted pursuant to the provisions of the Act is as marketable as title received at a judicial sale. ULSIA §§ 512–514.

3. Status

Although ULSIA and its ancestor, Article 3 of the Uniform Land Transactions Act, have generated considerable commentary in the legal literature, neither measure has been enacted anywhere. With the passage of time and increased federal involvement in the real estate finance area, widespread adoption of ULSIA is extremely unlikely.

C. RESTATEMENT OF PROPERTY— MORTGAGES

The American Law Institute, demonstrating concern about the current state of real estate finance law, undertook the task of preparing a restatement on the subject. The Restatement (Third) of Property (Mortgages) has been completed and is slated for publication in 1997. It presents an additional avenue for reform of land financing.

TABLE OF SECONDARY AUTHORITIES

Secondary authorities are listed by section within each chapter. Four of the sources cited in this table deserve special mention. My general approach to real estate finance has been significantly influenced by two casebooks: (1) the current and previous editions of Grant S. Nelson & Dale A. Whitman, Cases and Materials on Real Estate Transfer, Finance, and Development (4th ed. 1992) [hereinafter Nelson & Whitman casebook] and (2) an earlier edition of Norman Penney, Richard F. Broude, & Roger A. Cunningham, Cases and Materials on Land Financing (3d ed. 1985) [hereinafter Penney, Broude, & Cunningham]. Two other books served as key references: (1) Grant S. Nelson & Dale A. Whitman, Real Estate Finance Law (2 volume, Practitioner Treatise Series, 3d ed. 1994) [hereinafter Nelson & Whitman] (successor to George E. Osborne, Handbook on the Law of Mortgages (2d ed. 1970) [hereinafter Osborne]) and (2) Robert Kratovil & Raymond J. Werner, Modern Mortgage Law and Practice (2d ed. 1981) [hereinafter Kratovil & Werner].

CHAPTER 1. INTRODUCTION

I. A. 1 Nelson & Whitman § 1.1
    B. Kratovil & Werner § 32.01; 1 Nelson & Whitman §§ 5.27, 6.6
    C. Osborne, §§ 49–64 (1st ed. 1951 & 2d ed. 1970); 5 Herbert T. Tiffany & Basil Jones, The Law of Real Property § 1563 (3d ed. 1939 & Cum. Supp. 1995).

II. Kratovil & Werner §§ 1.2–1.5, 1.7, 41.08–41.08(a)(1), 41.09, 41.10; 1
     Nelson & Whitman §§ 1.1–1.4, 1.7, 3.1–3.2, 7.1, 7.9–7.11, 7.19, 8.4;
     Osborne §§ 5–10; 4 Richard R. Powell, *Powell on Real Property*
     ¶¶ 438, 462 (Patrick J. Rohan former revision ed., 1996–Release 77,
     Dec. 1996) [hereinafter Powell]; Howard E. Kane, *The Mortgagee's
     Option to Purchase Mortgaged Property* in Financing Real Estate in
     the 80s 123, 127–139 (Brian J. Strum ed., 1981) (reference for
     subsection B.2. only); Jeffrey L. Licht, *The Clog on the Equity of
     Redemption and Its Effect on Modern Real Estate Finance,* 60 St.
     John's L.Rev. 452 (1986) (reference for subsections A. & B. only).
III. Kratovil & Werner §§ 1.6, 1.8, 20.02; 1 Nelson & Whitman §§ 1.5,
     4.1–4.3; Osborne §§ 13–16.

CHAPTER 2. MORTGAGE MARKET

I. A. & B.   1. & 2.   Robert Kratovil, Modern Mortgage Law and
                        Practice §§ 207–209 (1972) [hereinafter Kratovil
                        (1972)]; Kratovil & Werner §§ 25.05–25.11,
                        25.35–25.38(a); Nelson & Whitman casebook
                        906; 2 Nelson & Whitman § 12.1.

           3.   a. & b.   Alvin A. Arnold, Construction and De-
                        velopment Financing ¶¶ 4.16, 4.17 (2d
                        ed. 1991 & Cum. Supp. 1996 No. 1)
                        [hereinafter Arnold]; Kratovil & Wer-
                        ner §§ 25.03–25.03(b)(2), 25.13, 25.17–
                        25.21, 25.27(f)–25.27(f)(5); Michael T.
                        Madison, Jeffry R. Dwyer, & Steven
                        Bender, The Law of Real Estate Financ-
                        ing ¶¶ 6.02[6][b][ii], 6.02[8][b] (revised
                        ed. 1996–Release 3, July 1996) [herein-
                        after Madison, Dwyer, & Bender]; 2
                        Nelson & Whitman §§ 12.1–12.2; B.C.
                        Hart & Howard E. Kane, *What Every
                        Real Estate Lawyer Should Know About
                        Payment and Performance Bonds,* 17
                        Real Prop., Prob. & Tr.J. 674 (1982);
                        Colin C. Livingston, *Current Business
                        Approaches–Commercial Construction
                        Lending,* 13 Real Prop., Prob. & Tr.J.
                        791 (1978).

              c.   Arnold ¶ 4.26[1]; Madison, Dwyer, &
                        Bender ¶ 6.04[7]; 2 Nelson & Whitman
                        § 12.11; Cindy A. Ferguson, *Lender's
                        Liability for Construction Defects,* 11
                        Real Est.L.J. 310 (1983); Comment, *Li-
                        ability of the Institutional Lender for
                        Structural Defects in New Housing,* 35
                        U.Chi.L.Rev. 739 (1968); Craig R. Thor-
                        stenson, Note, *Mortgage Lender Liabili-
                        ty to the Purchasers of New or Existing
                        Homes,* 1988 U.Ill.L.Rev. 191.

    C. Nelson & Whitman casebook 906–907.

II. D. Barlow Burke, Jr., Law of Federal Mortgage Documents §§ 7.4.2–7.5 (1989 & Supp. 1995) [hereinafter Burke]; Nelson & Whitman casebook 493–494, 904–906; 2 Nelson & Whitman § 11.1.

III. Allan Axelrod, Curtis J. Berger, & Quintin Johnstone, Land Transfer and Finance Cases and Materials 113–121, Supp. 12–15 (3d ed. 1986 & Supp. 1991); Curtis J. Berger & Quintin Johnstone, Land Transfer and Finance Cases and Materials 135–139 (4th ed. 1993); Kratovil & Werner §§ 7.03(d)–7.03(e); Madison, Dwyer, & Bender xv-xxvii, ¶¶ 3.03, 3.04[2]; 2 Nelson and Whitman §§ 11.1, 11.3; 4,Pt.1 Patrick J. Rohan, Real Estate Financing § 3.01 (1996— Release No. 52, Nov. 1996) [hereinafter Rohan]; U.S. Dept. of Hous. & Urb. Dev. Report, Housing in the Seventies 68–73, 140–145, 152–155 (1974) [hereinafter HUD Report]; Barbara Miles, *Housing Finance: Development and Evolution in Mortgage Markets* in Housing–A Reader 45, 55–65 (Cong. Research Service, Library of Congress, July, 1983) [hereinafter Miles]; Leonard Sahling & Elizabeth Lavin, *Will RTC Asset Dispositions Ruin the Real Estate Markets?*, 20:2 Real Est.Rev. 15 (Summer 1990); *RTC Raises $404 Million in Final Loan Auctions*, Housing & Dev. Rep., 23 Current Dev. 533 (Jan. 1, 1996); *Survey of Mortgage Lending Activity–1988*, HUD News Release, April 12, 1989; *Survey of Mortgage Lending Activity–Fourth Quarter/Annual, 1995*, HUD News Release, April 26, 1996.

IV. Kratovil & Werner §§ 4.01–4.06; 2 Nelson & Whitman § 12.3; Penney, Broude, & Cunningham 756–757; 4 Powell ¶ 441.3; L. Travis Brannon, Jr., *Enforceability of Mortgage Loan Commitments*, 18 Real Prop., Prob. & Tr.J. 724 (1983); Roger D. Groot, *Specific Performance of Contracts to Provide Permanent Financing*, 60 Cornell L.Rev. 718 (1975).

V. Kratovil & Werner §§ 29.04–29.04(c), 33.01–33.10(c); Madison, Dwyer, & Bender ¶¶ 4.04, 11.01; 1 & 2 Nelson & Whitman §§ 5.35, 11.3; Andrew Lance, *Balancing Private and Public Initiatives in the Mortgage–Backed Security Market*, 18 Real Prop., Prob. & Tr.J. 426 (1983); Walter M. Strine, Jr., *New Commercial Devices—Mortgage–Backed Securities*, 13 Real Prop., Prob. & Tr.J. 1011 (1978).

VI.   A. Nelson & Whitman casebook 1085–1086; 4C Rohan §§ 9A.01, 9A.02[1]–[2], 9A.03[1]–[2]; Julia Patterson Forrester, *Mortgaging the American Dream: A Critical Evaluation of the Federal Government's Promotion of Home Equity Financing*, 69 Tul.L.Rev. 373 (1994).

      B. Kratovil & Werner §§ 24.11–24.11(f); Nelson & Whitman casebook 886–903; 1 Nelson & Whitman § 9.8; 4C Rohan § 9A.03[3]; Francis P. Gunning, *The Wrap–Around Mortgage . . . Friend or U.F.O.?*, 2 Real Est.Rev. 35 (Summer 1972); Note, *Wrap–Around Financing: A Technique for Skirting the Usury Laws?*, 1972 Duke L.J. 785; Bill B. Caraway, Note, *Unwrapping the Wraparound Mortgage Foreclosure Process*, 47 Wash. & Lee L.Rev. 1025 (1990).

VII.   A. HUD Report 11–17, 83–137; Grace Milgram, *Housing the Urban Poor: Urban Housing Assistance Programs* in Housing–A Reader 114 (Cong.Research Service, Library of Congress, July 1983).

B. HUD Report 78–81; Nelson & Whitman casebook 942,
972–975, 985–988; 2 Nelson & Whitman § 11.2; 4,Pt.1
Rohan § 3.03; Miles 61, Robert Rothman, *Mortgages In-
sured by FHA Will Fluctuate With Market*, 42
Cong.Q.Weekly Report 20 (Jan. 7, 1984); 2 Housing &
Development Reporter 11:0011–11:0014 (1994–1995).

C. HUD Report 62–64, 73–78; 2 Nelson & Whitman § 11.3;
Miles 59–61.

D.   1. Paul Barron, Federal Regulation of Real Estate
and Mortgage Lending ¶¶ 10.01–10.09 (3d ed.
1992 & Cum.Supp.1996 No. 2) [hereinafter Bar-
ron]; David G. Epstein & Steve H. Nickles, Consumer Law in a Nutshell 80–85, 138–146, 198–
201 (2d ed. 1981) [hereinafter Epstein & Nick-
les]; 4 Powell § 37A.01; Gary Klein, *Preventing
Home Equity Lending Fraud: Special Truth in
Lending Protections Enacted*, 7 Loy. Consumer
L.Rep. 126 (1995); Stephen F.J. Ornstein, *Examining the Effect of New Legislation on Consumer
Protection for "High Cost Mortgages,"* 25 Real
Est.L.J. 40 (1996).

2. Barron ¶¶ 3.01–3.12; Epstein & Nickles 146–149;
Frank E. Catalina, *From the Legislatures: Inter-
state Land Sales—Tightening Consumer Protec-
tion*, 10 Real Est.L.J. 72 (1981); Robin Paul
Malloy, *The Interstate Land Sales Full Disclo-
sure Act: Its Requirements, Consequences, and
Implications for Persons Participating in Real
Estate Development*, 24 B.C.L.Rev. 1187 (1983);
Report of Comm. on Regulation of Land Sales,
Real Prop. Div., *Exemptions from the Registra-
tion Requirements of the Interstate Land Sales
Full Disclosure Act*, 15 Real Prop., Prob. & Tr.J.
334 (1980); Ronald A. Johnston, Comment, *The
Interstate Land Sales Full Disclosure Act: An
Analysis of Administrative Policies Implemented
in the Years 1968–1975*, 26 Cath.U.L.Rev. 348
(1977); Ralph Bellar, Jr., Comment, *Regulating
the Real Estate Industry: The Problem of Dual
Registration*, 37 U.Kan.L.Rev. 145 (1988).

3. Michael S. Baram & J. Raymond Miyares, *Man-
aging Flood Risk: Technical Uncertainty in the
National Flood Insurance Program*, 7 Co-
lum.J.Envt.L. 129 (1982); Leonard A. Bernstein,
Phillip H. Myers, & Daniel Steen, *Flood Insur-
ance Reform Act Engulfs Mortgage Lenders*, 112
Banking L.J. 238 (1995); Niles S. Campbell, *Reg-
ulators to Issue Flood Regulations; OCC Outlines
Flood Insurance Guidelines*, 65:12 BNA Banking
Report 529 (Oct. 2, 1995); Marilyn Cane & Paul
A. Caldarelli, *Apres le Deluge: National Flood
Insurance*, 17 Nova L.Rev. 1077 (1993); Oliver A.

Houck, *Rising Water: The National Flood Insurance Program and Louisiana,* 60 Tul.L.Rev. 61 (1985); Rod Sands, *A Refresher on Federal Flood Hazard Insurance Requirements,* 11:2 Prac. Real Est. Law. 85 (March, 1995); David E. Sturgess & John P. McHugh, *Flood Hazard Insurance: Requirements Imposed on Banks Extending Loans Secured by Real Property,* 16 Real Est.L.J. 226 (1988); Gerald M. Tierney, *The National Flood Insurance Program: Explanation and Legal Implications,* 8 Urb.Law 279 (1976); Bryant J. Spann, Note, *Going Down for the Third Time: Senator Kerry's Reform Bill Could Save the Drowning National Flood Insurance Program,* 28 Ga.L.Rev. 593 (1994); Charles T. Griffith, Note, *The National Flood Insurance Program: Unattained Purposes, Liability in Contract, and Takings,* 35 Wm. & Mary L.Rev. 727 (1994).

4. Barron ¶¶ 2.01–2.10; Epstein & Nickles 149–151; 4 Powell § 37A.02; Charles G. Field, *RESPA in a Nutshell,* 11 Real Prop., Prob. & Tr.J. 447 (1976).

5. Barron ¶¶ 11.01–11.07; Alfred J. Lechner, Jr., *National Banks and State Anti–Redlining Laws: Has Congress Preempted the Field?,* 99 Banking L.J. 388 (1982); Richard D. Marsico, *Fighting Poverty Through Community Empowerment and Economic Development: The Role of the Community Reinvestment and Home Mortgage Disclosure Acts,* 12 N.Y.L.Sch.J.Hum.Rts. 281 (1995); Barbara A. Kleinman & Katherine Sloss Berger, Note, *The Home Mortgage Disclosure Act of 1975: Will It Protect Urban Consumers from Redlining?,* 12 N.Eng.L.Rev. 957 (1977).

6. Madison, Dwyer, & Bender ¶ 13.06; 4,Pt.1 Rohan, Special Alert, *Summary of Lender Liability Legislation;* Paul A. Dominick & Leon C. Harmon, *Lender Limbo: The Perils of Environmental Lender Liability,* 41 S.C.L.Rev. 855 (1990); Marianne M. Jennings, *Lender Liability, CERCLA, and Other Things That Go Bump in the Night,* 24 Real Est.L.J. 372 (1996); Paul Katcher, *Lenders' Liability for Environmental Hazards,* 20:3 Real Est.Rev. 72 (Fall 1990); Michael B. Kupin, *New Alterations of the Lender Liability Landscape: CERCLA After The "Fleet Factors" Decision,* 19 Real Est.L.J. 191 (1991); Michael P. Last, *Superfund Liability Traps Affecting Developers and Lenders,* 3:3 Nat.Resources & Env't. 10 (Fall 1988); Roger J. Marzulla & Brett G. Kappel, *Lender Liability Under the Comprehensive Environmental Response, Compensation and Liability Act,* 41 S.C.L.Rev. 705 (1990); Jeffery

M. Sharp, *Of Politics, Principles, and Money: How Environmental Lender Liability Changed the Leopards' Spots*, 25 Real Est.L.J. 56 (1996); John M. Van Lieshout, *Bankers Beware: Liability of Lending Institutions Under Superfund*, 2 Hofstra Prop.L.J. 291 (1989); Alan P. Vollmann, *Double Jeopardy: Lender Liability Under Superfund*, 16 Real Est.L.J. 3 (1987); David J. Portelli, Comment, *SARA Slams the Door: The Effect of Superfund Amendments on Foreclosing Mortgagees*, 34 Wayne L.Rev. 223 (1987); Kathleen Hellevik, *Spending Package Contains Provision Clarifying Lender Liability for Cleanup of Contaminated Real Estate*, 10–11–96 WLN 10807.

CHAPTER 3. REAL ESTATE FINANCING DEVICES

I.   A. Kratovil & Werner §§ 19.01–19.09; 1 Nelson & Whitman §§ 1.1, 9.1.

       B. Mark Lee Levine, Real Estate Transactions—Tax Planning and Consequences (1995–1996 ed. 1995); Madison, Dwyer, & Bender ¶¶ 1.01, 12.03[5]; M. Madison & J. Dwyer, The Law of Real Estate Financing ¶¶ 12.01–12.02 (1981 & Cum. Supp. 1993).

II. Kratovil & Werner §§ 3.03–3.03(g); 1 Nelson & Whitman § 1.6; Osborne § 17.

III. Kratovil & Werner §§ 3.04–3.08; 1 Nelson & Whitman §§ 3.2–3.19, 3.38; 4 Powell ¶¶ 446–449, 450[2]–[3]; Roger A. Cunningham & Saul Tischler, *Disguised Real Estate Security Transactions as Mortgages in Substance*, 26 Rutgers L.Rev. 1 (1972); Comment Note, *Different Classes of "Vendors' Liens," So-Called, Upon Real Property*, 91 A.L.R. 148 (1934); W. R. Habeeb, Annotation, *Right of Vendee Under Executory Land Contract to Lien for Amount Paid on Purchase Price*, 33 A.L.R.2d 1384 (1954).

IV. A. & B. 1 Nelson & Whitman §§ 3.26–3.34; Penney, Broude & Cunningham 544–549; Eric T. Freyfogle, *Vagueness and the Rule of Law: Reconsidering Installment Land Contract Forfeitures*, 1988 Duke L.J. 609; John R. Lewis & John R. Reeves, *How the Doctrine of Equitable Conversion Affects Land Sale Contract Forfeitures*, 3 Real Est.L.J. 249 (1974); Allen E. Korpela, Annotation, *Specific Performance of Land Contract Notwithstanding Failure of Vendee to Make Required Payments on Time*, 55 A.L.R.3d 10 (1974).

       C. 1 Nelson & Whitman § 3.35; William M. Casey, Comment, *Real Estate Contracts—When Recording of a Lien Instrument is Not Notice to the Whole World—Actual Notice Required to Protect Second Lien on a Real Estate Contract: 'Shindledecker v. Savage,'* 13 N.M.L.Rev. 177 (1983); Thomas A. Henzler, Recent Case, *Mortgages—Mortgage of a Vendee's Interest in an Installment Land Contract—Mortgagee's Rights Upon Default*, 43 Mo.L.Rev. 371 (1978).

D. 1 Nelson & Whitman § 3.37; John F. Wagner, Jr., Annotation, *Applicability of Article 9 of Uniform Commercial Code to Assignment of Rights Under Real-Estate Sales Contract, Lease Agreement, or Mortgage as Collateral for Separate Transaction*, 76 A.L.R.4th 765 (1990).

V. A. & B. Kratovil & Werner §§ 20.10–20.11, 21.01–22.26, 30.07; 1 Milton R. Friedman, Friedman on Leases §§ 7.1–7.304e, 7.8–7.803, 8.3 (3d ed. 1990 & Cum.Supp. 1992); Nelson & Whitman casebook 1274–1276; Grant S. Nelson & Dale A. Whitman, Cases and Materials on Real Estate Finance and Development 972, 985–986 (1976); 4C Rohan §§ 7.01–7.06, 7A.01–7A.06; Jesse B. Heath, Jr., *Sale-Leasebacks and Leasehold Mortgages* in Financing Real Estate in the 80s 141 (Brian J. Strum ed., 1981); Martin Kobren, *Three Perspectives on Ground Lease Negotiations* 19 Real Est.L.J. 40 (1990); Report of Comm. on Leases, *Ground Leases and Their Financing*, 4 Real Prop., Prob. & Tr. J. 437 (1969).

C. Kratovil & Werner §§ 23.01–23.08; 4C Rohan §§ 6.01–6.05; Jesse B. Heath, Jr., *Sale-Leasebacks and Leasehold Mortgages* in Financing Real Estate in the 80s 141 (Brian J. Strum ed. 1981); Thomas C. Homburger & Gregory R. Andre, *Real Estate Sale and Leasebacks Transactions and the Risk of Recharacterization in Bankruptcy Proceedings*, 24 Real Prop., Prob. & Tr.J. 95 (1989).

CHAPTER 4. UNDERLYING OBLIGATION

I.–II. Kratovil & Werner §§ 10.01–10.07; 1 Nelson & Whitman §§ 2.1–2.3; U.C.C. § 3–106 comment 1 (1990); U.C.C. § 3–105 comments 3–4 (1972); Frank A. St. Claire, *Nonrecourse Debt Transactions: Limitations on Limitations of Liability*, 19 Real Est.L.J. 19 (1990).

III. Kratovil & Werner §§ 10.08–10.08(c); 1 Nelson & Whitman § 2.4; Osborne § 106.

IV. A. Osborne § 114; Grant S. Nelson & Dale A. Whitman, *Rethinking Future Advance Mortgages: A Brief for the Restatement Approach*, 44 Duke L.J. 657 (1995) [hereinafter Nelson & Whitman, *Rethinking Future Advance Mortgages*].

B. Kratovil & Werner §§ 11.01, 11.05; 2 Nelson & Whitman § 12.7.

C. 2 Grant Gilmore, Security Interests in Personal Property § 35.4 (1965) [hereinafter Gilmore]; Kratovil & Werner §§ 11.02–11.12; 2 Nelson & Whitman § 12.7; Osborne § 119; James B. Hughes, Jr., *Future Advance Mortgages: Preserving the Benefits and Burdens of the Bargain*, 29 Wake Forest L.Rev. 1101 (1994); Robert Kratovil & Raymond J. Werner, *Mortgages for Construction and the Lien Priorities Problem—The "Unobligatory" Advance*, 41 Tenn.L.Rev. 311 (1974) [hereinafter Kratovil & Werner, *The "Unobligatory" Advance*]; Nelson & Whitman, *Rethinking Future Advance Mortgages;* Benjamin E. Griffith & Crane Davis Kipp, Comment, *Mortgages to Secure Future Advances: Problems of Priority and the Doctrine of Economic Necessity*, 46 Miss.L.J. 433 (1975).

2. 2 Nelson & Whitman § 11.4; Nelson & Whitman casebook 1011–1012.

3. Kratovil & Werner §§ 13.18–13.18(a); Madison, Dwyer, & Bender ¶¶ 5.05[4][a], 8.02[5], 11.02; J. Cary Barton & Robert E. Morrison, *Equity Participation Arrangements Between Institutional Lenders and Real Estate Developers,* 12 St. Mary's L.J. 929 (1981); Levin & Roberts 40–43; Frank E. Roegge, Gerard J. Talbot, & Robert M. Zinman, *Real Estate Equity Investments and the Institutional Lender: Nothing Ventured, Nothing Gained,* 39 Fordham L.Rev. 579 (1971).

4. See sources cited in Ch. 6 § III.

C. 1.–3. Kratovil & Werner §§ 13.01–13.14(d); Madison, Dwyer, & Bender ¶ 5.05[4][e]; Marion Benfield, *Money, Mortgages, and Migraine—The Usury Headache,* 19 Case W.Res.L.Rev. 819 (1968); Robert P. Lowell, *A Current Analysis of the Usury Laws: A National View,* 8 San Diego L.Rev. 193 (1971).

4. Madison, Dwyer, & Bender ¶ 5.05[4][e]; Lynn M. Ewing, Jr. & Kendall R. Vickers, *Federal Pre-emption of State Usury Laws Affecting Real Estate Financing,* 47 Mo. L.Rev. 171 (1982); Samuel P. Merlo, *Federal Preemption of State Usury Statutes: Legislative and Judicial Modifications,* 99 Banking L.J. 585 (1982); Linda B. Samuels, *Usury Preemption: The Federal/State Scheme,* 98 Banking L.J. 892 (1981).

VI. Kratovil & Werner §§ 38.01–38.08; 1 Nelson & Whitman § 9.4; Robert P. Giesen, *"Routine" Mortgage Modifications: Lenders Beware,* 17 Real Est.L.J. 221 (1989).

VII. A. 1 Nelson & Whitman §§ 1.1, 6.6.

1. a. 2 Nelson & Whitman § 11.4.

   b. 2 Nelson & Whitman § 11.4; Celeste M. Hammond, *Reverse Mortgages: A Financial Planning Device for the Elderly,* 1 Elder L.J. 75 (1993); Susan M. Blumenstein & Gale Harmann, Comment, *The Effect of Reverse Annuity Mortgages on SSI,* 16 U.C.Davis L.Rev. 435 (1983).

   c. 2 Nelson & Whitman § 11.4; Stephen Barrett Kanner, *Growing Equity Mortgages,* 11 Real Est.L.J. 271 (1983).

2. Kratovil & Werner § 10.13; Robert Kratovil & Raymond J. Werner, Real Estate Law § 15.35(e) (8th ed. 1983), §§ 20.23, 23.08 (10th ed. 1993); 1 Nelson & Whitman § 1.1.

3. 1 Nelson & Whitman §§ 4.17–4.19; William B. Dunn, *Selected Current Legal Issues in Mortgage Financing,* 13 Real Prop., Prob. & Tr.J. 812, 814–820 (1978); Report of Comm. on Real Estate Financing, *Class Actions Under Anti–Trust Laws on Account of Escrow and Similar Practices,* 11 Real Prop., Prob. & Tr.J. 352 (1976); Henry C. Fader, Comment, *Payment of Interest on Mortgage Escrow Accounts: Judicial and Legislative Developments,* 23 Syracuse L.Rev. 845 (1972).

    4. Robert Kratovil, Modern Mortgage Law and Practice § 165 (1972) [hereinafter Kratovil (1972)]; Kratovil & Werner § 13.15(d); 1 Nelson & Whitman §§ 6.6–6.10; Gary D. Spivey, Annotation, *Validity and Construction of Provision Imposing "Late Charge" or Similar Exaction for Delay in Making Periodic Payments on Note, Mortgage, or Installment Sale Contract,* 63 A.L.R.3d 50 (1975).

B. 1 Nelson & Whitman §§ 6.1–6.5; Penney, Broude & Cunningham 341–342; Frank S. Alexander, *Mortgage Prepayment: The Trial of Common Sense,* 72 Cornell L. Rev. 288 (1987); Debra Pogrund Stark, *Prepayment Charges in Jeopardy: The Unhappy and Uncertain Legacy of "In Re Skyler Ridge,"* 24 Real Prop., Prob. & Tr.J. 191 (1989); Alan M. Weinberger, *Neither an Early Nor a Late Payor Be?—Presuming to Question the Presumption Against Mortgage Prepayment,* 35 Wayne L.Rev. 1 (1988); John G. Wharton, *Enforceability of Prepayment Penalties in Commercial Mortgages,* 20:2 Real Est.Rev. 35 (Summer 1990); Dale A. Whitman, *Mortgage Prepayment Clauses: An Economic and Legal Analysis,* 40 UCLA L.Rev. 851 (1993); Robert K. Baldwin, Note, *Prepayment Penalties: A Survey and Suggestion,* 40 Vand. L. Rev. 409 (1987); Michael T. McNelis, Note, *Prepayment Penalties and Due-on-Sale Clauses In Commercial Mortgages: What Next?,* 20 Ind.L.Rev. 735 (1987); Ellis J. Harmon, Comment, *Secured Real Estate Loan Prepayment and the Prepayment Penalty,* 51 Cal.L.Rev. 923 (1963).

C. Kratovil & Werner §§ 34.05, 34.05(g); 1 Nelson & Whitman § 6.6.

D. 1 Nelson & Whitman § 6.11; 4 Powell ¶ 461.

CHAPTER 5. MORTGAGED PROPERTY

I. A. & B. 4 Powell ¶¶ 443–443[1]; William F. Walsh, A Treatise on Mortgages § 10 (1934) [hereinafter Walsh].

     C. Kratovil & Werner § 8.01.

II.   A. Kratovil & Werner § 8.06; 1 Nelson & Whitman § 9.3; 4 Powell ¶ 443; Roger A. Cunningham & Saul Tischler, *Equitable Real Estate Mortgages,* 17 Rutgers L.Rev. 679, 715–723 (1963).

     B. Kratovil & Werner §§ 8.03, 8.05; 4 Powell ¶ 443.

     C. 2 Garrard Glenn, Mortgages, Deeds of Trust, and Other Security Devices as to Land § 350 (1943) [hereinafter Glenn]; Kratovil & Werner §§ 8.02–8.02(a); 1 Nelson & Whitman §§ 9.3, 9.5; 4 Powell ¶ 443.

     D. Kratovil & Werner § 6.07; 1 Nelson & Whitman § 4.12.

     E. 1 Nelson & Whitman §§ 4.13–4.15; Nelson & Whitman casebook 423; Derek Lisk, Comment, *Some Real Property Hazard Insurance Problems for Texas Mortgagors and Mortgagees,* 24 Hous.L.Rev. 717 (1987); Note, *Foreclosure, Loss, and the Proper Distribution of Insurance Proceeds Under Open and Standard Mortgage Clauses: Some Observations,* 7 Val.U.L.Rev. 485 (1973).

III. 1 Glenn §§ 34–34.3; 2 Glenn §§ 194–202.1; 1 Nelson & Whitman §§ 4.4, 4.10–4.11; Walsh § 22; David A. Leipziger, *The Mortgagee's Remedies For Waste*, 64 Cal.L.Rev. 1086 (1976).

CHAPTER 6. TRANSFER OF MORTGAGOR'S INTEREST

I. & II. A., B., & C. Kratovil & Werner §§ 15.01–15.12; 1 Nelson & Whitman §§ 5.1–5.20; Roger A. Cunningham & Saul Tischler, *Transfer of the Real Estate Mortgagor's Interest*, 27 Rutgers L.Rev. 24 (1973); Frederic P. Storke & Don W. Sears, *Transfer of Mortgaged Property*, 38 Cornell L.Q. 185 (1953); J. Louis Warm, *Some Aspects of the Rights and Liabilities of Mortgagee, Mortgagor and Grantee*, 10 Temple L.Q. 116 (1936).

D. 1 Nelson & Whitman §§ 3.1, 3.3, 6.18–6.19.

1. Arnold ¶ 6.05; Kratovil & Werner §§ 40.04–40.04(u); Madison, Dwyer, & Bender ¶ 12.02; 1 Nelson & Whitman §§ 3.3, 6.18–6.19; 4 Powell ¶ 469.1; Harvey Boneparth, *Taking a Deed in Lieu of Foreclosure: Pitfalls for the Lender*, 19 Real Est.L.J. 338 (1991); Michael F. Jones, *Structuring the Deed in Lieu of Foreclosure Transaction*, 19 Real Prop., Prob. & Tr.J. 58 (1984); Richard Kelley, *Foreclosure by Contract: Deeds in Lieu of Foreclosure in Missouri*, 56 UMKC L.Rev. 633 (1988).

2. Kratovil & Werner §§ 36.01–36.05; 1 Nelson & Whitman §§ 6.15–6.17; Ann M. Burkhart, *Freeing Mortgages of Merger*, 40 Vand.L.Rev. 283 (1987).

III. 1 Nelson & Whitman §§ 5.21–5.24, 5.26, 6.5; Edward N. Barad & Leon M. Layden, *Due-on-Sale Law as Preempted by the Garn–St. Germain Act*, 12 Real Est.L.J. 138 (1983); Kent D. Coleman, *Federal Preemption of State Law Prohibitions on the Exercise of Due-on-Sale Clauses*, 100 Banking L.J. 772 (1983); William B. Dunn & Thomas S. Nowinski, *Enforcement of Due-on-Transfer Clauses: An Update*, 16 Real Prop., Prob. & Tr.J. 291 (1981); Karl E. Geier, *Due-on-Sale Clauses Under the Garn–St. Germain Depository Institutions Act of 1982*, 17 U.S.F.L.Rev. 355 (1983); Grant S. Nelson & Dale A. Whitman, *Congressional Preemption of Mortgage Due-on-Sale Law: An Analysis of the Garn–St. Germain Act*, 35 Hastings L.J. 241 (1983); Ronald R. Volkmer, *The Application of the Restraints on Alienation Doctrine to Real Property Security Interests*, 58 Iowa L.Rev. 747 (1973); Joseph Gibson, III, Note, *Due-on-Sale Clauses: Separating Social Interests from Individual Interests*, 35 Vand.L.Rev. 357 (1982); Report of Subcomm. on "Due-on" Clauses of Comm. on Real Estate Financing, *Enforcement of Due-on-Transfer Clauses*, 13 Real Prop., Prob. & Tr.J. 891 (1978); FHLBB Regulations, *Preemption of State Due-on-Sale Laws*, 48 Fed.Regis. 21554–21563 (1983).

IV. See sources cited in § III above.

V. 2 Glenn §§ 300–307; Osborne § 251; 4 Powell ¶ 457[6]; J. Kraut, Annotation, *Right of Heir or Devisee to Have Realty Exonerated From Lien Thereon at Expense of Personal Estate*, 4 A.L.R.3d 1023 (1965).

CHAPTER 7. TRANSFER OF MORTGAGEE'S INTEREST

I. & II. A. & B. 1 Nelson & Whitman §§ 5.27–5.28; 4 Powell ¶¶ 455–455[3].

      C. Kratovil & Werner § 32.02; 1 Nelson & Whitman § 5.34.

      D. 1 Nelson & Whitman § 5.27; 4 Powell ¶ 455.

III. Kratovil & Werner §§ 32.05, 32.06; Fred H. Miller & Alvin C. Harrell, The Law of Modern Payments Systems and Notes §§ 3.03, 6.01–6.03 (2d ed. 1992) [hereinafter Miller & Harrell]; Nelson & Whitman §§ 5.27–5.32; Osborne §§ 227–228, 231; Richard E. Speidel & Steve H. Nickles, Negotiable Instruments and Check Collection (the new law) in a Nutshell 289–363 (4th ed. 1993); U.C.C. §§ 3–302, comments 1–3, 3–305, comments 1–2.

IV. 2 Baxter Dunaway, The Law of Distressed Real Estate § 19.23 (1995); Kratovil & Werner §§ 34.01–34.01(e); Miller & Harrell § 6.03[6][b]; 1 Nelson & Whitman §§ 5.33–5.34; Nelson & Whitman casebook 503–506; Grant S. Nelson & Dale A. Whitman, Real Estate Finance Law §§ 5.33–5.34 (Hornbook Series—2d ed. 1985); Osborne §§ 233–237; Annotation, *Recording Laws as Applied to Assignments of Mortgages on Real Estate*, 89 A.L.R. 171 (1934).

V. Kratovil & Werner § 32.10; 1 Nelson & Whitman § 5.34; Nelson & Whitman casebook 505–506.

VI. A. & B. Kratovil & Werner § 33.01; Madison, Dwyer, & Bender ¶ 11.01; 1 Nelson & Whitman 5.35; Nelson & Whitman casebook 510–513; Osborne § 243; 4 Powell ¶ 456.

      C. 2 Glenn §§ 318–318.3; 1 Nelson & Whitman § 5.35; Osborne §§ 244–246.

      D. 2 Glenn § 317; 1 Nelson & Whitman § 5.35; 4 Powell ¶ 456.

VII. Kratovil & Werner §§ 31.01–31.07; 2 Nelson & Whitman §§ 10.1–10.8; Osborne §§ 282, 284.

VIII. Kratovil & Werner § 32.14; 1 Nelson & Whitman § 5.28; Nelson & Whitman casebook 506–510.

IX. 2 Glenn § 311; 4 Powell ¶ 452.

CHAPTER 8. AFTER DEFAULT AND BEFORE FORECLOSURE

I. A. & B. Kratovil & Werner § 14.05; 1 Nelson & Whitman § 7.6; Osborne § 325.

      C. Kratovil & Werner § 14.04; 1 Nelson & Whitman § 7.7; E. J. Spires, Annotation, *Acceptance of Past–Due Interest as Waiver of Acceleration Clause in Note or Mortgage*, 97 A.L.R.2d 997 (1964).

II. Kratovil & Werner §§ 14.01–14.07, 14.09–14.10; 1 Nelson & Whit-
man §§ 7.6–7.8; Bruce J. Bergman, *Strict Acceleration in New York
Mortgage Foreclosure—Has the Doctrine Eroded?*, 8 Pace L.Rev.
475 (1988); Robert R. Rosenthal, *The Role of Courts of Equity in
Preventing Acceleration Predicated Upon a Mortgagor's Inadvertent
Default*, 22 Syracuse L.Rev. 897 (1971).

III. A. Kratovil & Werner, §§ 20.01–20.02; 1 Nelson & Whitman
§§ 1.5, 4.1–4.3, 4.20; Osborne, §§ 13–16; Report of
Comm. on Mortgage Law & Practice, *Disposition of Rents
and Profits After Mortgage Default*, 2 Real Prop., Prob. &
Tr.J. 601 (1967).

B. 1.–3. 1 Glenn § 33.3; 2 Glenn §§ 203–204.1; Kratovil &
Werner §§ 20.02–20.03(g); 1 Nelson & Whitman
§§ 4.24–4.32.

4. 1 Glenn § 33.4; Kratovil & Werner §§ 20.04–
20.05(c); 1 Nelson & Whitman §§ 4.20–4.23; 2 Nelson & Whitman § 12.9; Robert Kratovil, *Mortgages—Problems in Possession, Rents and Mortgagee
Liability*, 11 DePaul L.Rev. 1 (1961); Robert D.
Feinstein & Sidney A. Keyles, *Foreclosure: Subordination, Non–Disturbance and Attornment Agreements*, Prob. & Prop., July–Aug. 1989 at 38.

C. Kratovil & Werner §§ 20.07–20.07(a); Madison, Dwyer, &
Bender ¶ 12.03[2][b]; 1 Nelson & Whitman §§ 4.35, 4.39,
8.18; Julia Patterson Forrester, *A Uniform and More
Rational Approach to Rents as Security for the Mortgage
Loan*, 46 Rutgers L.Rev. 349 (1993).

D. Kratovil & Werner §§ 20.03, 20.06; 1 Nelson & Whitman
§§ 4.33–4.43; 4 Powell ¶ 465; J.P. Ludington, Annotation,
*Propriety of Appointing Receiver, At Behest of Mortgagee,
To Manage or Operate Property During Foreclosure Action*, 82 A.L.R.2d 1075 (1962).

IV. 1 Nelson & Whitman §§ 7.1–7.5.

V. A. & B. Arnold ¶¶ 6.05–6.07; Kratovil & Werner §§ 40.01(a)–
40.07; Madison, Dwyer, & Bender ¶¶ 12.01–12.02; Real
Estate Bankruptcies and Workouts (A. Kuklin & P. Rob-
erts eds. 1983); Paul E. Roberts & Howard J. Lazarus,
When the Workout Doesn't Work Out—An Outline, 12
Real Prop., Prob. & Tr.J. 437 (1977).

C. 1 Glenn §§ 73–73.1, 96; 1 Nelson & Whitman §§ 8.1–8.2.

CHAPTER 9. PRIORITIES

I. Walsh § 74.

II. William E. Burby, Handbook of the Law of Real Property §§ 130–
134 (3d ed. 1965); John E. Cribbet & Corwin W. Johnson, Principles of the Law of Property 306–326 (3d ed. 1989).

III. A. Kratovil & Werner §§ 19.01–19.09; 1 Nelson & Whitman, §§ 1.1, 9.1.

B. Kratovil & Werner, §§ 30.01–30.08; 2 Nelson & Whitman §§ 12.9–12.10; Osborne § 212; Gerald Korngold, *Construction Loan Advances and the Subordinated Purchase Money Mortgagee: An Appraisal, A Suggested Approach, and the ULTA Perspective*, 50 Fordham L.Rev. 313 (1981); Hugh B. Lambe, *Enforceability of Subordination Agreements*, 19 Real Prop., Prob. & Tr.J. 631 (1984); Warren H. McNamara, Jr., *Subordination Agreements as Viewed by Sellers, Purchasers, Construction Lenders, and Title Companies*, 12 Real Est.L.J. 347 (1984); Frederick D. Minnes, Note, *Purchase Money Subordination Agreements in California: An Analysis of Conventional Subordination*, 45 S.Cal.L.Rev. 1109 (1972); George Hollodick, Note, *Real Estate Finance—Subordination Clauses: North Carolina Subordinates Substance to Form—"MCB Ltd. v. McGowan,"* 23 Wake Forest L.Rev. 575 (1988); David J. Marchitelli, Annotation, *Construction Mortgagee–Lender's Duty to Protect Interest of Subordinated Purchase–Money Mortgagee*, 13 ALR5th 684 (1993); B. P. O'Byrne, Annotation, *Specific Performance: Requisite Definiteness of Provision in Contract for Sale or Lease of Land, That Vendor or Landlord Will Subordinate His Interest to Permit Other Party to Obtain Financing*, 26 A.L.R.3d 855 (1969).

C. Henry J. Bailey III & Richard B. Hagedorn, Secured Transactions in a Nutshell 282–290 (3d ed. 1988); Ray D. Henson, Handbook on Secured Transactions Under the Uniform Commercial Code, §§ 4–19, 8–1 to 8–3 (2d ed. 1979); Kratovil & Werner §§ 9.01–9.11; 1 Nelson & Whitman §§ 9.5–9.7; Daniel Fenton Adams, *Security Interests in Fixtures Under Mississippi's Uniform Commercial Code*, 47 Miss.L.J. 831 (1976); David Gray Carlson, *Fixture Priorities*, 4 Cardozo L.Rev. 381 (1983); U.C.C. §§ 9–313 comments 1–8, 9–403 comment 4 (1990).

D. 1.–3. Kratovil § 214 (1972); Kratovil & Werner §§ 25.27–25.27(c); Madison, Dwyer, & Bender ¶¶ 6.02[6]–6.02[a][i]; 2 Nelson & Whitman § 12.4; 5 Powell §§ 38.10–38.18; Uniform Simplification of Land Transfers Act, Article 5, Introductory Comment (1977).

4. 2 Nelson & Whitman § 12.5; Stephen C. Skubel, Note, *Mechanics' Liens Subject to Fourteenth Amendment Guarantees*, 26 Cath.U.L.Rev. 129 (1976); Denzil F. Lowry, Jr., Commentary, *Creditors' Rights: The Constitutionality of Oklahoma's Mechanics' Lien Law*, 31 Okla.L.Rev. 148 (1978).

5. Kratovil & Werner § 25.28: Madison, Dwyer, & Bender ¶ 6.02[6][a][iii]; 2 Nelson & Whitman § 12.6; 5 Powell § 38.19; Russell M. Blain, Note, *Lien Rights and Construction Lending: Responsibilities and Liabilities in Florida*, 29 U.Fla.L.Rev. 411 (1977); Richard Paroutaud, Note, *Mechanics' Liens: The "Stop Notice" Comes to Washington*, 49 Wash.L.Rev. 685 (1974).

E. 1. 3 Glenn §§ 434–435; 1 Nelson & Whitman § 4.17; 5 Powell ¶¶ 494–496.

2. Kratovil §§ 422–429 (1972); 5 Powell ¶ 497; 25 Fed.Tax Coordinator 2d ¶¶ V–6000 to V–6002, V–6300 to V–6456 (Res.Inst.Am. 1996).

F. 1 Nelson & Whitman § 7.13.

G. 2 Glenn §§ 289–296; Kratovil & Werner §§ 16.04, 34.05(h), 41.09(n); Madison, Dwyer, & Bender ¶ 8.01[3][e]; 2 Nelson & Whitman §§ 10.09–10.15; Walsh §§ 55–56; John J. Shalhoub, Note, *Marshaling: Equitable Rights of Holders of Junior Interests,* 38 Rutgers L.Rev. 287 (1986).

CHAPTER 10. FORECLOSURE

I. Kratovil & Werner § 41.09(c); 1 Nelson & Whitman § 7.12; 4 Powell ¶¶ 462, 463[6]; Walsh § 74.

II. 1 Nelson & Whitman §§ 6.11, 6.14.

III.
A. 1 Nelson & Whitman §§ 8.12–8.19; Madison, Dwyer, & Bender ¶ 12.04; Baxter Dunaway, *Effect of the Bankruptcy Reform Act of 1994 on Real Estate,* 30 Real Prop., Prob. & Tr.J. 601 (1996); Frank R. Kennedy, *Involuntary Fraudulent Transfers,* 9 Cardozo L.Rev. 531 (1987); Debra Pogrund Stark, *The Emperor Still Has Clothes: Fraudulent Conveyance Challenges After the BFP Decision,* 47 S.C.L.Rev. 563 (1996); Catherine M. Stites, Note, *A Palace for a Peppercorn: A Post–BFP Proposal to Resurrect Section 548(A)(2)(A),* 73 Wash.U.L.Q. 1747 (1995).

B. Kratovil & Werner §§ 41.05–41.05(c); 1 Nelson & Whitman §§ 8.9–8.11; Philip J. Bagley, III, *The Soldiers' and Sailors' Civil Relief Act—A Survey,* 45 Mil.L.Rev. 1 (1969); Kathleen H. Switzer, *Mortgage Defaults and the Soldiers' and Sailors' Civil Relief Act: Assigning the Burden of Proof When Applying the Material Effect Test,* 18 Real Est.L.J. 171 (1989); *Military and Civil Defense,* 54 Am.Jur.2d §§ 326–331 (1971); W. E. Shipley, Annotation, *Soldiers' and Sailors' Civil Relief Act of 1940, As Amended, As Affecting Foreclosure of Mortgages and Trust Deeds,* 40 A.L.R.2d 1262 (1955).

IV. Kratovil & Werner § 41.09; 1 Nelson & Whitman §§ 1.4, 7.11, 7.12; Osborne § 318; Foreclosure Law & Related Remedies: A State–By-State Digest (Sidney A. Keyles, ed., 1995).

A. 1. Kratovil & Werner § 41.09(c); 1 Nelson & Whitman §§ 7.12, 7.14; Osborne § 321; 4 Powell ¶ 463[6]; Walsh §§ 68, 74.

2. Kratovil & Werner § 20.05; 1 Nelson & Whitman § 7.12; Robert D. Feinstein & Sidney A. Keyles, *Foreclosure: Subordination, Non–Disturbance and Attornment Agreements,* Prob. & Prop., July–Aug. 1989 at 38.

3. 1 Nelson & Whitman § 7.13.

B. & C. Kratovil & Werner §§ 41.09(h)–41.09(*o*); 1 Nelson & Whitman § 7.16; 4 Powell ¶ 466; Robert M. Washburn, *The Judicial and Legislative Response to Price Inadequacy in Mortgage Foreclosure Sales,* 53 S.Cal.L.Rev. 843 (1980).

D. 1. 1 Glenn § 94; 1 Nelson & Whitman §§ 1.1, 7.17; Walsh § 74.
   2. 1 Nelson & Whitman § 7.15; George M. Platt, *The Dracula Mortgage: Creature of the Omitted Junior Lienholder,* 67 Or.L.Rev. 287 (1988).
   3. 1 Glenn § 94.1; Kratovil & Werner § 41.09(m).
   4. Kratovil & Werner § 41.16; 1 Nelson & Whitman § 4.44.

E. Kratovil & Werner § 41.10; 1 Nelson & Whitman §§ 1.1, 7.31–7.32; 4 Powell ¶ 467; Walsh § 79.

F. Kratovil & Werner § 41.10, 1 Nelson & Whitman §§ 8.1, 8.3; 4 Powell ¶¶ 462, 467; Walsh § 77; John Mixon, *Deficiency Judgments Following Home Mortgage Foreclosure: An Anachronism That Increases Personal Tragedy, Impedes Regional Economic Recovery, and Means Little to Lenders,* 22 Texas Tech.L.Rev. 1 (1991); Robert M. Washburn, *The Judicial and Legislative Response to Price Inadequacy in Mortgage Foreclosure Sales,* 53 S.Cal. L.Rev. 843 (1980).

V. Kratovil & Werner §§ 41.08–41.08(a)(1), 41.09; 1 Nelson & Whitman §§ 1.4, 7.9, 7.19; 4 Powell ¶ 468[1]–[6]; Foreclosure Law & Related Remedies: A State–By–State Digest (Sidney A. Keyles, ed., 1995).

A. Kratovil & Werner §§ 41.08–41.08(c), 41.08(e)–41.08(p); 1 Nelson & Whitman §§ 7.19–7.22, 8.1; Osborne §§ 342–344; 4 Powell ¶ 468[1]–[6].

B. 1 Nelson & Whitman §§ 7.23–7.30; James M. Pedowitz, *Current Developments in Summary Foreclosure,* 9 Real Prop., Prob. & Tr.J. 421 (1974); Donald L. Schwartz, Comment, *Power of Sale Foreclosure After Fuentes,* 40 U.Chi.L.Rev. 206 (1972).

VI. 1 Nelson & Whitman §§ 7.9–7.10; Osborne §§ 314–315; 4 Powell ¶ 469; James Geoffrey Durham, *In Defense of Strict Foreclosure: A Legal and Economic Analysis of Mortgage Foreclosure,* 36 S.C.Law Rev. 461 (1985).

VII. 2 Glenn §§ 227–243; Kratovil & Werner §§ 42.06–42.17; 1 Nelson & Whitman §§ 1.4, 7.1, 8.4–8.7; Osborne §§ 8, 307–310; Patrick B. Bauer, *Judicial Foreclosure and Statutory Redemption: The Soundness of Iowa's Traditional Preference for Protection Over Credit,* 71 Iowa L.Rev. 1 (1985); Patrick B. Bauer, *Statutory Redemption Reconsidered: The Operation of Iowa's Redemption Statute in Two Counties Between 1881 and 1980,* 70 Iowa L.Rev. 343 (1985); Catherine A. Gnatek, Note, *The New Mortgage Foreclosure Law: Redemption and Reinstatement,* 1989 U.Ill.L.Rev. 471; Benjamin Pitts, Comment, *Waiver of Redemption Rights in Tennessee Mortgages: Discarding the Contracts Clause and Common–Law Concepts,* 55 Tenn.L.Rev. 733 (1988); James Timothy Payne, Annotation, *Mortgages: Effect on Subordinate Lien of Redemption by Owner or Assignee From Sale Under Prior Lien,* 56 A.L.R.4th 703 (1987).

CHAPTER 11. FINANCING COOPERATIVES AND CONDOMINIUMS

I.–III. Arnold, ¶¶ 4.12–4.13; Kratovil & Werner §§ 26.01–26.14; Madison, Dwyer, & Bender ¶¶ 10.01–10.03; 2 Nelson & Whitman §§ 13.1–13.6; 4B Powell ¶¶ 631–632.1[6], 632.3, 632.4[2]-[3], 632.5[3]-[5]; Patrick J. Rohan & Melvin A. Reskin, 1,Pt.1 & 1,Pt.2 Condominium Law and Practice §§ 1.01–1.06, 3.01–3.04, 7.01–7.08, 9.01–9.09, 12.01–12.07 (1996—Release No. 61, Nov. 1996); Patrick J. Rohan & Melvin A. Reskin, 2 Cooperative Housing Law and Practice §§ 1.01–2.04, 5.01, 5A.01–5A.11 (1996—Release No. 41, Feb. 1996); Marvin Garfinkel, *The Uniform Condominium Act*, 28:8 Prac.Law. 43 (Dec., 1982); T. Bertram King, *Problems of Financing Condominiums*, 24 Bus.Law. 445 (1969); Thomas Pfeiler, *Condominium Financing: Some Legal Basics*, 38 U.S.Sav. & Loan League Legal Bull. 249 (1972); William Griffith Thomas, *The New Uniform Condominium Act*, 64 A.B.A.J. 1370 (1978); Uniform Condominium Act prefatory note and § 3–116 comment 2 (1980 version); *Table of Jurisdictions Wherein [Uniform Condominium] Act Has Been Adopted*, 7 U.L.A. 421 (1985) & 1996 Supp. at 335.

CHAPTER 12. REFORM

I. & II.   A.   Burke §§ 1.1.4–1.1.8, 1.3–1.5, 11.1–11.4; Kratovil & Werner §§ 6.02–6.03; 6.23–6.24(a); 37.02–37.03; 1 Nelson & Whitman §§ 7.19, 8.8; 2 Nelson & Whitman § 11.6; Frank S. Alexander, *Federal Intervention in Real Estate Finance: Preemption and Federal Common Law*, 71 N.C.L.Rev. 293 (1993); Eric T. Freyfogle, *The New Judicial Roles in Illinois Mortgage Foreclosures*, 19 Loy.U.Chi.L.J. 933 (1988); Alex M. Johnson, Jr., *Critiquing the Foreclosure Process: An Economic Approach Based on the Paradigmatic Norms of Bankruptcy*, 79 Va.L.Rev. 959 (1993); David M. Madway & Daniel D. Pearlman, *Mortgage Forms and Foreclosure Practices: Time for Reform,* 9 Real Prop., Prob. & Tr.J. 560 (1974); James M. Pedowitz, *Current Developments in Summary Foreclosure*, 9 Real Prop., Prob. & Tr.J. 421 (1974); Paul J. Prinzivalli, *Federal Legislation Preempts State Laws; Statutes Only Affect HUD Mortgages, N.Y.L.J.*, Aug. 21, 1995, S3; Patrick A. Randolph, Jr., *The New Federal Foreclosure Laws*, 49 Okla.L.Rev. 123 (1996); Steven Wechsler, *Through the Looking Glass: Foreclosure by Sale as "De Facto" Strict Foreclosure—An Empirical Study of Mortgage Foreclosure and Subsequent Resale*, 70 Cornell L.Rev. 850 (1985); Report of Comm. on Mortgage Law & Practice, *Cost and Time Factors in Foreclosure of Mortgages*, 3 Real Prop., Prob. & Tr.J. 413 (1968); Uniform Land Transaction Act introductory comment to Article 3 (1977); Uniform Land Security Interest Act prefatory note (1985); S. Rep. No. 103–307, 86–89 (1994); *Testimony Concerning Debt Collection Improvement Act of 1995 Before House Comm. on Gov't Mgmt., Info. & Tech.* (statement of Gerald Stern, Special Couns. for Fin. Institution Fraud, Off. of Deputy Att'y Gen.), 1995 WL 561205 (F.D.C.H.).

B. 4 Powell ¶¶ 435.1, 468[1]–[6]; Roger Bernhardt, *ULSIA's Remedies on Default—Worth the Effort?*, 24 Conn.L.Rev. 1001 (1992); Jon W. Bruce, *Mortgage Law Reform Under the Uniform Land Transactions Act,* 64 Geo.L.J. 1245 (1976); Norman Geis, *Escape From the 15th Century: The Uniform Land Security Interest Act,* 30 Real Prop., Prob. & Tr.J. 289 (1995); James M. Pedowitz, *Mortgage Foreclosure Under ULSIA (Uniform Land Security Interest Act),* 27 Wake Forest L.Rev. 495 (1992); James M. Pedowitz, *Mortgage Foreclosure Under the Uniform Land Transactions Act (As Amended),* 6 Real Est.L.J. 179 (1978); Patrick A. Randolph, Jr., *The Future of American Real Estate Law: Uniform Foreclosure Laws and Uniform Land Security Interest Act,* 20 Nova L.Rev. 1109 (1996); Uniform Land Transactions Act prefatory note, introductory comment to Article 3, & comments to §§ 3–101 to 3–513 (1977); Uniform Land Security Interest Act prefatory note & comments to §§ 101–514 (1985).

C. Restatement (Third) of Property (Mortgages)(Tentative Drafts No. 1, 1991; No. 2, 1992; No. 3, 1994; No.4, 1995; No.5, 1996); *Membership Gives Final Approval to Mortgages Restatement and Makes Significant Progress on Other Annual Meeting Drafts,* 18:4 ALI Rep. 1 (Summer, 1996).

APPENDIX A

NOTE AND MORTGAGE FORMS

The Federal National Mortgage Association (FNMA) and the Federal Home Loan Mortgage Corporation (FHLMC) have developed uniform note and mortgage instruments for use throughout the country. *See* Ch. 12, pp. 226–227 (discussing standard mortgage forms). The FNMA/FHLMC mortgage form contains a "uniform covenants" section which is the same in all states and a "nonuniform covenants" section which varies somewhat from jurisdiction to jurisdiction in order to accommodate differences in local law. Following are FNMA/FHLMC uniform multistate note and Indiana mortgage instruments.

NOTE

.... , 19......

[City]   [State]

[Property Address]

1. BORROWER'S PROMISE TO PAY

In return for a loan that I have received, I promise to pay U.S. $...................................... (this amount is called "principal"), plus interest, to the order of the Lender. The Lender is ....
.... I understand that the Lender may transfer this Note. The Lender or anyone who takes this Note by transfer and who is entitled to receive payments under this Note is called the "Note Holder."

2. INTEREST

Interest will be charged on unpaid principal until the full amount of principal has been paid. I will pay interest at a yearly rate of .... %.

The interest rate required by this Section 2 is the rate I will pay both before and after any default described in Section 6(B) of this Note.

3. PAYMENTS

(A) Time and Place of Payments

I will pay principal and interest by making payments every month.

I will make my monthly payments on the .... day of each month beginning on .... 19......... I will make these payments every month until I have paid all of the principal and interest and any other charges described below that I may owe under this Note. My monthly payments will be applied to interest before principal. If, on .... I still owe amounts under this Note, I will pay those amounts in full on that date, which is called the "maturity date."

I will make my monthly payments at ....
.... or at a different place if required by the Note Holder.

(B) Amount of Monthly Payments

My monthly payment will be in the amount of U.S. $...

4. BORROWER'S RIGHT TO PREPAY

I have the right to make payments of principal at any time before they are due. A payment of principal only is known as a "prepayment." When I make a prepayment, I will tell the Note Holder in writing that I am doing so.

I may make a full prepayment or partial prepayments without paying any prepayment charge. The Note Holder will use all of my prepayments to reduce the amount of principal that I owe under this Note. If I make a partial prepayment, there will be no changes in the due date or in the amount of my monthly payment unless the Note Holder agrees in writing to those changes.

5. LOAN CHARGES

If a law, which applies to this loan and which sets maximum loan charges, is finally interpreted so that the interest or other loan charges collected or to be collected in connection with this loan exceed the permitted limits, then: (i) any such loan charge shall be reduced by the amount necessary to reduce the charge to the permitted limit; and (ii) any sums already collected from me which exceeded permitted limits will be refunded to me. The Note Holder may choose to make this refund by reducing the principal I owe under this Note or by making a direct payment to me. If a refund reduces principal, the reduction will be treated as a partial prepayment.

6. BORROWER'S FAILURE TO PAY AS REQUIRED

(A) Late Charge for Overdue Payments

If the Note Holder has not received the full amount of any monthly payment by the end of .... calendar days after the date it is due, I will pay a late charge to the Note Holder. The amount of the charge will be .... % of my overdue payment of principal and interest. I will pay this late charge promptly but only once on each late payment.

(B) Default

If I do not pay the full amount of each monthly payment on the date it is due, I will be in default.

(C) Notice of Default

If I am in default, the Note Holder may send me a written notice telling me that if I do not pay the overdue amount by a certain date, the Note Holder may require me to pay immediately the full amount of principal which has not been paid and all the interest that I owe on that amount. That date must be at least 30 days after the date on which the notice is delivered or mailed to me.

(D) No Waiver By Note Holder

Even if, at a time when I am in default, the Note Holder does not require me to pay immediately in full as described above, the Note Holder will still have the right to do so if I am in default at a later time.

(E) Payment of Note Holder's Costs and Expenses

If the Note Holder has required me to pay immediately in full as described above, the Note Holder will have the right to be paid back by me for all of its costs and expenses in enforcing this Note to the extent not prohibited by applicable law. Those expenses include, for example, reasonable attorneys' fees.

7. GIVING OF NOTICES

Unless applicable law requires a different method, any notice that must be given to me under this Note will be given by delivering it or by mailing it by first class mail to me at the Property Address above or at a different address if I give the Note Holder a notice of my different address.

Any notice that must be given to the Note Holder under this Note will be given by mailing it by first class mail to the Note Holder at the address stated in Section 3(A) above or at a different address if I am given a notice of that different address.

8. OBLIGATIONS OF PERSONS UNDER THIS NOTE

If more than one person signs this Note, each person is fully and personally obligated to keep all of the promises made in this Note, including the promise to pay the full amount owed. Any person who is a guarantor, surety or endorser of this Note is also obligated to do these things. Any person who takes over these obligations, including the obligations of a guarantor, surety or endorser of this Note, is also obligated to keep all of the promises made in this Note. The Note Holder may enforce its rights under this Note against each person individually or against all of us together. This means that any one of us may be required to pay all of the amounts owed under this Note.

9. WAIVERS

I and any other person who has obligations under this Note waive the rights of presentment and notice of dishonor. "Presentment" means the right to require the Note Holder to demand payment of amounts due. "Notice of dishonor" means the right to require the Note Holder to give notice to other persons that amounts due have not been paid.

10. UNIFORM SECURED NOTE

This Note is a uniform instrument with limited variations in some jurisdictions. In addition to the protections given to the Note Holder under this Note, a Mortgage, Deed of Trust or Security Deed (the "Security Instrument") dated the same date as this Note, protects the Note Holder from possible losses which might result if I do not keep the promises which I make in this Note. That Security Instrument describes how and under what conditions I may be required to make immediate payment in full of all amounts I owe under this Note. Some of those conditions are described as follows:

Transfer of the Property or a Beneficial Interest in Borrower. If all or any part of the Property or any interest in it is sold or transferred (or if a beneficial interest in Borrower is sold or transferred and Borrower is not a natural person) without Lender's prior written consent, Lender may, at its option, require immediate payment in full of all sums secured by this Security Instrument. However, this option shall not be exercised by Lender if exercise is prohibited by federal law as of the date of this Security Instrument.

If Lender exercises this option, Lender shall give Borrower notice of acceleration. The notice shall provide a period of not less than 30 days from the date the notice is delivered or mailed within which Borrower must pay all sums secured by this Security Instrument. If Borrower fails to pay these sums prior to the expiration of this period, Lender may invoke any remedies permitted by this Security Instrument without further notice or demand on Borrower.

WITNESS THE HAND(S) AND SEAL(S) OF THE UNDERSIGNED

....(Seal)
Borrower

....(Seal)
Borrower

....(Seal)
Borrower

[Sign Original Only]

—————————————————— [Space Above This Line For Recording Data] ——————————————————

MORTGAGE

THIS MORTGAGE ("Security Instrument") is given on ....
19 .... The mortgagor is ....
.... ("Borrower"). This Security Instrument is given to ....
.... , which is organized and existing
under the laws of .... , and whose address is ....
.... ("Lender").
Borrower owes Lender the principal sum of ....
.... Dollars (U.S. $ ....). This debt is evidenced by Borrower's note
dated the same date as this Security Instrument ("Note"), which provides for monthly payments, with the full debt, if not
paid earlier, due and payable on .... This Security Instrument
secures to Lender: (a) the repayment of the debt evidenced by the Note, with interest, and all renewals, extensions and
modifications of the Note; (b) the payment of all other sums, with interest, advanced under paragraph 7 to protect the security
of this Security Instrument; and (c) the performance of Borrower's covenants and agreements under this Security Instrument
and the Note. For this purpose, Borrower does hereby mortgage, grant and convey to Lender the following described property
located in .... County, Indiana:

which has the address of .... , ... ,
                                        [Street]   [City]
Indiana .... ("Property Address");
               [Zip Code]

TOGETHER WITH all the improvements now or hereafter erected on the property, and all easements, appurtenances,
and fixtures now or hereafter a part of the property. All replacements and additions shall also be covered by this Security
Instrument. All of the foregoing is referred to in this Security Instrument as the "Property."

BORROWER COVENANTS that Borrower is lawfully seised of the estate hereby conveyed and has the right to mortgage,
grant and convey the Property and that the Property is unencumbered, except for encumbrances of record. Borrower warrants
and will defend generally the title to the Property against all claims and demands, subject to any encumbrances of record.

THIS SECURITY INSTRUMENT combines uniform covenants for national use and non-uniform covenants with limited
variations by jurisdiction to constitute a uniform security instrument covering real property.

INDIANA—Single Family—**Fannie Mae/Freddie Mac UNIFORM INSTRUMENT**   **Form 3015   9/90** *(page 1 of 6 pages)*
                                                                                             [G4085]

UNIFORM COVENANTS. Borrower and Lender covenant and agree as follows:

1. Payment of Principal and Interest; Prepayment and Late Charges. Borrower shall promptly pay when due the principal of and interest on the debt evidenced by the Note and any prepayment and late charges due under the Note.

2. Funds for Taxes and Insurance. Subject to applicable law or to a written waiver by Lender, Borrower shall pay to Lender on the day monthly payments are due under the Note, until the Note is paid in full, a sum ("Funds") for: (a) yearly taxes and assessments which may attain priority over this Security Instrument as a lien on the Property; (b) yearly leasehold payments or ground rents on the Property, if any; (c) yearly hazard or property insurance premiums; (d) yearly flood insurance premiums, if any; (e) yearly mortgage insurance premiums, if any; and (f) any sums payable by Borrower to Lender, in accordance with the provisions of paragraph 8, in lieu of the payment of mortgage insurance premiums. These items are called "Escrow Items." Lender may, at any time, collect and hold Funds in an amount not to exceed the maximum amount a lender for a federally related mortgage loan may require for Borrower's escrow account under the federal Real Estate Settlement Procedures Act of 1974 as amended from time to time, 12 U.S.C. § 2601 *et seq.* ("RESPA"), unless another law that applies to the Funds sets a lesser amount. If so, Lender may, at any time, collect and hold Funds in an amount not to exceed the lesser amount. Lender may estimate the amount of Funds due on the basis of current data and reasonable estimates of expenditures of future Escrow Items or otherwise in accordance with applicable law.

The Funds shall be held in an institution whose deposits are insured by a federal agency, instrumentality, or entity (including Lender, if Lender is such an institution) or in any Federal Home Loan Bank. Lender shall apply the Funds to pay the Escrow Items. Lender may not charge Borrower for holding and applying the Funds, annually analyzing the escrow account, or verifying the Escrow Items, unless Lender pays Borrower interest on the Funds and applicable law permits Lender to make such a charge. However, Lender may require Borrower to pay a one-time charge for an independent real estate tax reporting service used by Lender in connection with this loan, unless applicable law provides otherwise. Unless an agreement is made or applicable law requires interest to be paid, Lender shall not be required to pay Borrower any interest or earnings on the Funds. Borrower and Lender may agree in writing, however, that interest shall be paid on the Funds. Lender shall give to Borrower, without charge, an annual accounting of the Funds, showing credits and debits to the Funds and the purpose for which each debit to the Funds was made. The Funds are pledged as additional security for all sums secured by this Security Instrument.

If the Funds held by Lender exceed the amounts permitted to be held by applicable law, Lender shall account to Borrower for the excess Funds in accordance with the requirements of applicable law. If the amount of the Funds held by Lender at any time is not sufficient to pay the Escrow Items when due, Lender may so notify Borrower in writing, and, in such case Borrower shall pay to Lender the amount necessary to make up the deficiency. Borrower shall make up the deficiency in no more than twelve monthly payments, at Lender's sole discretion.

Upon payment in full of all sums secured by this Security Instrument, Lender shall promptly refund to Borrower any Funds held by Lender. If, under paragraph 21, Lender shall acquire or sell the Property, Lender, prior to the acquisition or sale of the Property, shall apply any Funds held by Lender at the time of acquisition or sale as a credit against the sums secured by this Security Instrument.

3. Application of Payments. Unless applicable law provides otherwise, all payments received by Lender under paragraphs 1 and 2 shall be applied: first, to any prepayment charges due under the Note; second, to amounts payable under paragraph 2; third, to interest due; fourth, to principal due; and last, to any late charges due under the Note.

4. Charges; Liens. Borrower shall pay all taxes, assessments, charges, fines and impositions attributable to the Property which may attain priority over this Security Instrument, and leasehold payments or ground rents, if any. Borrower shall pay these obligations in the manner provided in paragraph 2, or if not paid in that manner, Borrower shall pay them on time directly to the person owed payment. Borrower shall promptly furnish to Lender all notices of amounts to be paid under this paragraph. If Borrower makes these payments directly, Borrower shall promptly furnish to Lender receipts evidencing the payments.

Borrower shall promptly discharge any lien which has priority over this Security Instrument unless Borrower: (a) agrees in writing to the payment of the obligation secured by the lien in a manner acceptable to Lender; (b) contests in good faith the lien by, or defends against enforcement of the lien in, legal proceedings which in the Lender's opinion operate to prevent the enforcement of the lien; or (c) secures from the holder of the lien an agreement satisfactory to Lender subordinating the lien to this Security Instrument. If Lender determines that any part of the Property is subject to a lien which may attain priority over this Security Instrument, Lender may give Borrower a notice identifying the lien. Borrower shall satisfy the lien or take one or more of the actions set forth above within 10 days of the giving of notice.

5. Hazard or Property Insurance. Borrower shall keep the improvements now existing or hereafter erected on the Property insured against loss by fire, hazards included within the term "extended coverage" and any other hazards, including floods or flooding, for which Lender requires insurance. This insurance shall be maintained in the amounts and for the periods that Lender requires. The insurance carrier providing the insurance shall be chosen by Borrower subject to Lender's approval which shall not be unreasonably withheld. If Borrower fails to maintain coverage described above, Lender may, at Lender's option, obtain coverage to protect Lender's rights in the Property in accordance with paragraph 7.

All insurance policies and renewals shall be acceptable to Lender and shall include a standard mortgage clause. Lender shall have the right to hold the policies and renewals. If Lender requires, Borrower shall promptly give to Lender all receipts of paid premiums and renewal notices. In the event of loss, Borrower shall give prompt notice to the insurance carrier and Lender. Lender may make proof of loss if not made promptly by Borrower.

Unless Lender and Borrower otherwise agree in writing, insurance proceeds shall be applied to restoration or repair of the Property damaged, if the restoration or repair is economically feasible and Lender's security is not lessened. If the restoration or repair is not economically feasible or Lender's security would be lessened, the insurance proceeds shall be applied to the sums secured by this Security Instrument, whether or not then due, with any excess paid to Borrower. If Borrower abandons the Property, or does not answer within 30 days a notice from Lender that the insurance carrier has offered to settle a claim, then Lender may collect the insurance proceeds. Lender may use the proceeds to repair or restore the Property or to pay sums secured by this Security Instrument, whether or not then due. The 30-day period will begin when the notice is given.

Unless Lender and Borrower otherwise agree in writing, any application of proceeds to principal shall not extend or postpone the due date of the monthly payments referred to in paragraphs 1 and 2 or change the amount of the payments. If under paragraph 21 the Property is acquired by Lender, Borrower's right to any insurance policies and proceeds resulting from damage to the Property prior to the acquisition shall pass to Lender to the extent of the sums secured by this Security Instrument immediately prior to the acquisition.

6. Occupancy, Preservation, Maintenance and Protection of the Property; Borrower's Loan Application; Leaseholds. Borrower shall occupy, establish, and use the Property as Borrower's principal residence within sixty days after the execution of this Security Instrument and shall continue to occupy the Property as Borrower's principal residence for at least one year after the date of occupancy, unless Lender otherwise agrees in writing, which consent shall not be unreasonably withheld, or unless extenuating circumstances exist which are beyond Borrower's control. Borrower shall not destroy, damage or impair the Property, allow the Property to deteriorate, or commit waste on the Property. Borrower shall be in default if any forfeiture action or proceeding, whether civil or criminal, is begun that in Lender's good faith judgment could result in forfeiture of the Property or otherwise materially impair the lien created by this Security Instrument or Lender's security interest. Borrower may cure such a default and reinstate, as provided in paragraph 18, by causing the action or proceeding to be dismissed with a ruling that, in Lender's good faith determination, precludes forfeiture of the Borrower's interest in the Property or other material impairment of the lien created by this Security Instrument or Lender's security interest. Borrower shall also be in default if Borrower, during the loan application process, gave materially false or inaccurate information or statements to Lender (or failed to provide Lender with any material information) in connection with the loan evidenced by the Note, including, but not limited to, representations concerning Borrower's occupancy of the Property as a principal residence. If this Security Instrument is on a leasehold, Borrower shall comply with all the provisions of the lease. If Borrower acquires fee title to the Property, the leasehold and the fee title shall not merge unless Lender agrees to the merger in writing.

7. Protection of Lender's Rights in the Property. If Borrower fails to perform the covenants and agreements contained in this Security Instrument, or there is a legal proceeding that may significantly affect Lender's rights in the Property (such as a proceeding in bankruptcy, probate, for condemnation or forfeiture or to enforce laws or regulations), then Lender may do and pay for whatever is necessary to protect the value of the Property and Lender's rights in the Property. Lender's actions may include paying any sums secured by a lien which has priority over this Security Instrument, appearing in court, paying reasonable attorneys' fees and entering on the Property to make repairs. Although Lender may take action under this paragraph 7, Lender does not have to do so.

Any amounts disbursed by Lender under this paragraph 7 shall become additional debt of Borrower secured by this Security Instrument. Unless Borrower and Lender agree to other terms of payment, these amounts shall bear interest from the date of disbursement at the Note rate and shall be payable, with interest, upon notice from Lender to Borrower requesting payment.

8. Mortgage Insurance. If Lender required mortgage insurance as a condition of making the loan secured by this Security Instrument, Borrower shall pay the premiums required to maintain the mortgage insurance in effect. If, for any reason, the mortgage insurance coverage required by Lender lapses or ceases to be in effect, Borrower shall pay the premiums required to obtain coverage substantially equivalent to the mortgage insurance previously in effect, at a cost substantially equivalent to the cost to Borrower of the mortgage insurance previously in effect, from an alternate mortgage insurer approved by Lender. If substantially equivalent mortgage insurance coverage is not available, Borrower shall pay to Lender each month a sum equal to one-twelfth of the yearly mortgage insurance premium being paid by Borrower when the insurance coverage lapsed or ceased to be in effect. Lender will accept, use and retain these payments as a loss reserve in lieu of mortgage insurance. Loss reserve payments may no longer be required, at the option of Lender, if mortgage insurance coverage (in the amount and for the period that Lender requires) provided by an insurer approved by Lender again becomes available and is obtained. Borrower shall pay the premiums required to maintain mortgage insurance in effect, or to provide a loss reserve, until the requirement for mortgage insurance ends in accordance with any written agreement between Borrower and Lender or applicable law.

9. Inspection. Lender or its agent may make reasonable entries upon and inspections of the Property. Lender shall give Borrower notice at the time of or prior to an inspection specifying reasonable cause for the inspection.

10. Condemnation. The proceeds of any award or claim for damages, direct or consequential, in connection with any condemnation or other taking of any part of the Property, or for conveyance in lieu of condemnation, are hereby assigned and shall be paid to Lender.

In the event of a total taking of the Property, the proceeds shall be applied to the sums secured by this Security Instrument, whether or not then due, with any excess paid to Borrower. In the event of a partial taking of the Property in which the fair market value of the Property immediately before the taking is equal to or greater than the amount of the sums secured by this Security Instrument immediately before the taking, unless Borrower and Lender otherwise agree in writing, the sums secured by this Security Instrument shall be reduced by the amount of the proceeds multiplied by the following fraction: (a) the total amount of the sums secured immediately before the taking, divided by (b) the fair market value of the Property immediately before the taking. Any balance shall be paid to Borrower. In the event of a partial taking of the Property in which the fair market value of the Property immediately before the taking is less than the amount of the sums secured immediately before the taking, unless Borrower and Lender otherwise agree in writing or unless applicable law otherwise provides, the proceeds shall be applied to the sums secured by this Security Instrument whether or not the sums are then due.

If the Property is abandoned by Borrower, or if, after notice by Lender to Borrower that the condemnor offers to make an award or settle a claim for damages, Borrower fails to respond to Lender within 30 days after the date the notice is given, Lender is authorized to collect and apply the proceeds, at its option, either to restoration or repair of the Property or to the sums secured by this Security Instrument, whether or not then due.

Unless Lender and Borrower otherwise agree in writing, any application of proceeds to principal shall not extend or postpone the due date of the monthly payments referred to in paragraphs 1 and 2 or change the amount of such payments.

11. Borrower Not Released; Forbearance By Lender Not a Waiver. Extension of the time for payment or modification of amortization of the sums secured by this Security Instrument granted by Lender to any successor in interest of Borrower shall not operate to release the liability of the original Borrower or Borrower's successors in interest. Lender shall not be required to commence proceedings against any successor in interest or refuse to extend time for payment or otherwise modify amortization of the sums secured by this Security Instrument by reason of any demand made by the original Borrower or Borrower's successors in interest. Any forbearance by Lender in exercising any right or remedy shall not be a waiver of or preclude the exercise of any right or remedy.

12. Successors and Assigns Bound; Joint and Several Liability; Co-signers. The covenants and agreements of this Security Instrument shall bind and benefit the successors and assigns of Lender and Borrower, subject to the provisions of paragraph 17. Borrower's covenants and agreements shall be joint and several. Any Borrower who co-signs this Security Instrument but does not execute the Note: (a) is co-signing this Security Instrument only to mortgage, grant and convey that Borrower's interest in the Property under the terms of this Security Instrument; (b) is not personally obligated to pay the sums secured by this Security Instrument; and (c) agrees that Lender and any other Borrower may agree to extend, modify, forbear or make any accommodations with regard to the terms of this Security Instrument or the Note without that Borrower's consent.

13. Loan Charges. If the loan secured by this Security Instrument is subject to a law which sets maximum loan charges, and that law is finally interpreted so that the interest or other loan charges collected or to be collected in connection with the loan exceed the permitted limits, then: (a) any such loan charge shall be reduced by the amount necessary to reduce the charge to the permitted limit; and (b) any sums already collected from Borrower which exceeded permitted limits will be refunded to Borrower. Lender may choose to make this refund by reducing the principal owed under the Note or by making a direct payment to Borrower. If a refund reduces principal, the reduction will be treated as a partial prepayment without any prepayment charge under the Note.

14. Notices. Any notice to Borrower provided for in this Security Instrument shall be given by delivering it or by mailing it by first class mail unless applicable law requires use of another method. The notice shall be directed to the Property Address or any other address Borrower designates by notice to Lender. Any notice to Lender shall be given by first class mail to Lender's address stated herein or any other address Lender designates by notice to Borrower. Any notice provided for in this Security Instrument shall be deemed to have been given to Borrower or Lender when given as provided in this paragraph.

15. Governing Law; Severability. This Security Instrument shall be governed by federal law and the law of the jurisdiction in which the Property is located. In the event that any provision or clause of this Security Instrument or the Note conflicts with applicable law, such conflict shall not affect other provisions of this Security Instrument or the Note which can be given effect without the conflicting provision. To this end the provisions of this Security Instrument and the Note are declared to be severable.

16. Borrower's Copy. Borrower shall be given one conformed copy of the Note and of this Security Instrument.

17. Transfer of the Property or a Beneficial Interest in Borrower. If all or any part of the Property or any interest in it is sold or transferred (or if a beneficial interest in Borrower is sold or transferred and Borrower is not a natural person) without Lender's prior written consent, Lender may, at its option, require immediate payment in full of all sums secured by this Security Instrument. However, this option shall not be exercised by Lender if exercise is prohibited by federal law as of the date of this Security Instrument.

If Lender exercises this option, Lender shall give Borrower notice of acceleration. The notice shall provide a period of not less than 30 days from the date the notice is delivered or mailed within which Borrower must pay all sums secured by this Security Instrument. If Borrower fails to pay these sums prior to the expiration of this period, Lender may invoke any remedies permitted by this Security Instrument without further notice or demand on Borrower.

18. Borrower's Right to Reinstate. If Borrower meets certain conditions, Borrower shall have the right to have enforcement of this Security Instrument discontinued at any time prior to the earlier of: (a) 5 days (or such other period as applicable law may specify for reinstatement) before sale of the Property pursuant to any power of sale contained in this Security Instrument; or (b) entry of a judgment enforcing this Security Instrument. Those conditions are that Borrower: (a) pays Lender all sums which then would be due under this Security Instrument and the Note as if no acceleration had occurred; (b) cures any default of any other covenants or agreements; (c) pays all expenses incurred in enforcing this Security Instrument, including, but not limited to, reasonable attorneys' fees; and (d) takes such action as Lender may reasonably require to assure that the lien of this Security Instrument, Lender's rights in the Property and Borrower's obligation to pay the sums secured by this Security Instrument shall continue unchanged. Upon reinstatement by Borrower, this Security Instrument and the obligations secured hereby shall remain fully effective as if no acceleration had occurred. However, this right to reinstate shall not apply in the case of acceleration under paragraph 17.

19. Sale of Note; Change of Loan Servicer. The Note or a partial interest in the Note (together with this Security Instrument) may be sold one or more times without prior notice to Borrower. A sale may result in a change in the entity (known as the "Loan Servicer") that collects monthly payments due under the Note and this Security Instrument. There also may be one or more changes of the Loan Servicer unrelated to a sale of the Note. If there is a change of the Loan Servicer, Borrower will be given written notice of the change in accordance with paragraph 14 above and applicable law. The notice will state the name and address of the new Loan Servicer and the address to which payments should be made. The notice will also contain any other information required by applicable law.

20. Hazardous Substances. Borrower shall not cause or permit the presence, use, disposal, storage, or release of any Hazardous Substances on or in the Property. Borrower shall not do, nor allow anyone else to do, anything affecting the Property that is in violation of any Environmental Law. The preceding two sentences shall not apply to the presence, use, or storage on the Property of small quantities of Hazardous Substances that are generally recognized to be appropriate to normal residential uses and to maintenance of the Property.

Borrower shall promptly give Lender written notice of any investigation, claim, demand, lawsuit or other action by any governmental or regulatory agency or private party involving the Property and any Hazardous Substance or Environmental Law of which Borrower has actual knowledge. If borrower learns, or is notified by any governmental or regulatory authority, that any removal or other remediation of any Hazardous Substance affecting the Property is necessary, Borrower shall promptly take all necessary remedial actions in accordance with Environmental Law.

As used in this paragraph 20, "Hazardous Substances" are those substances defined as toxic or hazardous substances by Environmental Law and the following substances: gasoline, kerosene, other flammable or toxic petroleum products, toxic pesticides and herbicides, volatile solvents, materials containing asbestos or formaldehyde, and radioactive materials. As used in this paragraph 20, "Environmental Law" means federal laws and laws of the jurisdiction where the Property is located that relate to health, safety or environmental protection.

NON-UNIFORM COVENANTS. Borrower and Lender further covenant and agree as follows:

21. Acceleration; Remedies. Lender shall give notice to Borrower prior to acceleration following Borrower's breach of any covenant or agreement in this Security Instrument (but not prior to acceleration under paragraph 17 unless applicable law provides otherwise). The notice shall specify: (a) the default; (b) the action required to cure the default; (c) a date, not less than 30 days from the date the notice is given to Borrower, by which the default must be cured; and (d) that failure to cure the default on or before the date specified in the notice may result in acceleration of the sums secured by this Security Instrument, foreclosure by judicial proceeding and sale of the Property. The notice shall further inform Borrower of the right to reinstate after acceleration and the right to assert in the foreclosure proceeding the non-existence of a default or any other defense of Borrower to acceleration and foreclosure. If the default is not cured on or before the date specified in the notice, Lender at its option may require immediate payment in full of all sums secured by this Security Instrument without further demand and may foreclose this Security Instrument by judicial proceeding. Lender shall be entitled to collect all expenses incurred in pursuing the remedies provided in this paragraph 21, including, but not limited to, reasonable attorneys' fees and costs of title evidence.

22. Release. Upon payment of all sums secured by this Security Instrument, Lender shall release this Security Instrument without charge to Borrower.

23. Waiver of Valuation and Appraisement. Borrower waives all right of valuation and appraisement.

24. Riders to this Security Instrument. If one or more riders are executed by Borrower and recorded together with this Security Instrument, the covenants and agreements of each such rider shall be incorporated into and shall amend and supplement the covenants and agreements of this Security Instrument as if the rider(s) were a part of this Security Instrument. [Check applicable box(es)]

☐ Adjustable Rate Rider   ☐ Condominium Rider   ☐ 1—4 Family Rider

☐ Graduated Payment Rider   ☐ Planned Unit Development Rider   ☐ Biweekly Payment Rider

☐ Balloon Rider   ☐ Rate Improvement Rider   ☐ Second Home Rider

☐ Other(s) [specify]

BY SIGNING BELOW, Borrower accepts and agrees to the terms and covenants contained in this Security Instrument and in any rider(s) executed by Borrower and recorded with it.

Witnesses:

....(Seal)
                                                                    —Borrower

Social Security Number...

....(Seal)
                                                                      —Borrower

Social Security Number...

————————————————— [Space Below This Line For Acknowledgment] —————————————————

APPENDIX B

ADJUSTABLE RATE NOTE AND MORTGAGE RIDER FORMS

The Federal National Mortgage Association (FNMA) has developed a uniform Adjustable Rate Note and a uniform Adjustable Rate Rider to the FNMA/FHLMC standard mortgage. The FNMA uniform instruments under which interest may be adjusted annually are reproduced below.

ADJUSTABLE RATE NOTE
(1 Year Treasury Index—Rate Caps—Fixed Rate Conversion Option)

THIS NOTE CONTAINS PROVISIONS ALLOWING FOR CHANGES IN MY INTEREST RATE AND MY MONTHLY PAYMENT. THIS NOTE LIMITS THE AMOUNT MY ADJUSTABLE INTEREST RATE CAN CHANGE AT ANY ONE TIME AND THE MAXIMUM RATE I MUST PAY. THIS NOTE ALSO CONTAINS THE OPTION TO CONVERT MY ADJUSTABLE RATE TO A FIXED RATE.

.... 19..... ....
                                               [City]   [State]

....
                                  [Property Address]

1. BORROWER'S PROMISE TO PAY

In return for a loan that I have received. I promise to pay U.S. $ .... (this amount is called "principal"), plus interest, to the order of the Lender. The Lender is ....

....

I understand that the Lender may transfer this Note. The Lender or anyone who takes this Note by transfer and who is entitled to receive payments under this Note is called the "Note Holder."

2. INTEREST

Interest will be charged on unpaid principal until the full amount of principal has been paid. I will pay interest at a yearly rate of .... %. The interest rate I will pay will change in accordance with Section 4 of this Note.

The interest rate required by this Section 2 and Sections 4 or 5 of this Note is the rate I will pay both before and after any default described in Section 8(B) of this Note.

3. PAYMENTS

A) Time and Place of Payments

I will pay principal and interest by making payments every month.

I will make my monthly payments on the first day of each month beginning on ....
19 .... I will make these payments every month until I have paid all of the principal and interest and any other charges described below that I may owe under this Note. My monthly payments will be applied to interest before principal. If, on ...., 20...... I still owe amounts under this Note, I will pay those amounts in full on that date, which is called the "Maturity Date."

I will make my monthly payments at ....

.... or at a different place if required by the Note Holder.

(B) Amount of My Initial Monthly Payments

Each of my initial monthly payments will be in the amount of U.S. $ .... This amount may change.

(C) Monthly Payment Changes

Changes in my monthly payment will reflect changes in the unpaid principal of my loan and in the interest rate that I must pay. The Note Holder will determine my new interest rate and the changed amount of my monthly payment in accordance with Sections 4 or 5 of this Note.

4. ADJUSTABLE INTEREST RATE AND MONTHLY PAYMENT CHANGES

(A) Change Dates

The adjustable interest rate I will pay may change on the first day of ...., 19......, and on that day every 12th month thereafter. Each date on which my adjustable interest rate could change is called a "Change Date."

(B) The Index

Beginning with the first Change Date, my adjustable interest rate will be based on an Index. The "Index" is the weekly average yield on United States Treasury securities adjusted to a constant maturity of 1 year, as made available by the Federal Reserve Board. The most recent Index figure available as of the date 45 days before each Change Date is called the "Current Index."

If the Index is no longer available, the Note Holder will choose a new index that is based upon comparable information. The Note Holder will give me notice of this choice.

(C) Calculation of Changes

Before each Change Date, the Note Holder will calculate my new interest rate by adding .... percentage points (............%) to the Current Index. The Note Holder will then round the result of this addition to the nearest one-eighth of one percentage point (0.125%). Subject to the limits stated in Section 4(D) below, this rounded amount will be my new interest rate until the next Change Date.

The Note Holder will then determine the amount of the monthly payment that would be sufficient to repay the unpaid principal that I am expected to owe at the Change Date in full on the Maturity Date at my new interest rate in substantially equal payments. The result of this calculation will be the new amount of my monthly payment.

(D) Limits on Interest Rate Changes

The interest rate I am required to pay at the first Change Date will not be greater than .... % or less than ....%. Thereafter, my adjustable interest rate will never be increased or decreased on any single Change Date by more than two percentage points (2.0%) from the rate of interest I have been paying for the preceding 12 months. My interest rate will never be greater than ....%, which is called the "Maximum Rate."

(E) Effective Date of Changes

My new interest rate will become effective on each Change Date. I will pay the amount of my new monthly payment beginning on the first monthly payment date after the Change Date until the amount of my monthly payment changes again.

MULTISTATE ADJUSTABLE RATE NOTE—ARM PLANS 721-521 & 652 611—Single Family—Fannie Mae Uniform Instrument   Form 3503 12 87
                                                                                                            (04001)

Bruce, Real Est Fin 4th NS —10

(F) Notice of Changes

The Note Holder will deliver or mail to me a notice of any changes in my adjustable interest rate and the amount of my monthly payment before the effective date of any change. The notice will include information required by law to be given me and also the title and telephone number of a person who will answer any question I may have regarding the notice.

5. FIXED INTEREST RATE OPTION

(A) Option to Convert to Fixed Rate

I have a Conversion Option that I can exercise unless I am in default or this Section 5(A) will not permit me to do so. The "Conversion Option" is my option to convert the interest rate I am required to pay by this Note from an adjustable rate with interest rate limits to the fixed rate calculated under Section 5(B) below.

The conversion can only take place on the (1) if the first Change Date is 21 months or less from the date of this Note, the third, fourth or fifth Change Date, or (2) if the first Change Date is more than 21 months from the date of this Note, the first, second or third Change Date. Each Change Date on which my interest rate can convert from an adjustable rate to a fixed rate also is called the "Conversion Date." **I can convert my interest rate only on one of these three Conversion Dates.**

If I want to exercise the Conversion Option, I must first meet certain conditions. Those conditions are that: (i) I must give the Note Holder notice that I want to do so at least 15 days before the next Conversion Date; (ii) on the Conversion Date, I must not be in default under the Note or the Security Instrument; (iii) by a date specified by the Note Holder, I must pay the Note Holder a conversion fee of U.S. $..............................; and (iv) I must sign and give the Note Holder any documents the Note Holder requires to effect the conversion.

(B) Calculation of Fixed Rate

My new, fixed interest rate will be equal to the Federal National Mortgage Association's required net yield as of a date and time of day specified by the Note Holder for (1) if the original term of this Note is greater than 15 years, 30-year fixed rate mortgages covered by applicable 60-day mandatory delivery commitments, plus five-eighths of one percentage point (0.625%), rounded to the nearest one-eighth of one percentage point (0.125%), or (ii) if the original term of this Note is 15 years or less, 15-year fixed rate mortgages covered by applicable 60-day mandatory delivery commitments, plus five-eighths of one percentage point (0.625%), rounded to the nearest one-eighth of one percentage point (0.125%). If this required net yield cannot be determined because the applicable commitments are not available, the Note Holder will determine my interest rate by using comparable information. My new rate calculated under this Section 5(B) will not be greater than the Maximum Rate stated in Section 4(D) above.

(C) New Payment Amount and Effective Date

If I choose to exercise the Conversion Option, the Note Holder will determine the amount of the monthly payment that would be sufficient to repay the unpaid principal I am expected to owe on the Conversion Date in full on the Maturity Date at my new fixed interest rate in substantially equal payments. The result of this calculation will be the new amount of my monthly payment. Beginning with my first monthly payment after the Conversion Date, I will pay the new amount as my monthly payment until the Maturity Date.

6. BORROWER'S RIGHT TO PREPAY

I have the right to make payments of principal at any time before they are due. A payment of principal only is known as a "prepayment." When I make a prepayment, I will tell the Note Holder in writing that I am doing so.

I may make a full prepayment or partial prepayments without paying any prepayment charge. The Note Holder will use all of my prepayments to reduce the amount of principal that I owe under this Note. If I make a partial prepayment, there will be no changes in the due dates of my monthly payments unless the Note Holder agrees in writing to those changes. My partial prepayment may reduce the amount of my monthly payments after the first Change Date following my partial prepayment. However, any reduction due to my partial prepayment may be offset by an interest rate increase.

7. LOAN CHARGES

If a law, which applies to this loan and which sets maximum loan charges, is finally interpreted so that the interest or other loan charges collected or to be collected in connection with this loan exceed the permitted limits, then: (i) any such loan charge shall be reduced by the amount necessary to reduce the charge to the permitted limit; and (ii) any sums already collected from me that exceeded permitted limits will be refunded to me. The Note Holder may choose to make this refund by reducing the principal I owe under this Note or by making a direct payment to me. If a refund reduces principal, the reduction will be treated as a partial prepayment.

8. BORROWER'S FAILURE TO PAY AS REQUIRED

(A) Late Charges for Overdue Payments

If the Note Holder has not received the full amount of any monthly payment by the end of .... calendar days after the date it is due, I will pay a late charge to the Note Holder. The amount of the charge will be ....% of my overdue payment of principal and interest. I will pay this late charge promptly but only once on each late payment.

(B) Default

If I do not pay the full amount of each monthly payment on the date it is due, I will be in default.

(C) Notice of Default

If I am in default, the Note Holder may send me a written notice telling me that if I do not pay the overdue amount by a certain date, the Note Holder may require me to pay immediately the full amount of principal that has not been paid and all the interest that I owe on that amount. That date must be at least 30 days after the date on which the notice is delivered or mailed to me.

(D) No Waiver By Note Holder

Even if, at a time when I am in default, the Note Holder does not require me to pay immediately in full as described above, the Note Holder will still have the right to do so if I am in default at a later time.

(E) Payment of Note Holder's Costs and Expenses

If the Note Holder has required me to pay immediately in full as described above, the Note Holder will have the right to be paid back by me for all of its costs and expenses in enforcing this Note to the extent not prohibited by applicable law. Those expenses include, for example, reasonable attorneys' fees.

9. GIVING OF NOTICES

Unless applicable law requires a different method, any notice that must be given to me under this Note will be given by delivering it or by mailing it by first class mail to me at the Property Address above or at a different address if I give the Note Holder a notice of my different address.

Any notice that must be given to the Note Holder under this Note will be given by mailing it by first class mail to the Note Holder at the address stated in Section 3(A) above or at a different address if I am given a notice of that different address.

10. OBLIGATIONS OF PERSONS UNDER THIS NOTE

If more than one person signs this Note, each person is fully and personally obligated to keep all of the promises made in this Note, including the promise to pay the full amount owed. Any person who is a guarantor, surety or endorser of this Note is also obligated to do these things. Any person who takes over these obligations, including the obligations of a guarantor, surety or endorser of this Note, is also obligated to keep all of the promises made in this Note. The Note Holder may enforce its rights under this Note against each person individually or against all of us together. This means that any one of us may be required to pay all of the amounts owed under this Note.

11. WAIVERS

I and any other person who has obligations under this Note waive the rights of presentment and notice of dishonor. "Presentment" means the right to require the Note Holder to demand payment of amounts due. "Notice of dishonor" means the right to require the Note Holder to give notice to other persons that amounts due have not been paid.

12. UNIFORM SECURED NOTE

This Note is a uniform instrument with limited variations in some jurisdictions. In addition to the protections given to the Note Holder under this Note, a Mortgage, Deed of Trust or Security Deed (the "Security Instrument"), dated the same date as this Note, protects the Note Holder from possible losses that might result if I do not keep the promises which I make in this Note. That Security Instrument describes how and under what conditions I may be required to make immediate payment in full of all amounts I owe under this Note. Some of those conditions are described as follows:

(A) Until I exercise my Conversion Option under the conditions stated in Section 5 of this Adjustable Rate Note, Uniform Covenant 17 of the Security Instrument is described as follows:

Transfer of the Property or a Beneficial Interest in Borrower. If all or any part of the Property or any interest in it is sold or transferred (or if a beneficial interest in Borrower is sold or transferred and Borrower is not a natural person) without Lender's prior written consent, Lender may, at its option, require immediate payment in full of all sums secured by this Security Instrument. However, this option shall not be exercised by Lender if exercise is prohibited by federal law as of the date of this Security Instrument. Lender also shall not exercise this option if: (a) Borrower causes to be submitted to Lender information required by Lender to evaluate the intended transferee as if a new loan were being made to the transferee; and (b) Lender reasonably determines that Lender's security will not be impaired by the loan assumption and that the risk of a breach of any covenant or agreement in this Security Instrument is acceptable to Lender.

To the extent permitted by applicable law, Lender may charge a reasonable fee as a condition to Lender's consent to the loan assumption. Lender also may require the transferee to sign an assumption agreement that is acceptable to Lender and that obligates the transferee to keep all the promises and agreements made in the Note and in this Security Instrument. Borrower will continue to be obligated under the Note and this Security Instrument unless Lender releases Borrower in writing.

If Lender exercises the option to require immediate payment in full, Lender shall give Borrower notice of acceleration. The notice shall provide a period of not less than 30 days from the date the notice is delivered or mailed within which Borrower must pay all sums secured by this Security Instrument. If Borrower fails to pay these sums prior to the expiration of this period, Lender may invoke any remedies permitted by this Security Instrument without further notice or demand on Borrower.

(B) If I exercise my Conversion Option under the conditions stated in Section 5 of this Adjustable Rate Note, Uniform Covenant 17 of the Security Instrument described in Section 12(A) above shall then cease to be in effect, and Uniform Covenant 17 of the Security Instrument shall instead be described as follows:

Transfer of the Property or a Beneficial Interest in Borrower. If all or any part of the Property or any interest in it is sold or transferred (or if a beneficial interest in Borrower is sold or transferred and Borrower is not a natural person) without Lender's prior written consent, Lender may, at its option, require immediate payment in full of all sums secured by this Security Instrument. However, this option shall not be exercised by Lender if exercise is prohibited by federal law as of the date of this Security Instrument.

If Lender exercises this option, Lender shall give Borrower notice of acceleration. The notice shall provide a period of not less than 30 days from the date the notice is delivered or mailed within which Borrower must pay all sums secured by this Security Instrument. If Borrower fails to pay these sums prior to the expiration of this period, Lender may invoke any remedies permitted by this Security Instrument without further notice or demand on Borrower.

WITNESS THE HAND(S) AND SEAL(S) OF THE UNDERSIGNED.

.... (Seal)
                                               -Borrower

.... (Seal)
                                               -Borrower

.... (Seal)
                                               -Borrower

[Sign Original Only]
[G4093]

ADJUSTABLE RATE RIDER
1 Year Treasury Index—Rate Caps—Fixed Rate Conversion Option

THIS ADJUSTABLE RATE RIDER is made this .... day of .... 19 ...., and is incorporated into and shall be deemed to amend and supplement the Mortgage, Deed of Trust or Security Deed (the "Security Instrument") of the same date given by the undersigned (the "Borrower") to secure Borrower's Adjustable Rate Note (the "Note") to ....

.... (the "Lender") of the same date and covering the property described in the Security Instrument and located at:

....
Property Address

THE NOTE CONTAINS PROVISIONS ALLOWING FOR CHANGES IN THE INTEREST RATE AND THE MONTHLY PAYMENT. THE NOTE LIMITS THE AMOUNT THE BORROWER'S ADJUSTABLE INTEREST RATE CAN CHANGE AT ANY ONE TIME AND THE MAXIMUM RATE THE BORROWER MUST PAY. THE NOTE ALSO CONTAINS THE OPTION TO CONVERT THE ADJUSTABLE RATE TO A FIXED RATE.

ADDITIONAL COVENANTS. In addition to the covenants and agreements made in the Security Instrument, Borrower and Lender further covenant and agree as follows:

A. ADJUSTABLE RATE AND MONTHLY PAYMENT CHANGES

The Note provides for an initial interest rate of ....%. The Note provides for changes in the adjustable interest rate and the monthly payments, as follows:

4. ADJUSTABLE INTEREST RATE AND MONTHLY PAYMENT CHANGES

(A) Change Dates

The adjustable interest rate I will pay may change on the first day of .... 19 ...... and on that day every 12th month thereafter. Each date on which my adjustable interest rate could change is called a "Change Date."

(B) The Index

Beginning with the first Change Date, my adjustable interest rate will be based on an Index. The "Index" is the weekly average yield on United States Treasury securities adjusted to a constant maturity of 1 year, as made available by the Federal Reserve Board. The most recent Index figure available as of the date 45 days before each Change Date is called the "Current Index."

If the Index is no longer available, the Note Holder will choose a new index that is based upon comparable information. The Note Holder will give me notice of this choice.

(C) Calculation of Changes

Before each Change Date, the Note Holder will calculate my new interest rate by adding .... percentage points (................%) to the Current Index. The Note Holder will then round the result of this addition to the nearest one-eighth of one percentage point (0.125%). Subject to the limits stated in Section 4(D) below, this rounded amount will be my new interest rate until the next Change Date.

The Note Holder will then determine the amount of the monthly payment that would be sufficient to repay the unpaid principal that I am expected to owe at the Change Date in full on the Maturity Date at my new interest rate in substantially equal payments. The result of this calculation will be the new amount of my monthly payment.

(D) Limits on Interest Rate Changes

The interest rate I am required to pay at the first Change Date will not be greater than ....% or less than ....%. Thereafter, my adjustable interest rate will never be increased or decreased on any single Change Date by more than two percentage points (2.0%) from the rate of interest I have been paying for the preceding 12 months. My interest rate will never be greater than ....%, which is called the "Maximum Rate."

(E) Effective Date of Changes

My new interest rate will become effective on each Change Date. I will pay the amount of my new monthly payment beginning on the first monthly payment date after the Change Date until the amount of my monthly payment changes again.

(F) Notice of Changes

The Note Holder will deliver or mail to me a notice of any changes in my adjustable interest rate and the amount of my monthly payment before the effective date of any change. The notice will include information required by law to be given me and also the title and telephone number of a person who will answer any question I may have regarding the notice.

B. FIXED INTEREST RATE OPTION

The Note provides for the Borrower's option to convert from an adjustable interest rate with interest rate limits to a fixed interest rate, as follows:

5. FIXED INTEREST RATE OPTION

(A) Option to Convert to Fixed Rate

I have a Conversion Option that I can exercise unless I am in default or this Section 5(A) will not permit me to do so. The "Conversion Option" is my option to convert the interest rate I am required to pay by this Note from an adjustable rate with interest rate limits to the fixed rate calculated under Section 5(B) below.

The conversion can only take place on (1) if the first Change Date is 21 months or less from the date of this Note, the third, fourth or fifth Change Date, or (2) if the first Change Date is more than 21 months from the date of this Note, the first, second or third Change Date. Each Change Date on which my interest rate can convert from an adjustable rate to a fixed rate also is called the "Conversion Date." **I can convert my interest rate only on one of these Conversion Dates.**

If I want to exercise the Conversion Option, I must first meet certain conditions. Those conditions are that: (i) I must give the Note Holder notice that I want to do so at least 15 days before the next Conversion Date; (ii) on the Conversion Date, I must not be in default under the Note or the Security Instrument; (iii) by a date specified by the Note

Holder, I must pay the Note Holder a conversion fee of U.S. $..; and (iv) I must sign and give the Note Holder any documents the Note Holder requires to effect the conversion.

(B) Calculation of Fixed Rate

My new, fixed interest rate will be equal to the Federal National Mortgage Association's required net yield as of a date and time of day specified by the Note Holder for (i) if the original term of this Note is greater than 15 years, 30-year fixed rate mortgages covered by applicable 60-day mandatory delivery commitments, plus five-eighths of one percentage point (0.625%), rounded to the nearest one-eighth of one percentage point (0.125%), or (ii) if the original term of this Note is 15 years or less, 15-year fixed rate mortgages covered by applicable 60-day mandatory delivery commitments, plus five-eighths of one percentage point (0.625%), rounded to the nearest one-eighth of one percentage point (0.125%). If this required net yield cannot be determined because the applicable commitments are not available, the Note Holder will determine my interest rate by using comparable information. My new rate calculated under this Section 5(B) will not be greater than the Maximum Rate stated in Section 4(D) above.

(C) New Payment Amount and Effective Date

If I choose to exercise the Conversion Option, the Note Holder will determine the amount of the monthly payment that would be sufficient to repay the unpaid principal I am expected to owe on the Conversion Date in full on the Maturity Date at my new fixed interest rate in substantially equal payments. The result of this calculation will be the new amount of my monthly payment. Beginning with my first monthly payment after the Conversion Date, I will pay the new amount as my monthly payment until the Maturity Date.

C. TRANSFER OF THE PROPERTY OR A BENEFICIAL INTEREST IN BORROWER

1. Until Borrower exercises the Conversion Option under the conditions stated in Section B of this Adjustable Rate Rider, Uniform Covenant 17 of the Security Instrument is amended to read as follows:

Transfer of the Property or a Beneficial Interest in Borrower. If all or any part of the Property or any interest in it is sold or transferred (or if a beneficial interest in Borrower is sold or transferred and Borrower is not a natural person) without Lender's prior written consent, Lender may, at its option, require immediate payment in full of all sums secured by this Security Instrument. However, this option shall not be exercised by Lender if exercise is prohibited by federal law as of the date of this Security Instrument. Lender also shall not exercise this option if: (a) Borrower causes to be submitted to Lender information required by Lender to evaluate the intended transferee as if a new loan were being made to the transferee; and (b) Lender reasonably determines that Lender's security will not be impaired by the loan assumption and that the risk of a breach of any covenant or agreement in this Security Instrument is acceptable to Lender.

To the extent permitted by applicable law, Lender may charge a reasonable fee as a condition to Lender's consent to the loan assumption. Lender also may require the transferee to sign an assumption agreement that is acceptable to Lender and that obligates the transferee to keep all the promises and agreements made in the Note and in this Security Instrument. Borrower will continue to be obligated under the Note and this Security Instrument unless Lender releases Borrower in writing.

If Lender exercises the option to require immediate payment in full, Lender shall give Borrower notice of acceleration. The notice shall provide a period of not less than 30 days from the date the notice is delivered or mailed within which Borrower must pay all sums secured by this Security Instrument. If Borrower fails to pay these sums prior to the expiration of this period, Lender may invoke any remedies permitted by this Security Instrument without further notice or demand on Borrower.

2. If Borrower exercises the Conversion Option under the conditions stated in Section B of this Adjustable Rate Rider, the amendment to Uniform Covenant 17 of the Security Instrument contained in Section C 1 above shall then cease to be in effect, and the provisions of Uniform Covenant 17 of the Security Instrument shall instead be in effect, as follows:

Transfer of the Property or a Beneficial Interest in Borrower. If all or any part of the Property or any interest in it is sold or transferred (or if a beneficial interest in Borrower is sold or transferred and Borrower is not a natural person) without Lender's prior written consent, Lender may, at its option, require immediate payment in full of all sums secured by this Security Instrument. However, this option shall not be exercised by Lender if exercise is prohibited by federal law as of the date of this Security Instrument.

If Lender exercises this option, Lender shall give Borrower notice of acceleration. The notice shall provide a period of not less than 30 days from the date the notice is delivered or mailed within which Borrower must pay all sums secured by this Security Instrument. If Borrower fails to pay these sums prior to the expiration of this period, Lender may invoke any remedies permitted by this Security Instrument without further notice or demand on Borrower.

By SIGNING BELOW, Borrower accepts and agrees to the terms and covenants contained in this Adjustable Rate Rider.

.... (Seal)
-Borrower

.... (Seal)
-Borrower

APPENDIX C

CONDOMINIUM RIDER

The Federal National Mortgage Association and the Federal Home Loan Mortgage Corporation have created a Condominium Rider to their standard mortgage instrument. It is reproduced below.

CONDOMINIUM RIDER

THIS CONDOMINIUM RIDER is made this .... day of ...., 19.........
and is incorporated into and shall be deemed to amend and supplement the Mortgage, Deed of Trust or Security Deed (the "Security Instrument") of the same date given by the undersigned (the "Borrower") to secure Borrower's Note to ....
.... (the "Lender")
of the same date and covering the Property described in the Security Instrument and located at:

....
[Property Address]

The Property includes a unit in, together with an undivided interest in the common elements of, a condominium project known as:

....
[Name of Condominium Project]

(the "Condominium Project"). If the owners association or other entity which acts for the Condominium Project (the "Owners Association") holds title to property for the benefit or use of its members or shareholders, the Property also includes Borrower's interest in the Owners Association and the uses, proceeds and benefits of Borrower's interest.

CONDOMINIUM COVENANTS. In addition to the covenants and agreements made in the Security Instrument, Borrower and Lender further covenant and agree as follows:

A. Condominium Obligations. Borrower shall perform all of Borrower's obligations under the Condominium Project's Constituent Documents. The "Constituent Documents" are the: (i) Declaration or any other document which creates the Condominium Project; (ii) by-laws; (iii) code of regulations; and (iv) other equivalent documents. Borrower shall promptly pay, when due, all dues and assessments imposed pursuant to the Constituent Documents.

B. Hazard Insurance. So long as the Owners Association maintains, with a generally accepted insurance carrier, a "master" or "blanket" policy on the Condominium Project which is satisfactory to Lender and which provides insurance coverage in the amounts, for the periods, and against the hazards Lender requires, including fire and hazards included within the term "extended coverage," then:

(i) Lender waives the provision in Uniform Covenant 2 for the monthly payment to Lender of one-twelfth of the yearly premium installments for hazard insurance on the Property; and

(ii) Borrower's obligation under Uniform Covenant 5 to maintain hazard insurance coverage on the Property is deemed satisfied to the extent that the required coverage is provided by the Owners Association policy.

Borrower shall give Lender prompt notice of any lapse in required hazard insurance coverage.

In the event of a distribution of hazard insurance proceeds in lieu of restoration or repair following a loss to the Property, whether to the unit or to common elements, any proceeds payable to Borrower are hereby assigned and shall be paid to Lender for application to the sums secured by the Security Instrument, with any excess paid to Borrower.

C. Public Liability Insurance. Borrower shall take such actions as may be reasonable to insure that the Owners Association maintains a public liability insurance policy acceptable in form, amount, and extent of coverage to Lender.

D. Condemnation. The proceeds of any award or claim for damages, direct or consequential, payable to Borrower in connection with any condemnation or other taking of all or any part of the Property, whether of the unit or of the common elements, or for any conveyance in lieu of condemnation, are hereby assigned and shall be paid to Lender. Such proceeds shall be applied by Lender to the sums secured by the Security Instrument as provided in Uniform Covenant 10.

E. Lender's Prior Consent. Borrower shall not, except after notice to Lender and with Lender's prior written consent, either partition or subdivide the Property or consent to:

(i) the abandonment or termination of the Condominium Project, except for abandonment or termination required by law in the case of substantial destruction by fire or other casualty or in the case of a taking by condemnation or eminent domain;

(ii) any amendment to any provision of the Constituent Documents if the provision is for the express benefit of Lender;

(iii) termination of professional management and assumption of self-management of the Owners Association; or

(iv) any action which would have the effect of rendering the public liability insurance coverage maintained by the Owners Association unacceptable to Lender.

F. Remedies. If Borrower does not pay condominium dues and assessments when due, then Lender may pay them. Any amounts disbursed by Lender under this paragraph F shall become additional debt of Borrower secured by the Security Instrument. Unless Borrower and Lender agree to other terms of payment, these amounts shall bear interest from the date of disbursement at the Note rate and shall be payable, with interest, upon notice from Lender to Borrower requesting payment.

BY SIGNING BELOW, Borrower accepts and agrees to the terms and provisions contained in this Condominium Rider.

.... (Seal)
-Borrower

.... (Seal)
-Borrower

MULTISTATE CONDOMINIUM RIDER—Single Family—Fannie Mae/Freddie Mac UNIFORM INSTRUMENT   Form 3140 9/90

INDEX

References are to Pages

267

†